The Parson Knows

For my father, mother and family, and for all who heard and read, or will read the words of the Vicar

The Parson Knows

. . . from the *Parish Notes,* 1953–1968

Rev. Oliver Willmott (1910–1996)

Edited by Michael Willmott
Illustrations by Andy James

Acknowledgements

Family and friends	–	for information, and inspiration
Sub-editors	–	for close criticism
Choir Press	–	for professionalism

First published by Bishop Street Press September, 1999
2nd impression November, 1999

ISBN 0-9531802-1-2

Produced by Action Publishing Technology Limited, Gloucester
Printed in Great Britain

Contents

Chapter 1	Part One	**The thirty-nine articles**	1
	Part Two	**Spreading the faith**	10
		A brief biography	43
Chapter 2		**Country calendar**	44
Chapter 3		**Loders Court**	89
Chapter 4		**From the font to the grave**	110
		The Aylmers of Askerswell	111
		Granny Hyde	116
		P. C. Edrich	127
Chapter 5		**Outside world**	146
Chapter 6		**Of birds, bees, beasts and flowers**	177
Chapter 7		**Ring out the old, ring in the new**	197
		Harry Crabb	220
Chapter 8		**Wit and mystic**	225
		Historical background	225

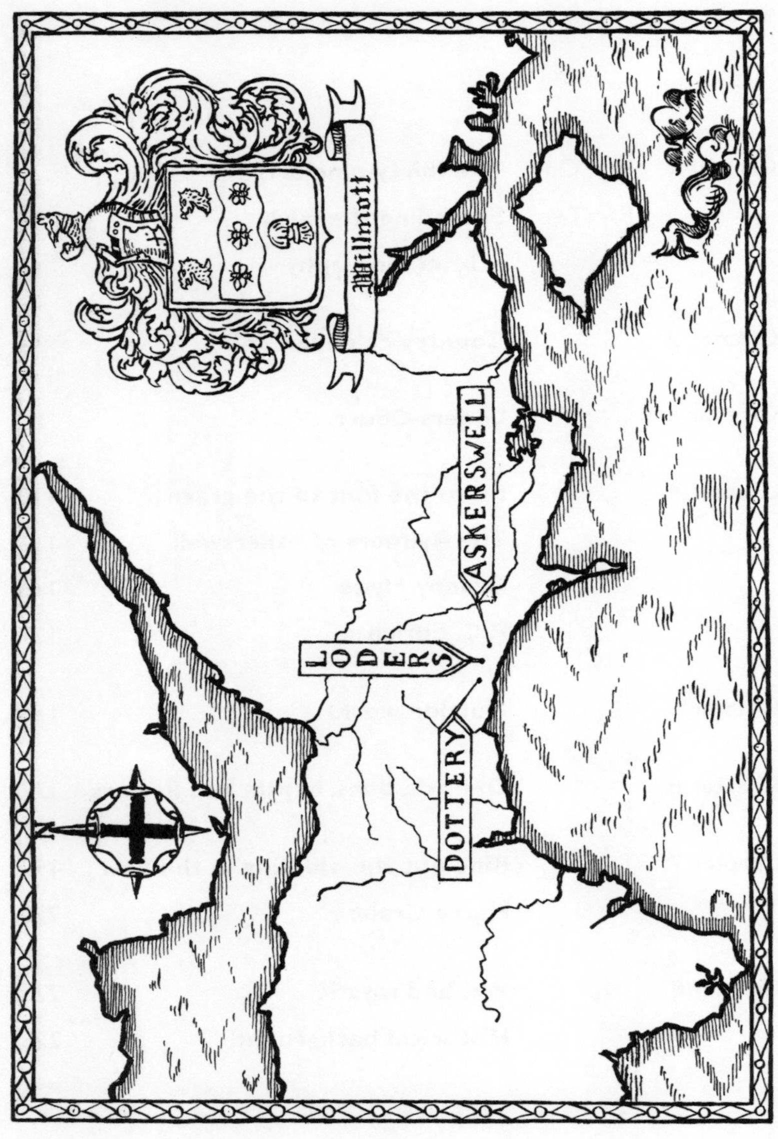
Willmott
ASKERSWELL
LODERS
DOTTERY

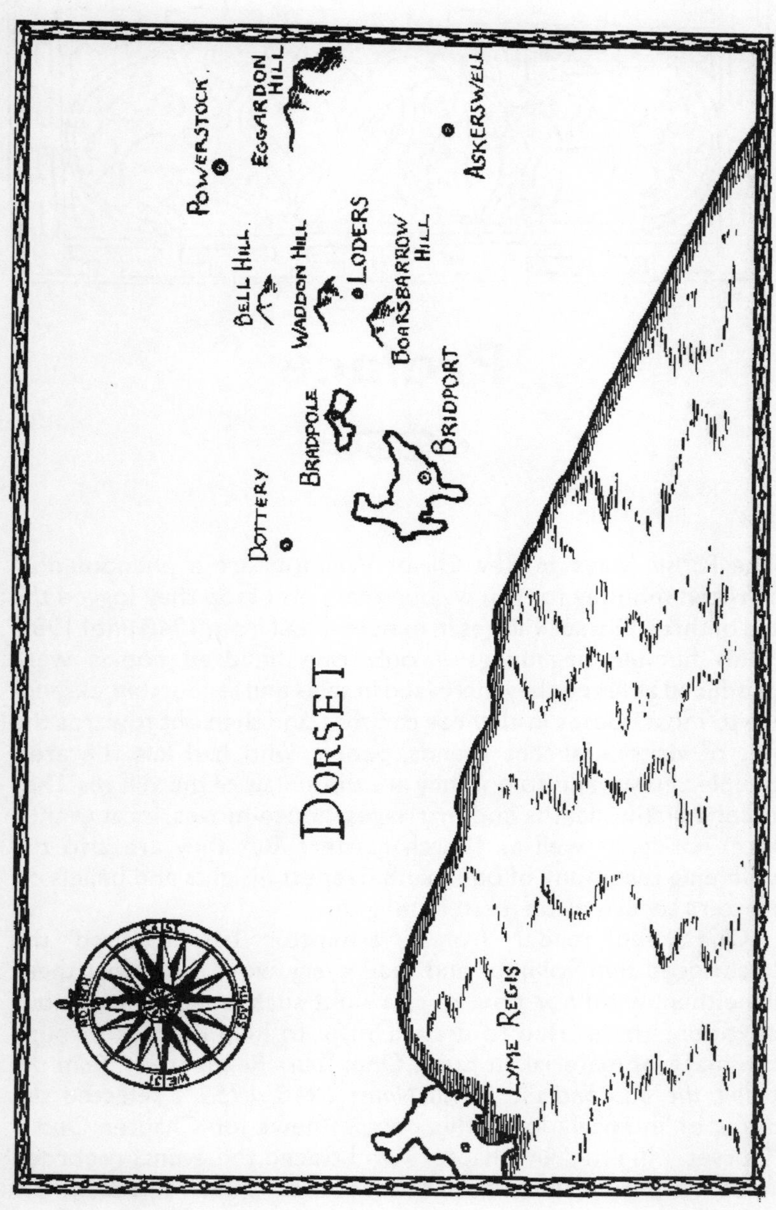
DORSET
POWERSTOCK
EGGARDON HILL
ASKERSWELL
BELL HILL
WADDON HILL
LODERS
BOARSBARROW HILL
BRADPOLE
BRIDPORT
DOTTERY
LYME REGIS
NORTH
EAST
SOUTH
WEST

Preface

The *Parish Notes* of Rev. Oliver Willmott are a phenomenon. Written monthly for thirty-four years non-stop they logged the life of three Dorset villages in minute detail from 1948 until 1982. With humble beginnings – only one hundred copies were produced at first – they increased in sales and readership, extending to most houses in all three parishes, and then out towards the net of visitors, absent friends, people who had left the area, people abroad, and so on. They are the annals of the villages. They record births, deaths and marriages, house-moves, local events, local gossip, as well as church matters. But they are also the unfolding testimony of one man's deepest insights and beliefs on matters secular as on matters religious.

One keen reader from Warminster has acquired the unabridged two volumes and read every word. For most there is neither world nor time to carry out such an act of tenacious devotion. I have tried to draw a 'map' to help readers through the maze of material. In Book One, *Yours Reverently … from the pulpit, the pub and the Parish Notes 1948–1953*, I selected the items of 'intensely local' (his phrase) news for Chapter One – 'Dorset – In little'. In Chapter Two I traced the events recorded over the period until the Coronation of Queen Elizabeth the

Second in 'Dorset – At large'. Chapter Three followed – 'The church's year' – with short homilies on the different saints' days and holy days. Chapter Four was bizarrely entitled 'Of campanology, male chauvinism and bibulousness', registering some of the wide interests (and prejudices) he had beyond the merely ecclesiastical. He was a maverick: he had a wilful enjoyment of independent personality in himself and others.

Chapter Five gave special attention to his 'Wit and wisdom' that percolate all the *Parish Notes* whether in a weather report or an obituary. He was a conscious stylist with a very idiosyncratic voice. 'Voice' is the word, for he used the organ of the *Notes* to continue talking to his parishioners. He talked with the club of opening-time drinkers at his village pubs, and to the people he met on the lanes as he went on his pastoral visits, or 'sermonised' with his dogs. Chapter Six traced 'The diurnal round' of village and country life. Chapter Seven switched attention to the 'Gentlemen, officers and foreigners' whom he delighted in reporting on because this extended the range of the *Parish Notes* beyond the rural backwater. Finally, in Chapter Eight I returned to 'The parish pump' from whence all his observations emanated.

I have drawn this map of the first book to give a feel of its organisation, and to explain how the second book of the trilogy is inevitably more of the same, but different. A remarkable feature of the *Parish Notes* is that they are so regular and disciplined that they give the mysterious feeling of having been written at one go. They are 'as constant as the Northern star'. But to repeat the format of *Yours Reverently* would be tedious, so I have placed a slightly different pattern on the second book. The period covered is longer – 1953–1968. It spans the period from the Coronation to the year of revolutions – (except in Dorset). More has been excised, though with extreme difficulty. Items which merely record some fact of family history have been left to the research volumes in Bridport Museum, with the Somerset and Dorset Family History Society, the British Library, etc. One or two items that might be seen as hobby-horses of the Vicar have been pruned. Arguments about who trims the mounds in the churchyard, or who really controls the school may still be lively subjects of debate. At the time the number of words devoted to them was sometimes too many.

Chapter One starts with his 'Articles of faith' – his pronouncements on matters of deepest theology as well as his decided views on matters as diverse as home childbirth or British Rail. Chapter Two gives a feel of how the 'Country Calendar' unfolded, with the services at church intertwined with secular events. There is not space for every account of Harvest, but it is hoped that this format will stir memories of how season followed season in an unashamedly rustic environment. Chapter Three sets the scene at 'Loders Court' – the feudal centre of the village. Chapter Four travels to the other end of the valley with a portrait of the Aylmers of Askerswell, followed by some shorter sketches of country people. Chapter Five 'Outside world' – speaks for itself. I have held back some material that focuses on the private entries about the Vicar and his family until Book Three. There I will integrate them into the final period of 1968–1982. This may disappoint some keen readers, but there was too much good stuff, and it needs to be seen in the total context of the *Parish Notes*. These are not the *Diaries of Rev. Oliver Willmott*. In a peculiar way they are the diaries for the trio of parishes. His own family matters do start to impinge more prominently in this second phase. In Book One there are only the briefest mentions of the birth of a son, or private gratitude from the Vicar for Easter Offerings of cash in the collection plate, or manure.

Chapter Six contains the sorts of things that Francis Kilvert and Gilbert White of Selborne made country parsons famous for: 'Birds, Bees, Beasts and Flowers', observed with that eye for detail and a certain kind of rural serenity (apart from some harsher encounters with foxes and badgers). 'Ring out the old, ring in the new' celebrates the Vicar's tendency to maintain the past and cultivate good traditions, whilst fostering the enthusiasms of newcomers and exciting ventures – anything that enhanced the quality of village life. Ringers and pub friends were the inevitable source of much of this traditional energy and innovation, though there were many others, of both sexes. Harry Crabb gets a full portrait in this chapter. He was one of the Vicar's deepest friends, and his 'tarmenter'.

Finally, the 'Wit and Wisdom' of Book One is transformed into 'Wit and Mysticism' in Chapter Eight of Book Two. The profound observations of the first phase are expressed in ways that make you realise that the Vicar was more than a mere journalist, or even a mere parish priest. He had an infinite capacity with words, and his words quite regularly touched upon the infinite. He was a poet in prose. Whilst having his feet firmly on the ground in matters of church finance, gardening or local government, he occasionally reached heights of spiritual intensity that only his six years' training as a monk can account for.

The sheer bulk of his output prevented him from seeing what were the central threads in his work. He had no word-processor. He was his own word-processor. He couldn't write a book. I have inherited the humble but daunting task of transforming his monthly linear lists of inclusions into what may eventually be recognised as his lasting work. The Welsh, the poet Gillian Clarke tells me, describe such works as this as a *cofiante*, or tribute from a son. Such a work in the nineteenth century would be accompanied by several examples of sermons. Unfortunately, and remarkably, he didn't write his thousands down, except one he had to time for a BBC broadcast. So there are no sermons here. Only serious fun.

At Loders Vicarage the stern profile of Girolamo Savonarola (p. xii) kept watch over the dining-table behind the Vicar's chair. He was his hero, having been hanged in 1498 for being 'the puritan of Catholicism'. The little hills of Dorset and in particular the 'benign brow of Boarsbarrow' mellowed Savonarola's rigour brought from Kelham College. The soft yellow sandstone of the church and cottages all conspired to make the valleys laugh and sing.

Girolamo Savonarola

Editorial notes

1. The words of the Vicar are in normal type. Any editorial comment is as typed on this page, or in square brackets [ ].

2. The Vicar's headings have been used where possible: where not, the Editor has endeavoured to make up an appropriate introduction.

3. On pages 255–8 there are some background facts about the period covered by the book, with cross-references to the text where possible.

4. The typing customs of the 1950s and 1960s were not the same as the typing customs of 1999. If there are any anomalies, we apologise. (£. s. d. was particularly difficult to regularise.)

CHAPTER I

Articles of faith

Part One: The Thirty-Nine Articles

The Thirty-nine Articles of the Church of England were composed by Thomas Cranmer in 1553 and ratified by King Charles as Head of the Church and State in 1562 (after Cranmer had been burnt at the stake). They were intended to prevent schism and used as the basis of the constitution of the Church of England until 1865. Even during that period, it is doubtful that any two Anglicans might subscribe to the same articles, let alone them all. Then a more general affirmation was substituted to which all ordinands had to subscribe. At Kelham Theological College where he trained as a monk for six years (p. 43, A brief biography) the Articles would have been chewed over as an historical document amongst many, before a more universal Christianity based on the scriptures, tradition and reason was accepted. Oliver Willmott's favourite subject – though he loved Literature and dabbled in Psychology – was Logic. He would accept no article of faith on any subject without severe personal scrutiny.

With training also in the Bristol Christian Missionary Society,

and with war experience as an Army Chaplain, Rev. Oliver Willmott's Christian base was broad. Prebendary Brooke Lunn of St. Paul's Cathedral wrote in, ironically, the *Catholic Messenger* (February 1998):
'In a world where *catholic* meant what it does in the creed, and was not a sectarian term to denote a denominational demarcation, one might describe Oliver Willmott as a good *catholic* parish priest – a near-papist encouraging the Wesleyan Chapel, married, seven children, in the same parish from the forties to the eighties, at home in his parish in both the good times and the uncomfortable times (the frustrations of the parish priest surface from time to time in these *Parish Notes*), holding fast to fundamental Christian belief ... you can't pigeon-hole someone like this.'

The muscularity of his certainty went well beyond matters of faith. In his meditations as he walked round the country lanes he hammered out his principles in matters political, agricultural, and sociological, even branching out into the world of fashion, transport and local government. He viewed sport as an unnecessary addition to human activity when physical outlets could be found in digging in manure or chopping up beech. In this chapter I have selected thirty-nine of his most challenging statements from the period covered by this book as an introduction to an extended survey of his own articles of faith. He enjoyed following a statement of deep seriousness with a remark of pithy outrageousness.

1. Sir Francis Drake

We should all do well to make our own the prayer prayed by Sir Francis Drake on the day he sailed into Cadiz in 1587: 'O Lord God, when Thou movest Thy servants to attempt any great matter, grant them to know that it is not the beginning, but the continuing of the thing, until it be thoroughly finished, that yieldeth the true glory.' Dogged perseverance is a virtue badly needed in these days of butterfly-flitting from one brief interest to another.

January 1953

2. Confirmation

The way in which the Dottery candidates are trying to live up to their promise is inspiriting in these days when vows mean nothing.

October 1953

3. The eighteenth century

The eleven o'clock service on Christmas morning has more of the spirit of the eighteenth century – 'the rising of the sun, the running of the deer, the playing of the merry organ, sweet singing in the choir'.

December 1953

4. Loders giving

No parish beats Loders at giving.

January 1955

5. Fred Vacher

He is one of those rare beings who thinks for himself.

March 1955

6. The authorised version

New versions of the Bible have the paradoxical effect of making the hearer approve their freshness and relevance – and of doubling his devotion to the Authorised Version.

October 1955

7. The constable's word

So, in the phrase of our constable, we must 'soldier on'.

May 1956

8. Country ways

The National Farmers' Union of all people (p. 20, Growing in popularity) should have known that you must always order a countryman to do the opposite of what you want him to do.

June 1957

9. To serve the Esquimaux

In these days of self-seeking it is an inspiration to see a most valuable member of our community giving her skill and care to humanity less fortunate than ourselves.

July 1957

10. Behind the times

Your Vicar is usually behind the times, and is not always sorry to be so, seeing what the times are.

November 1957

11. Ladies

A lady's legs may fail her, but her tongue never.

May 1958

12. The after-life

The people of Dottery were grieved to lose their oldest inhabitant, Mrs. Agnes Gibbs, within two months of her ninety-seventh birthday. Her belief in the knitting-up of severed friendships after death was strong and matter-of-fact.

September 1961

13. Giving

The test of giving is that it hurts. (pp. 32–33, Fêtes)

August 1962

14. Sermons

Sermons are merciless self-revelations of the preacher. (pp. 239–240, The return of a native)

September 1962

15. In-laws

The difficulty of living with in-laws is notorious.

January 1963

16. The Bishop of Sherborne [Victor Pike]

He is 'honest to God' in a way that does not befuddle and bemuse, and is warmly appreciated by people of common sense.

June 1963

17. Fête-collecting

May I ask my clients only to bestow on me what is saleable? (p. 34 Taking the initiative)

August 1963

18. The Vicar

One who knows the virtue of striking while the iron is hot (p. 34, Taking the initiative).

January 1964

19. Boy at school

Group-Captain Newall tells us that his son Robert, who broke a leg skiing, is doing well, and hopes (hardly the word for a boy) to be back at school before long.

February 1964

20. Dorset parishes

It is the recognised form for Dorset parishes to maintain an outward show of contempt for each other.

June 1964

21. Topless dresses

One of the ringers' ladies remarked that distinguishing between the sexes made topless dresses a necessity nowadays, and Mr. Harry Crabb agreed (p. 223, Ringers' outing).

August 1964

22. Confirmands

This will be the first Christmas communion for the candidates confirmed in October. The dark winter mornings are already putting them to the test, and shewing whether their spiritual name is Percy Vere or Peter Out.

December 1964

23. Loders

Loders is a wee bit like Nazareth: unexpected good comes out of it at time (p. 250).

February 1965

24. Badges

Not many youngsters will flock to where He is to be found, nor scream with ecstacy, for His badge is not a hair style but a cross (p. 36, Christ's badge).

March 1965

25. Brawls

Brawls with somebody in authority have been your parson's lot ever since he came to these parts. One fears you will never have the honour of being ministered to by Canon or Archdeacon Willmott.

April 1965

26. An episcopal astronaut

We are all agog at the spectacle of a Russian astronaut attached to an airship by a kind of umbilical cord, floating high above the world in space. But let it be recognised that religion in the person of the Bishop of Woolwich anticipated this achievement of science by several months when he published his book 'Honest to God' (p. 172, An episcopal astronaut).

April 1965

27. Cathedral music

The musical tradition of English cathedrals is second to none in the world. It makes wonderful use of air, but cannot live on it (p. 218, Recital on the Vicarage lawn).

June 1965

28. Saint Mary Magdalene

Country people even more than townspeople are governed by habit, and it is the habit of Loders people not to turn out for the dedication festival to thank God for a church which fills the visitors' book with praise not unmixed with envy. Old habits are tending to pass away. Cannot this one?

July 1965

29. Musical Loders

Loders people as a whole are not musical.

July 1965

30. Spiritual exercises

The English find spiritual exercises terribly exhausting and this year the day after Christmas was a Sunday. Empty churches that day would not have been surprising, but services were well attended.

January 1966

31. Lived out

The clamant need of religion is to be lived out rather than talked about (p. 38, The clamant need of religion).

February 1966

32. Religion

Religion is essentially a family affair (p. 38, Religion – a family affair).

April 1966

33. Gaol

I would not be above juggling with the accounts if that were to improve them, for another friend tells me that life in Dorchester Gaol isn't to be sneezed at nowadays.

July 1966

34. Television

The reluctance of people with television to turn out at night has changed the pattern of social life in most villages, denuded village halls of most of their activities and made hall maintenance something of a headache.

October 1967

35. Dark days

Life is always happier when there is something to look forward to and work for, as was proved even in the dark days of the war.

December 1967

36. Competition

Competition in good works is an excellent thing.

December 1967

37. Beauty

If the face be the mirror of the soul then the bride is in no need of a eulogy from us.

(Of Miss Christine Edwards) April 1968

38. Newcomers

In a Dorset village it is the normal lot of newcomers to be under grave suspicion for the first twenty-five years.

39. The Vicar's fold

The Vicar is also deeply grateful for the support the churchyard got from certain good folk, non-churchgoers, of whom he said to himself, 'Other sheep I have, which are not of this fold.'

The pulpit at Loders

Part Two: Spreading the Faith

Enterprise

Herewith a word of appreciation of the local branch of the South-Western Electricity Authority. Shortly before Loders harvest evensong, the nave lights were found to be defunct. Answering the call with their usual promptness, the electricians discovered that the wiring in the pipes under the roof had been corroded by rain water which had come through the former lead covering. To repair this at short notice was a considerable job, but the electricians obliged us by getting it done in time for harvest. Which poses the question: what matters it whether enterprise is private or public, as long as it is enterprise?

November 1953

Less and less of more and more

The Young People of Askerswell kept up their Christmas partying well into January, and Miss Edwards' cottage was the venue for most of it. There she entertained first the Brownies and Cubs, then the Guides and the boys whose company the Guides are able to bear. The Brownies' party was honoured by a visit from the District Commissioner, Lady Crutchley. The choir spent an enjoyable evening at Loders Vicarage. In a general knowledge quiz, the older members left the junior members standing, a point which may be useful to those who contend that the only result of the huge sum spent on education is that the children know less and less about more and more.

February 1954

Our schools

To the regret of the scholars of Askerswell, Miss Robinson is ill again, and off-duty. We wish her a speedy recovery. Her place is being taken by Mr. Wake, who has often done supply duty in this district. Mr. Wake tells us that with the present shortage of teachers, and with so many of them falling sick, the County is at its wits' end for supplies. At Loders Miss Bryan is fortunate in having the help of a student teacher for three weeks. Loders school has risen to 28 children, whose ages range from 5 to 11, and we are hoping against hope that the county may be able to produce a second teacher, so that infants and juniors may be divided into two classes. No teacher can be expected to teach at the same time tots of five who know nothing, and children of eleven who are preparing for the passing-out examination. While on the subject of Loders Schools, we would like to rouse the interest of a kindly man who is handy with cement, and ready to do the school a good turn. Miss Bryan is arranging to have some wire netting fitted to the school wall, to prevent balls used in physical training from going into adjoining gardens, but before this can be done the wall needs pointing. Money can be found for the materials, but that is about all. In a couple of Saturday afternoons a Good Samaritan could save the school a builder's account of double figures.

February 1954

Anglican worship

One of the beauties of Anglican worship is that it is impersonal in the sense that it is ordered more by a liturgy than by the personal whims of a minister. Yet on occasion Anglican worship can be too impersonal. In June a choral festival was held in Salisbury Cathedral. The cathedral was packed from end to end with church choirs from all over the diocese (including Loders) who had shewn their keenness by weeks of practice beforehand, and coming, some of them, considerable distances. The service was sung magnificently, but it was all over in forty minutes, and just as the choristers were beginning to feel the spell of the service, they found themselves outside the cathedral. The service had contained no word of welcome from the cathedral authorities, and although this vast congregation of singers was in the mood to hear a sermon on some such theme as the part to be played by music in the service of God, no sermon was given notwithstanding the number of preachers present.

Many of the choirs must have come away feeling like our own that a great opportunity had been missed.

July 1954

A smell of Nazidom

Saturday, Dec. 4th, is the date of Loders children's annual mission sale. As usual, it will be held in the school, beginning at 2 o'clock, and it promises to be a pleasant social afternoon. The children have collected and also made themselves, useful articles which will doubtless find ready buyers, and business is to be brightened by cups of tea and a few items of entertainment by the children. The need for the sale to raise a goodly sum is specially great this year. The missionary societies which we support have had war declared on them by the South African Government, and battle is already joined. In England church and state have long known how to work together, and the Church of England missions in South Africa are sympathetic towards the problems of government there, but they cannot allow themselves to be made instruments of the unchristian doctrine that the destiny of the African is to be merely a hewer of wood and a drawer of water for the white man. The *Daily Telegraph* reports that when the English Bishop of Johannesburg gave away the prizes in a big mission school, plain clothes policemen were there in force, and his speech was taken down. A smell of Nazidom there. What the South African Government regarded as sedition on the Bishop's part was only reiteration of the New Testament doctrine: 'There can be neither Jew nor Greek ... bond or free ... for ye are all one man in Christ Jesus'.

December 1954

A word in jest often comes true

When the Rev. Joost de Blank was senior chaplain of the 61st. Division he said to his staff chaplain (your present vicar): 'The Roman Catholics and the Free Churches have decent church newspapers, that keep their people interested in their church as a whole. The Church of England hasn't got one. If I were a bishop I'd make it my job to give the Church of England a decent newspaper'. The Reverend Joost de Blank is now the Right Reverend Joost de Blank, Lord Bishop of Stepney, and he is chairman of the new Church of England periodical to be launched in January. Launching a periodical of good taste when magazines like *John o' London*'s have just gone under is an act of faith calling for no small courage. We hope our three parishes will help the new venture by becoming readers. It will be an illustrated monthly, on the lines of *Picture Post*, costing 6d. More about it in the next *Notes*.

December 1954

[*Church Illustrated* went under]

'Spare the rod, spoil the child.'

St. Paul, the Bible in general, and the public schools, are firm believers of this doctrine. But it seems that some parents are not, and that some County Education Committees aren't either. Hence, an intriguing situation in Northampton. A teacher there gave 37 naughty children a stroke each, on the hand, with a blackboard pointer. A parent of one of the naughty children summoned the teacher for assault, and she was fined £1 by the local magistrates. She appealed to the Quarter Sessions, and this higher court, holding that it is no crime for a teacher to cane naughty children, quashed the conviction. But it seems that by caning the naughty children the teacher was infringing the regulations of her County Education Committee, and rendered herself liable to disciplinary action. All of which indicates that the County Education Committee and the Law may be at variance. If the Northampton Education Committee's rules are anything like the Dorset Education Committee's, which they probably are, then people of commonsense would support the Law every time. Here are some of the Dorset Committee's regulations on corporal punishment, quoted from the 1954 Handbook:- '(a) Corporal punishment may only be administered by the head-teacher and by certificated assistant teachers to whom the head-teacher will have specially entrusted such power. (b) Corporal punishment with the cane may only be inflicted, save for a grave offence, after other methods have been tried and have failed. (c) The instrument used must only be a proper cane supplied for the purpose by the committee's school contractor ... (d) Corporal punishment must not be inflicted until the name of the offender and the nature of the offence and of the punishment have been entered in the Punishment Book'.

It is clear from this that if the Vicar is taking Scripture lesson in Loders School, and he tells Billy Jones to stop talking, and Billy says 'Shan't', and sticks his tongue out, whereupon the Vicar puts Billy across his knee and warms Billy's seat with his bare hand, then the Vicar is breaking all the rules of the Dorset Education Committee and is rendering himself liable to disciplinary action. What he should do according to the Committee's regulations, is, first, try to reason Billy into an obedient frame of mind; if that fails, to give him a hundred lines; if that fails, to speak to his father; if that fails, to proceed to the last resort, and fetch the head teacher. She will solemnly inform Billy that he is about to be chastised; she will get out the Punishment Book and write in it Billy's name, the nature of his offence and the extent of the punishment she is about to administer, then she will give him a stroke on the hand with the cane supplied by the school contractor.

One wonders whether the Committee who drew up these precious rules have children of their own, or have ever taught in school. It may well be that the rules reflect the morbid fear that some education authorities have of being proceeded against in Court. Now that the Courts are making it clear that they will protect teachers against silly parents, isn't it time that the Education Committees scrapped these silly regulations?

February 1955

In hospital

Mrs. Knight, of Cuckholds' Corner, is in the Weymouth and District Hospital, and Mr. Saunders has been moved from Weymouth Portwey to Bridport Hospital. By all accounts Mr. Saunders is lucky to be alive. He jumped to avoid a car which skidded into him as he was walking on the verge of the main road, and sustained a broken leg. It seems a pity that so often local patients have to go to distant hospitals for the appropriate treatment. Nowadays the sick are whisked off to Dorchester, Weymouth, and even Salisbury, which makes visiting difficult for their friends.

February 1955

The one true Church

The good wishes of Dottery, and especially of the young communicants, were with Miss Doris Parker at her marriage to Mr. Frank Oxenbury, of Bridport. Nobody regretted it more than Miss Parker that the wedding was away from her own parish church. Her fiancé is a Roman Catholic, and the fancy which Roman Catholics have, in common with Plymouth Brethren and Jehovah's Witnesses, that they are the only true Church, had to be humoured. It is gratifying to know that Miss Parker remains a member of the Church of England, and hopes, when she is home, to be at Dottery Church, with the friends with whom she was confirmed. She is sure of a welcome.

November 1955

Better than Ovaltine

Uploders pensioner, to Vicar, making pastoral call: 'I be glad you be come, sir. Life don't seem right if passon don't call. I shall sleep like a little topper tonight.'

December 1955

The baiting of public servants

Is there a change, and a change for the worse, coming over English character? We seem to be growing more and more indulgent of our own personal shortcomings, and less and less tolerant of any mistakes or signs of human fallibility in our public servants, who were once the nation's pride. Take British Railways as a case in point. At the close of last year there were three accidents in succession. The public got alarmed, the appropriate minister was obliged to make extraordinary investigations, and the sensational press more than suggested that the British railwayman was losing his sense of responsibility for the safety of the travelling public. It is only right, of course, that a vigilant eye should be kept on the public services, but no stranger to our now nagging mood would have guessed that British Railways really have something to be proud of. They struck a bad patch in 1955, but in 1954 they carried their enormous traffic without one person being killed. A comparison of road casualties with rail is startling. Between 1946 and 1952, 331 passengers were killed in rail accidents; in the same period 34,197 people were killed on the roads. The terrible monthly figures of road casualties are tucked away in inconspicuous corners of the newspapers, and we take them from the wireless as a matter of course. But let there be an accident on the railways and at once there is a universal howl. Is it because we, the general public, have a part to play in road safety, and the road casualties are a sign of our own shortcomings, to be treated indulgently, whereas rail safety is the railwayman's business and he, being a public servant, must be altogether infallible, and above making mistakes? That admiration of the world, the English policeman and the English judiciary, have also come in for a nagging. Because the odd policeman had shewn his humanity by doing what he ought not to, the whole police force is suspected of corruption, and the criminal gets all the sympathy. Because three men got wrongly imprisoned, and because there is just a possibility that Evans was wrongly hanged, the English judges are a thoroughly bad lot, the death penalty must be abolished, and the wrongly imprisoned men handsomely compensated. It matters not that Evans told the police three times that he had done the murder, and could not blame anybody but himself if he got hanged. It matters not that the three men who were wrongfully imprisoned were convicted on their own false evidence; were, on their own showing, on their way to crack a safe when they were supposed to be elsewhere attacking a policeman; and were men with previous convictions. All this matters not one bit – policemen and judges are public servants, and therefore not allowed to make one mistake. It is high time that the great British public stopped measuring their servants by the standard expected of the Almighty, and turned the searchlight of criticism on themselves.

February 1956

'Wiser than the children of light'

As the Loders minute bell for matins was sounding on a recent Sunday morning, the stragglers saw a car pull up near the police station. Four people got out of it, armed with literature, and began a door to door canvas. They were Jehovah's Witnesses, trying to sell the publications of their founder, Judge Rutherford. He was an American, and the strength of this sect is in America. He claimed, before he died, to have sold 13 million pieces of literature. We leave it to our readers to work out the Judge's profit if he made only a penny on each piece. The House of Lords has lately rejected a claim by the purveyors of this literature to be exempt from national service. Mistaken as Jehovah's Witnesses may be, one cannot but admire their zeal for their religion. They, like the Communists, put heaps more effort into propagating a false faith than we Christians do into spreading the true one. Jesus Christ aptly summed up the situation when he said, 'The children of this world are in their generation wiser than the children of light.'

August 1956

Harvest produce

A difficult harvest, and a summer of gales and floods, might have lowered the temperature of harvest festival, but it seems to have had the opposite effect. Which means, we hope, that our people know that whether we receive little or much, it all derives from the Almighty. At Dottery the changing of the weeknight service from Thursday to Friday, so as not to clash with the ploughing match, seemed to produce an even bigger congregation. It was very pleasing to have the scattered members of the Harris family, lately of Bilshay, back in strength, and to have several families complete from grand-parents to grand-children. At first sight, three babes in arms augured ill for the peace of the service, but they knew by instinct that sermons were meant to be slept through, so the preacher proceeded without competition. Somebody's cat tried to attend the service, but this Mrs. Gale would not tolerate. Finding himself shut out in the churchyard, the cat mounted a tombstone and charged a window repeatedly. Fortunately for the thinly-thatched heads in the pew beneath, the glass held. At Askerswell there was a great gathering of the clans for evensong, and the old familiar faces included those of Mr. & Mrs. Studley, from up country. Practically every family in the parish was represented, giving a delightful taste of what Sunday worship could be. On the following day those who wanted the harvest decorations came to church and took them, and left a contribution to church funds. The contributions came to £6. 16s. It seemed to be agreed that this was a better way of dealing with the produce than to take it to the hospitals. Even before the hospitals were nationalised they found it hard to assimilate the harvest offerings of the urban and the rural districts, and the writer well remembers arriving at a hospital with sacks of fruit and vegetables, and being told to empty them on a big and decaying heap of harvest produce in the backyard. At Loders the church was well filled for morning service, and in the evening the presence of many of the Askerswell Young Farmers made it necessary for some of the congregation to be seated in the chancel. At each service the choir sang an anthem upon which they have not yet ceased to be congratulated. It was all that a harvest anthem should be – lively, crisp, full-bodied, and with plenty of light and shade. Thanks to an absence of frosts, plenty of flowers of fine quality were available for the decorations, and our ladies excelled themselves.

November 1956

Toning in

The new council houses at Well Plot have now come to life. Smoke rises from the chimneys, curtains grace the windows, and the milkman calls. Everybody in Loders who wanted a council house has got one, and seems well pleased with it. The architect is to be congratulated on toning the new houses to their surroundings. There are no dazzling whites or shocking reds. The houses pass the test of being quiet and unobtrusive when one looks down on them from Waddon or Boarsbarrow.

December 1956

All for it

Askerswell Church is heated – and sometimes scented – by a Gurney stove, consuming coal and coke. The gentlemen of the parish look askance at her, like hen-pecked husbands, when they come into church. And with good reason. In return for her winter warmth, she exacts a heavy toll of stoking and water carrying, which the gentlemen discharge by rota. She is their bête noir. She makes the house of prayer a house of bondage. One of the gentlemen, with an eye to the future, has gone so far as to clean her out voluntarily every week. He does not say so, but our surmise is that he trusts this may reduce his time in purgatory. Our readers can imagine the ray of hope that flickered on the beaten brows of these gentlemen when it was announced at the Easter Vestry that it might be possible to convert the Gurney to oil, and dispense with the stoking. Never were churchmen so sure that the necessary funds would be forthcoming, and the secretary was asked to investigate the possibility without delay.

May 1957

Growing in popularity

When the ancient Rogationtide service of prayer for the growing crops was revived in Loders Church ten years ago, there was not, to our knowledge, any comparable service in the neighbourhood. But the idea has since 'caught on', and every year sees an increase in the number of churches observing Rogationtide, which is all to the good. This year a chapel, the Bridport Congregational, made history by taking a leaf out of the Church's calendar. It arranged a special agricultural service for the evening of Rogation Sunday, and invited the local branch of the N.F.U. and the Askerswell Y.F.C. – which together comprise most of the local farming community – to attend. Apparently the promoters of this service saw nothing incongruous in bringing country people into town for a country occasion, but it struck us as odd that farming people who for the past ten years had been in the habit of attending Rogation in Loders Church should be requested by their local N.F.U., and by the Askerswell Y.F.C., to attend the Bridport Congregational service. The N.F.U. of all people should have known that you must always order a countryman to do the opposite of what you really want him to do. The effect of this request to attend service in Bridport was to make the Loders service more crowded than ever and to make the collection a record. The service was memorable for its singing, and for excellent reading of the lessons by Mr. C. Gale (Chairman, Loders Discussion Club), Mr. R Dennett, and Mr. P. Baker (Vice-Chairman, Askerswell Y.F.C.). Once again we are indebted to Mr. Wilfred Crabb for the loan of his old horse plough for the chancel.

June 1957

A famous man

Dr. Martin Niemoller is already in the history books as a U-boat commander in the last war who rebelled against the Nazis, was thrown into a concentration camp, was ordained a minister in, and is now a leader of, the German Church. He is to speak in the Bridport Methodist Church at 4.15 p.m. and again at 7.30 p.m. on Thursday, June 13th, and our readers ought not to miss this opportunity of meeting one of the heroic protagonists of Christianity against Nazism. The chair will be taken by Lady North, wife of the Admiral whose career has lately been the subject of much discussion in and out of parliament.

June 1957

A birthday party

Our local Women's Institute celebrated their tenth birthday by inviting Litton Cheney W.I. to a party. The birthday cake had been made by Mrs. Knight, and we can vouch personally for its excellence – although we ourselves being of the superior sex are not W.I., Mrs. Harry Legg [p. 47 portrait] and Mrs Carver gave us a piece for seeing them home after the party. (We leave our readers to guess whether it was themselves or their load of W.I. utensils that they were glad to have seen home.)

July 1957

Saint Mary Magdalene

Loders' choice of a patron saint when they built their parish church was Mary Magdalene, whose day is July 22nd. Loders feast, the fair which for centuries was associated with Mary Magdalene's day, is now only a childhood memory of some of our octagenarians, but we still keep the Sunday nearest Mary Magdalene – July 21st this year – as our dedication festival. It is sometimes said that strangers who look on the beauty of our church for the first time appreciate it more than we who live round it. But we can give the lie to this by crowding the ancient place on July 21st to thank God for it. In Loders Church we have a treasure without price.

July 1957

The true character of Christmas

Some of the shops were dressed up for Christmas at the beginning of November, and one at least had a display of Christmas cards in mid-October. This anxiety of some tradesmen to cash in early on the Christmas spending ought to set us thinking about the true character of Christmas. It all began because on the first Christmas Day God became man, to shew us what God is, and what we must be. The shepherds of Bethlehem had no turkey nor plum pudding, yet theirs was a real Christmas because they went to the manger and paid their joyful respects to Him whose birthday it was. If ours is to be a real Christmas, too, we must be like them. The manger is out of reach, but every parish has its house of God, and there God's family should pay their respects on this auspicious day.

December 1957

Lecturers versus T.V.

The Askerswell lectures finished this year's session shortly before Christmas. The subject had been the appreciation of painting. This had seemed to some who attended to be not 'up their street', but the reward of bowing to the majority was to find the course entertaining as well as interesting. The lectures were illustrated by filmstrips. The company found that television cannot really better the pleasure of meeting a live lecturer (who can be questioned, or disagreed with, or put in his place) in the amiable fellowship of one's friends. It is hoped that this year's lectures may be on the notable buildings of Dorset.

January 1958

A lesson to newcomers

A lady who has lately pitched her tabernacle amongst us, and charmed us in every way, had her electric light fail at an awkward time. Neighbours opposite, with their wonted kindness, put her in touch with the Electricity Authority, but the time was when the Authority did not function. She was then put in touch with another friendly neighbour who dabbled in electricity, and after an exhaustive examination of the entire wiring system he was at his wits' end to find nothing wrong. In a final gesture of despair, he looked at the meter. His eyes lighted up. He called for a shilling, put it in the slot, and the mystery was solved.

February 1958

Focus on Salisbury

The mother church of Wiltshire and Dorset, Salisbury Cathedral, attains her seven hundredth birthday this year. There is to be a series of celebrations, which will allow of every parish in the diocese taking part. The young people of the diocese will set the ball rolling by gathering at Old Sarum on April 12th, marching to the Cathedral, and handing the Dean a bag of silver coins as a birthday present from their parish to the mother church. Some of the young pilgrims will walk all the way to Old Sarum, disdaining forms of conveyance other than Shanks' pony; some will do the pilgrimage on bicycles; and some, according to *The Times*, hope to start a new fashion by arriving in helicopters. The names of the young pilgrims who are to represent our parishes will be given in our March number; meanwhile, parishioners may begin to put by the silver coins for the birthday bag. Musical parishioners may like to know that in March the Bournemouth Symphony

Orchestra, with the Salisbury Musical Society, will give a performance of Handel's 'Samson' in the Cathedral – an apt reminder that Handel lived for a time in the Cathedral Close. On June 28th, bishops from all over the world, attending the Lambeth Conference, will take part in a commemoration service at which the preacher will be the Archbishop of Canterbury. On September 29th and 30th there will be festival services in the Cathedral for the parishes of the diocese. Scores of our parishioners will wish to take part in one of these. We hope to arrange transport, and make a day-to-be-remembered of it. The uninitiated may wonder what Old Sarum is (where the pilgrims are to gather on April 12th). It is a big rocky mound, two miles out on the road from Salisbury to Stonehenge. It is the site of the former capital city of the diocese of Salisbury, and it holds the remains of the original cathedral, begun in 1057. By the thirteenth century the bishop and burgesses of Old Sarum were tired of this barren spot. They decided to move south, to the rich meadows where four rivers met, and there, in 1220, they began to build the present Cathedral which in the setting of the Close, is one of the loveliest buildings in the whole world. Except for the spire, which was carried to its extreme height of 404 feet in 1274, the Cathedral was completed and consecrated in 1258. In our mother church we Dorset people have a goodly heritage, and we should find no difficulty in echoing the words of the Psalmist, 'Lord, I have loved the habitation of thy house, and the place where thine honour dwelleth'.

February 1958

Uncomfortable words

Those who are familiar with the Communion Service know that the most solemn part of it is introduced by a recital of certain words of comfort spoken by Our Lord, and these are called The Comfortable Words. But Our Lord also said some most uncomfortable things, which human nature, left to itself, will avoid listening to. The Archbishop of Cape Town has collected some of these, and published them for Lent reading under the title of Uncomfortable Words. Your Editor has not yet seen the Archbishop's book, so he is wondering whether the collection will include a group of Our Lord's sayings which ought to make the Englishman of to-day positively ill with discomfort, namely, the sayings about almsgiving. Our Lord takes it for granted that all who claim to be Christians will be givers of alms – 'Therefore, when thou doest thine alms...'. In the Sermon on the Mount he goes as far as to enjoin selling one's personal possessions if one lacks cash for almsgiving – 'Sell that ye have and give alms, provide yourselves bags which wax not old'. This admonition is as uncomfortable a word as any, but those who are trying to follow the Master must heed it. Now is the appropriate time to understand what alms are, and what they are not. None of the collections taken nowadays in our three churches is an alms. The collections are spent on ourselves, because they pay for the running of our churches for our own use. Easter Offerings are not an alms; they are a voluntary payment for services rendered; the Poppy Day collections are not an alms, but the payment of a due to those who gave their all for us; the ringers' collection is not an alms, but a payment we make to those who give us pleasure by ringing our bells; the money raised at fêtes is not alms, but pays for the repair of our own churches. This catalogue of what alms are not should have given the attentive reader an inkling of what they are. Alms are what we give to those who have a claim on our compassion. Gifts of money and clothing to refugees or victims of disasters are alms; money spent on taking the gospel to the heathen and supplying them with hospitals is an alms; helping discharged prisoners to rehabilitate themselves is an alms; providing police-court missioners to try to prevent the shipwreck of lives and homes is an alms. And so on. The disturbing feature about the giving in our three parishes is that so small a proportion of it is alms. With the exception of the children's mission sale, the Lent boxes, and an annual donation from Askerswell Church to missions, none of our giving is alms. Church collections and fêtes have their work cut out to pay the running expenses and repairs of the churches, and leave no margin for alms. Compared with some parishes, our giving is very good. The comparison, however, should not be with other parishes. It should be a personal matter – what is my income, and how much of it do I give to God? ('Give' is hardly the right word, for all things are God's). In the old days people thought that a tenth of one's income was the appropriate amount to give to God. Nowadays a half-crown a week would be less than one eightieth of the average wage. It behoves those of us who attend service to see whether our contribution to the plate has risen with our income, and those of us who have lost the habit to see the wrongness of not pulling our weight. One of the joys of these parishes is that they contain some people who, if they are unable to attend service, either send along God's portion by somebody else, or put it by until they can come again. How good it would be if everybody were of the same mind. Financial clouds would evaporate, and God's work, of which the world is in such dire need, would go vigorously ahead.

March 1958

Defender of Church and State

Easter in our churches was very inspiring. The decorators had done wonders despite the shortage of flowers, the singing was excellent, and the congregations were large, especially the eleven o'clock at Loders, which was packed tight. The Jehovah's Witnesses of Bridport chose Easter morning to do a blitz on the householders of Loders and Uploders. As the Vicar drove up to Loders Church from Askerswell, he chuckled to see a Witness tackling the landlord of the Loders Arms, on the latter's doorstep. The Witness could not have found a tougher defender of Church and State in all Loders.

May 1958

Saturday August 2nd

The sun has been quixotic this summer, but we are looking to him to shine down on Loders Court on fête day. The fête has become a kind of family reunion of Loders people, and we are fortunate in being able still to have it in the pleasant grounds of the manor, which has been for centuries the focal point of the social life of the village. We recollect being told last year that the fête brought together on that occasion some thirty scattered members of one particular family, who greatly enjoyed their get-together in the setting of their childhood. It is not easy to devise something new in the entertainment line year after year, but at least the fête committee have succeeded in producing variations on the old theme. Our faithful standby, Mr. Bernard Gale, has devised a woodland ballet which we have not seen before, and our friends in the Women's Institute have kindly promised their pageant of hair-styles from the cradle to the grave – a pure delight hitherto enjoyed by ladies only. For children of all ages there is a fancy dress competition of what they would like to be, real or imaginary, comic or serious. For the handy people (whom we have in plenty in this neighbourhood) there will be a chance to display new things that they have made out of old (within the bounds of decorum, of course). For gardeners there is something easier than growing fine vegetables and flowers – a competition for the biggest weed grown in a garden. Such has been the season, violent rain alternating with violent heat, that the eternal battle with the jungle has inclined to the jungle this year, and it would not surprise us if both Vicar and Squire were keeping their eye on some exotic plant with which they hope to achieve a walkover in this competition. The really new item in the afternoon's entertainment is a 'Bedstead Relay' for ladies and gentlemen, married or unmarried. The committee were somewhat exercised as to whether this was entirely proper to a church fête, but other fêtes have put it on without repercussions in the Lord Chamberlain's Office. It should be THE laughter-maker of the afternoon.

August 1958

Home delivery

Congratulations to Mr. and Mrs. Francis, of Yondover, on the birth of their first child, a daughter. Before her marriage Mrs. Francis was a sister at Bridport Hospital. Her preference for home for this important event rather shews that informed opinion regards hospital as a mere runner-up.

November 1958

Confirmation

The Lord Bishop of Sherborne [John Key] will take the Confirmation service at Loders Church on Sunday, Oct. 18th, at 3 p.m. As the number of candidates is large, and confirmations in these parishes are comparatively few and far between, we advise the godparents, parents and friends of the candidates to come early. The Bishop would like to meet them, and the candidates, on the vicarage lawn after service. Here it may be explained, for the benefit of those who do not know, that in this service the candidates, standing before the Bishop as Jesus Christ's representative, confirm with their own lips what their godparents did in enlisting them as Christ's soldiers, and receive his blessing.

In the good old days of the eighteenth century, according to the churchwardens' accounts, the cost of entertaining 'ye lorde Bishoppe when he did take ye Confirmacione' fell on the parish, and embraced several 'pottles of Canary'.

October 1959

A bit thick

Dorset County Council have increased the charge for light and heat to non-charitable bodies using school premises to £2 per time. At their last meeting the managers of Askerswell School considered this unreasonable and unsympathetic, and asked the Voluntary Schools Association to take it up with the Local Education Authority. Nobody, if they tried their hardest, could burn two pounds worth of coke and electricity in three hours in Askerswell School. And a surcharge of two pounds, coming on top of the hire of the school premises, would be the end of the village whist drive, which, as things are already, does not easily pay its way. If this sort of thing were not a threat to village social life, it would be amusing to note how the bureaucrats spend a million without turning a hair, and shudder over a pound.

October 1959

The Authorized Version

The Sunday School Mission Sale was a great success, and for once was blest with reasonable weather. Proceedings began with a most impressive nativity play, produced by the day school mistress, Mrs. Scott. The children were word-perfect, and reverent, in passages of the Authorized Version Bible (which, by the way, was infinitely preferable to the fashionable modern playlets), and the singing revealed a reserve of future talent for the church choir.

January 1960

Strength in weakness

Dottery Church has suffered a grievous loss by the death of one of its most faithful members, Mrs. Annie Hopkins, of Pymore. Yet the sense of loss is tempered by pride in the magnificent way in which she contrived to live for ten years with a major disease. She carried on with her work at the mill, the running of her home, her few simple pleasures, and her church, as if she had no worries, and wherever she saw the need of a helping hand she offered hers. To the Vicar, and possibly to some of her many friends, she was a living commentary on the text, 'My strength is made perfect in weakness.'

February 1960

Conscience money

A tall stranger came into Loders Church and put two sixpences in the guide book box. He did not take a book. He told the verger it was the price of two guides he had taken earlier in the week and forgotten to pay for. He had made a special journey, to clear his conscience. Good to know that some tender consciences survive the present moral climate!

March 1960

The cost of living

An ambulance was parked outside Loders School when parishioners trooped into the school for the Easter Vestry. This was pure coincidence, and not a precaution against a rowdy meeting (the ambulance driver, Mr. Herbert, happens to live opposite). Yet the ambulance outside the vestry meeting could well be a portent, if the cost of running a church – which is the vestry's main business – keeps rising. Everybody knows the cost of living, and of running a home, but few people realise, when they look at a peaceful country church, that that too is bedevilled by a cost of living.

May 1960

Whitsuntide

Ascension Day saw practically all the young people of Loders who were confirmed last year at the communion service. They went on to school fortified by breakfast at the Vicarage, and recognising, we hope, that the Ascension, though not a public holiday, is the third great festival in the Church's year. Which is a reminder that the fourth and last of the great festivals, Whitsuntide, is upon us. She is distinguished by a public holiday, but remains a cinderella of religious observance, which is all wrong, seeing that Whitsun is the birthday anniversary of the Christian Church.

June 1960

The United Nations

We contributed £40.7.8d to the Christian Aid Week for Refugees. Our church collections were £32. 6s. (Loders £25. 14s. 6d., Dottery £3, Askerswell £3. 11s. 6d.), and the house-to-house collections £8.1s.8d. (Loders £4. 9s. 5d., Dottery £2. 13s. 6d., Askerswell 18s. 9d.). One feels about the refugees that private charity is left to play the Good Samaritan while Governments, whose misdeeds made refugees of these poor people, pass by on the other side. Nothing shews up so well the impotence of the United Nations, for they have not the unity nor the will to do anything really effective, even in a humanitarian cause to which all nations do lip-service.

June 1960

A bottle in the smoke

Some divine is on record as having said that the true nature of a parsonage is to be the public house *par excellence* of the parish. Loders Vicarage would have qualified for his approval in June, when it was so public that its regular inmates would have remained unsurprised at meeting anybody on earth within its venerable precincts. On Whit Tuesday the lawn was edged around with adoring young mothers, watching the multitudinous toddlers of the parish at their Whitsun frolic. Mothers and children loved to have an unorganised couple of hours of play, tea and buns, and the mothers a good old gossip. They warmly thanked Mrs. Willmott for renewing the annual opportunity. The second publicanising of the vicarage was after the Mothers' Union Deanery Festival Service in Loders Church, when well over two hundred members of that venerable institution took possession of the lawn for tea, our own M.U., whose function it was to prepare the tea, having been embattled in the kitchen and the dining-room from ten o'clock that morning. Bravo for the Mothers' Union! thought a mere man, as he peeped through the kitchen window and saw so many women milling round the sink, where the nice women know they belong. What would have happened had the unfriendly-looking sky translated looks into action we were saved from trying to picture, for the rain kept off, the tea was up to the best Loders reputation, and the members boarded their buses feeling that their journey had been worthwhile. Not so the Vicar of Toller. He had been the only man among all those women for most of the tea. He said that when next he recited in the psalm, 'I am become like a bottle in the smoke,' he would know what it meant.

June 1960

Early to bed

Children, unlike adults, are not given to burning the candle at both ends. If they do not get the proper amount of sleep by night, they take it, or rather it takes them, by day, which means in lesson time. Bright morning faces are now a thing of the pre-television past. The teachers at our two schools find themselves confronted by yawns, gapes, a stretching of arms, and an atmosphere of hangover. A question round the class elicits a time of going to bed which would make any responsible parent squirm. One tot of eight confessed that she went to bed between ten and eleven, and wondered what was strange about that. We are sure that all our parents want their children to get on at school, but how can they if they only go there to sleep? Parents who allow such late hours are unfair to the children, to the teachers, and to the taxpayer.

August 1961

Sunday duty

The Clough family, who, though living at Salwayash were very often at church at Dottery, have moved to Chideock. They were a fine example of parents and children doing their Sunday duty together, and will be missed.

November 1961

Ash Wednesday

Lent begins on March 7th, Ash Wednesday. Like New Year's Day, Ash Wednesday is a time for good resolutions. You could not make a better one than to keep the Fourth Commandment, and join in the worship of God, in His house, every Sunday.

March 1962

Looking back

This month, space allows us to quote from the Loders Magazine of December, 1881, kindly loaned by Miss Madge Marsh. The Vicar, Dr. Edersheim, writes: 'We have been able to provide a church for a part of our parishioners whose distance from the parish church had in great measure deprived them of its ordinances. Ever since my institution I had endeavoured to provide a service for our friends at Pymore and Dottery. They have shewn their full appreciation of this by their regular attendance. At last this attendance had outgrown the capacities of any cottage, and it became necessary to think of erecting an iron church. I laid it down as a principle that, if possible, this should be done exclusively by the landowners, farmers, and inhabitants of Dottery and Pymore, and that I should try to enlist in it every landowner, farmer and family in the district, so that this church might be truly their own. I am deeply thankful we have succeeded, by the blessing of God. I must here express my warmest thanks, to the landowners, farmers and all the families in the district, whose liberality, according to their means, has been very great, and has enabled me to provide the handsome iron church, called St. Saviour's Mission Church, where I hope for generations to come the Gospel will be preached and the ordinances of our Church administered to the people of the district.' The building of the Church was begun in November 1881, and finished at the end of January, 1882. It was consecrated on Saturday, Feb. 4th, 1882 [p. 109, illustration].

March 1962

Weddings

There were two at Loders in March. The brides were very beautiful, but apprehensive when they heard of snow all over the rest of the country that their weddings might be too white. They were spared the snow, the east wind eased, and the sun beamed on them as they processed to and from the church to the pealing of the bells. The congregation of each occasion was large, and it was a pleasure to have them taking their part in the service reverently (alas, so often at big weddings the atmosphere is more akin to Saturday night music hall than church).

April 1962

Fêtes

Giving to the fête is nothing like the mental agony of choosing a wedding present. There is no limit to what may be given – anything eatable, anything drinkable, anything wearable, anything useful in the home or nursery, and cash from them who prefer the easiest way. Above all, let nobody confuse the words 'give' and 'discard'. Getting rid of something that is no use to you or anybody else is not giving. A member of Loders Choir, just back from a holiday in Eire, was in a parish where the church fête made nearly £500. The cake stall alone took

£51. The almost incredible thing about this fête was that it had been organised by a country church consisting of eighteen families! These people understand the meaning of giving. The test of giving is that it hurts.

August 1962

Early birds

When the Vicar went down to Loders Church shortly after eight the other morning he found Reggie Drake and his sister Sheila, whose family left Loders ten years ago, showing a party round. They had called at Loders en route from Portsmouth, to Charmouth. Reggie is now a grown man, and had his fiancée with him. Sheila is married, and had her husband and son with her. When the Vicar last saw them they were Sunday School children. Before they left the church of their childhood, the party knelt down of their own accord, which rather shows that Sunday Schools achieve more than is always apparent.

August 1962

Growing popularity

A recent newspaper article contends that Mothering Sunday has now become the third most popular festival, Christmas being first, and Easter second. The observance of Mothering Sunday originated by Mother Church, but commercial interests have done more than Mother Church to raise it to its present eminence. The newspaper article said that the makers of greeting cards hoped to sell twenty nine million Mothering cards this year, and that Mothering Sunday is now a considerable item in the calculations of chocolate and cosmetic manufacturers, and also of florists. The commercialisation of the Christian festivals is often bemoaned, but is it really the evil that it is made out to be? On Mothering Sunday Dottery Church was pleasingly full of mothers, children, and grown-up children who had come home for the day. One large family had even got father there. The vicar was agreeably surprised, and a little conscience-stricken by the thought that Woolworths had done all the advertising. At Loders the advertising is not all left to Woolworths. It has long been the custom to send out notes beforehand, inviting the mothers. This year there was nearly a hundred-percent response, and a splendid service. But the nice Uploders father who eschewed his Sunday nap to drive to church a load of children could not screw up enough courage to go in. He sat outside enveloped in the Sunday newspaper – whether a respectable one we could not see. As the Sunday arrangements at Askerswell did not allow of a Mothering service in church, Miss Grigg held one in school on the Friday before, which the mothers say they greatly enjoyed.

April 1963

Taking the initiative

When something for the public weal needs doing, some people's reaction is 'to bring it up' at a public meeting; others' is to do something about it themselves. We like those people better whose disposition is to do something rather than 'bring it up'. Church seats, for example, are hard to sit on. We admire the do-it-yourself type who says nothing, but comes to worship armed with cushion as well as prayer book. We admire still more the person who upholsters the entire pew, *pro bono publico*. But the truly devout use their knees as well as their seats in the divine service, and these are ill catered for in Loders Church. Mrs. Doris Rudd (with perhaps the example of the Askerswell ladies in mind) asked if she might do something about it, and was swiftly given permission by one who knows the virtue of striking while the iron's hot. The outcome is the appearance on your editor's desk of a charming little paragraph for insertion in this month's *Notes*:- 'General and Mrs. Rome invite anyone interested to a coffee morning at Uploders Place on Thursday, Jan. 9th, 1964, from 10.40 a.m. onwards, to inaugurate a scheme for making hassocks for Loders Church. Coffee & Biscuits 2s. Bring and Buy Stall. Footnote – I don't know whether you think 2s. too much for coffee – perhaps you need not say a price.'

January 1964

Getting to church before time

Sean and Melvin Skipp are to be congratulated on clocking in at Sunday School on their first Sunday in Loders. It is nice these days to find new arrivals getting to church before church, in the shape of the vicar, gets to them. After all, the obligation is on both parties.

February 1964

Inter-church aid

Mr. John Shoobridge writes to tell us that Inter-Church Aid Week will be from the 25th–30th May, and asking for volunteers to sell flags in Askerswell, Loders and Dottery. The work of Inter-Church Aid is to help feed the millions who are short of food, and to equip them to grow their own. It is high time Inter-church Aid changed their name. Unlike 'Oxfam', the name gives no clue to the work of the movement. Inter-Church Aid could just as well mean an effort among churches to go to each other's rescue.

April 1964

Inter-parish aid

It is the recognised form for Dorset country parishes to maintain an outward show of contempt for each other, but they are not such bad neighbours at heart. We have sympathised with our neighbour, the Vicar of Bradpole, in his long and exacting illness, with his wife for the noble way in which she kept the wheels turning, and with the Bradpole congregation for rising to a difficult occasion. Mr. Gibb is now back on light duty, and we hope his health will continue to improve. The Loders vicar was deeply touched to receive from the Bradpole congregation not only a nice letter of thanks for the help he had been able to give, but a handsome book-token which rather defeated his aim of saving them expense.

June 1964

Christ's badge

Spring cleaning ought not to be necessary in a well ordered house. That's what one husband at least tells his wife when the annual urge to turn him inside out comes upon her. But the subconscious reasoning that lies behind spring cleaning has a religious significance. The good housewife looks at her home, and measures what it is against what it ought to be. Then she gets out her dustpan and paintpot, and brings the actual up to the ideal, as much as in her lies. There you have the meaning of the Church's season of Lent, which is now upon us. Everybody has an ideal of himself, which he is always tending to make actual (some people's ideal is quite obvious, as that post office engineer knows who was 'carpited' for driving the van with a blonde beside him, and the blonde turned out to be his mother with hair a foot long). One of the reasons why Jesus Christ came to this earth was to give us the ideal of human nature which alone can bring well-being and happiness. He is the model: Lent is the time to measure ourself by Him. Not many youngsters will flock to where He is to be found, nor scream with ecstasy, for His badge is not a hair style but a cross.

March 1965

The time of Sunday school

We are sorry that the normal time for Loders Sunday School has to be the rather inconvenient one of 2 p.m. As long as the Vicar & Mrs. Willmott have to take it, with Juliet playing, there is no alternative because of the other services which have to be fitted in. We hope those good mothers who find this time in conflict with Sunday dinners will do what they can to help. Most of them promised solemnly at their children's baptism that they should be brought up in the faith of the church, and Sunday School is usually the only means by which this solemn promise is fulfilled.

March 1965

Askerswell school

The tussle with the Department of Education and Science languished for many weeks simply because the Department did not answer letters. Then the battle chose the eve of the Vicar's departure to Kuwait to flare up with the Diocesan Board of Education, the Diocesan Board of Finance and the Archdeacon of Sherborne joining the fray. They thought they had us on toast and are finding they haven't. Mr. William Harrison's legal knowledge has been of great assistance.

September 1965

Grave business

Unexpected incidents are no strangers to services in Dottery church [p. 109, illustration], as the faithful well know. On the fifth Sunday after Trinity the Vicar was preaching on St. Peter's admonition to be courteous. As so often happens at Dottery, people chose the one hour in the week when there is a service to come and tend a grave. The church windows are clear glass, at eye level, and activity in the churchyard at service time is bound to distract the congregation. On this occasion, not only was there drawing of water from the butt adjacent to the pulpit, but a noisy conversation between ladies well aware that a service was in progress. (They had done this kind of thing before and been asked to avoid service time.) As if this were not distraction enough on the preacher's left hand, another group of people under the churchyard hedge on his right began to hold forth in loud voices, with no consideration for the church. It became clear that the homily on courtesy was needed more without than within, so he left the pulpit and went out. It was hardly necessary for him to say anything. A nice man among those under the hedge said he was sorry. The tongues of the others were paralysed by the mere sight of a surpliced preacher bearing down on them and there was great calm. It doesn't seem as widely known as it should be that disturbing a church service is not only a matter of courtesy: it is against the law of the land.

August 1965

Unsuspected talent

A vicar faced with the task of organising a social would not normally think of entrusting the job to his Mothers' Union, whose public image as staid supporters of the sanctity of marriage does not readily link up with frolics. But since January 14th one vicar, at any rate, would not hesitate; for the social put on by Loders Mothers' Union in aid of the Hut improvement fund was one of the best anybody could remember. And that is the opinion, not of this journal only, but of the 120 folks who braved the winter's cold to get their 3s. 6d. worth and vowed that what they had was worth 10s. On entering the Hut their eye was caught immediately by the magnificent spread of the buffet supper, whose centre-piece was a jorum of fresh-fruit salad and farmhouse cream. How that banquet, plus sherry, ale and cider, could be served up for 3s. 6d. and yet make a profit of £40 for the Hut, only the M.U. knows. As a religious publication we must not wax too lyrical about the flesh pots, so we pass on to the entertainment. A group of young instrumentalists who call themselves 'The Vicarage Five' led off with light music. Our organist played for games and dancing, proving that he could cope as well with the secular as the sacred, and those saints, the Askerswell Young Farmers, put on their rustic – and most enjoyable – play for the nth time in a good cause.

February 1966

The clamant need of religion

Lent begins on Ash Wednesday, February 24th. The services for that day will be found in the timetable below. Lent commemorates the time of prayer and planning spent by our Lord in the wilderness before he began his ministry. The Church has always kept it as a season of prayer, self-sacrifice and renewed study of God's will, as given in the Bible. In our parishes we never seem to rise to the Lent observances that other parishes impose upon themselves. It may be that our people have no problems in religion that they would like resolved. If so, blessed are they. It does not further the cause of religion to create difficulties and doubts where none existed. The clamant need of religion is to be lived out rather than talked about.

February 1966

Leaving Easter to the moon

As Easter draws near, church decorators usually find themselves asking whether there will be enough flowers out for church. This year daffodils and primroses have been brought on quickly by the mild weather and the question being asked is whether there will be any left for Easter. The fixing of the date of Easter might make life easier for educational establishments and seaside landladies, but, the English climate being what it is, would not guarantee a sunny Easter and abundance of flowers. It looks likely that Easter may be fixed before long. Even the Roman Catholic Church is now agreeable to this. But we 'squares' are not enthusiastic. Easter as at present regulated is the only festival whose timing coincides with the event it commemorates. Christmas is only Our Lord's official birthday. The actual date, in common with the birthdays of other great men of antiquity, is unknown. But for upwards of two thousand years Easter has been determined by the moon. We know that the paschal moon looked down on the agony among the olive trees in Gethsemane. The paschal moon shone on the sepulchre that first Easter morning when the crucified Christ became gloriously alive. A pity that the age old link between Easter and the moon should be broken. Must everything always be subordinated to commercial and secular interests?

April 1966

Religion – a family affair

Askerswell is sorry to lose Mr. and Mrs. Walsh and family, who stayed at Church Farm in the winter, and are now returned to their home in Gloucestershire. Mr. Walsh is a fairly rare bird, a combination of atomic scientist and lay reader. He preached at evensong during the winter, and gave us much food for thought. At communion he and his wife used to bring their two little boys with them to the altar rail. This is the custom in some churches. If from an early age it gets infants used to the communion service, and impresses on them that religion is essentially a family affair, then the custom is surely a good one, and to be copied.

April 1966

The modern way of life

Outings, like other old institutions, are finding it hard to survive in the modern way of life, but that of Loders' Sunday School is an exception. It always attracts a good following. This year the coach set off with forty-five souls aboard. Previous to that, Mrs. Christine Newberry, Mrs. Gladys Newberry and Mrs. Willmott had gone collecting, not minding that they were in the wake of the Fête. They had been kindly received and had been given £16. 12s. (some of which will go to Christmas prizes). The weather was perfect but the boat which was to have taken them down the river from Wareham to Poole was anything but perfect and the obliging coach took them to Swanage instead, where the sea enticed the most unlikely matrons of the party into swim-suits. At Dorchester, on the way home, they found a fish-and-chip shop that didn't keep them waiting and so got to bed tired, but completely satisfied. The children wish to thank all the kind subscribers and the three brave collectors.

September 1966

'Forgive us our Christmasses.'

A teacher in a Sunday School in London got this instead of 'Forgive us our trespasses' when she asked her children to write out the Lord's Prayer. An inspired mistake on the child's part; for the Christmases need forgiving which are all feasting and present-giving and leave out of the picture Him whose birthday it is. To make sure that they keep Christmas properly, the children of Askerswell are coming to church at ten on Christmas morning and singing, 'Happy birthday to you' before the Communion service begins. At Loders the children – and we hope, parents – will come at eleven. They will sing carols at the tree on the chancel step, in place of a sermon, and doubtless they will go back to their pews clutching the packet of sweets put on the tree by the Mothers' Union. The first service of Christmas in Loders will be what is now called 'The Midnight' at twelve on Christmas Eve. The hold this has on our people was demonstrated last year, when wind and icy rain were doing their worst, and yet the church was full. Dottery need little reminding that their Christmas Day service has to be earlier than usual – at nine.

December 1966

The late Mr. Gilbert Miller

We recently recorded a donation from Mr. Miller to Loders Church roof fund, not suspecting that we should soon be recording his sudden death, or that he who seemed so young in mind had reached the ripe age of seventy-seven. The Marshwood Vale where he and his widow had spent most of their married life, was his first love, but he generated quite a love for Loders in his two and a half years here. The Vicar remembers with gratitude the hours he worked for nothing in the churchyard, and the further hours he spent in licking the glebe into shape. But he will best be remembered because his daily life was a fine advertisement for daily prayer, daily Bible reading, and regular Sunday worship. We feel deeply for Mrs. Miller in this time of adjustment. But this is where the doctrine of the communion of saints is a comfort.

May 1967

Comment

Mr. Wilfred Crabb's belief that tithe goes to the Church Commissioners is mistaken. Tithe was nationalised thirty years ago, in 1936. Like railway fares and electricity charges, it goes to the Government. It is to be hoped the Council will not delay a decision too long, for grass grows, the men have to be paid and the congregation refuse to be saddled with the entire upkeep of a public utility. After all, they are few in number, and they already pay the running expenses of the Church. If they (and several of them are not Loders people) are ready to pay half the cost of the churchyard, cannot the Council give in to the Parish Assembly? Who would guess from all the palaver that the parish are only being asked to pay an average of a penny-farthing per household per week, and for the care of their own dead!

May 1967

Post script

A patient – a widow – in Bridport Hospital has just told me that her late husband is buried in Yeovil municipal cemetery. It cost her £11 to open the ground and she gets a bill of £2 each year towards cemetery expenses which she gladly pays. How trifling by comparison is the penny-farthing per household per week from the rate that we are asking!

June 1967

Remembrance Day

The big parade service in Bridport inevitably robs us of some of our congregation, but all our three services were well attended. We sent £28. 3s. to Earl Haig's Fund, which is still working to mitigate some of the evil consequences of the two wars, and we were pleased to be congratulated by the local organiser of the Fund on having sent more even than the Bridport parade.

December 1967

Christmas arrangements

The cold and frequently fog-bound days of December are to many people pleasanter than the physically more attractive days of spring because they lead up to Christmas. Turkey and plum pudding taste better in the dead of English winter than they do in the tropics. In the joy of feasting and family re-union let us not miss the target of the operation, to celebrate the shining forth of God's light in the darkness of men's souls. Our Christmas programme will follow the usual lines. First, a fusillade of carols.

December 1967

Lent

Lent comes again! The springtime of the soul
When heavy soil of sin must all be ploughed,
The seed cast in, and rain of tears
With sunshine of new faith and hope to ripen it
Against the harvest time.

March 1968

A thought for life

About 70% of the electors voted, which is very high for a local government election and equal to a general election. It had an energising effect on the sick of the parish. Mr. Charlie Gale and Mr. George Randall rose up from their couches to vote and Mrs. Frank Gill forsook her wheeled chair. The oldest inhabitant, Mrs. Beatrice Clark, now in her ninetieth year, came from Uploders with the roses of June already in her cheeks and with the express intent of voting for Mr. Wilfred Crabb 'because he is a very nice man,' and for the Vicar, 'because he ain't all that bad'.

June 1968

A brief biography

Oliver Leonard Willmott was born in 1910 in Frome, Somerset, and educated there. He took a great interest in the parish church, St. John's, becoming a server and also taking up his lifetime interest in bellringing. At first a career in journalism seemed ahead of him as he started working for the *Somerset Standard*, but he changed course and spent seven years in the Anglican monastery of Kelham. Again he changed course, tempering the strict high church training of Kelham, cut off from the world, with two further years' training at the Bristol Church Missionary Society. There his ministry was on the streets of Bristol, and in contact with missionary work across the world. After ordination as an Anglican priest at Exeter Cathedral he became curate of Totnes, briefly. But war broke out, and he became an Army Chaplain. At first he was posted to Northern Ireland. Soon after, he was put in charge of the chapel of the Duke of York's Military School at Dover, and then of the chapel of Dover Castle, where services continued despite heavy shelling as our forces invaded France. At that time he was Chaplain at Fort Darland, the Army's toughest prison.

All of this was before he 'retired to the country' to look after the souls of his flock of 1,100 villagers, from squire to humble widow. He was much more than a vicar: he was a countryman, and a person who helped create a special sense of community in the post-war years. He ran a small-holding with pigs, turkeys, geese, hens and a cow to support his wife and family of seven children. He chopped trees for his Tudor fireplace which had attracted him to the place first of all. He mowed the churchyard, assisted by his faithful wife. He held forth at early sessions in the local hostelries – the Marquis of Lorne and the Crown Inn, Uploders. He visited the sick, and collected tirelessly for the yearly Fête which earned huge sums for the maintenance of the church fabric – he saw this as a mission in itself. But he kept in contact with the outside world by talking to all newcomers, while scanning *The Times* and *The Daily Telegraph* voraciously to keep up with national and international events. He listened to, and later watched the News, five or six times a day.

The Parish Notes, which he wrote monthly for thirty-four years record local news of church, parish and locality in meticulous detail, but they are much more than a chronicle: they are a testimony to his Christian practice, to his deep theological convictions, to his Anglicanism based on a firm belief in practised ecumenicalism – 'Unity without union', he preached; to his love of all people (apart from a few opponents, with whom he was fair, but ruthless); to his love of flowers, beasts and birds; and above all to his deep rootedness in the quietessentially English life of 'the little hills of Dorset'.

CHAPTER 2

Country calendar

It is highly unlikely that any other one person has written so many words about such riveting country topics as jumble sales, the job of churchwarden, the weather, the position of tombstones, and the christenings, weddings and funerals of literally hundreds of country people. But the yearly round was always a novelty. This chapter has been designed to give a flavour of how a reader would have the ordinary and the extraordinary reported regularly with subtle changes each year. The whole adds up to a rustic symphony of the year.

Instead of following the years from 1953–1968 as in other chapters I have followed the seasonal entries month by month taken from the most memorable entries over the period. With a journalist's eye for the novel, if not the sensational, the Vicar worked hard on the mundane and repetitious. Claims could be made for his weather coverage, though he himself started from the point of view that 'the weather … is normally a topic of conversation when one has nothing else to dwell on'. (p. 54) He referred all his observations, anonymously, to 'The Clerk of the Weather'.

As well as celebrating present customs, the Vicar devoted a lot of space to highlighting past traditions, good and bad. The

Shrove Tuesday 'threshing the hen' (p. 51) is a stark reminder of how cruel some country pastimes can be. If there wasn't a tradition, he with the help of the-opening-time-at-The Crown-team manufactured one. These traditions are given prominence in Chapter Seven – 'Ring out the old, ring in the new'. He drip-fed history into the present. An odd quotation from his wide range of antiquarian books was always to hand. Dr. Edersheim's writings enriched the sparse present of Dottery. Dr. Edersheim was Vicar of Loders from 1876–1873. He had Dottery Church built (pp. 31–32; illustration p. 109) as a missionary church. He also wrote a once yearly magazine. The Askerswell Log Book added to any current study of the school and parish hall. Although he was entangled in the day-by-day of the village, he was the glue by which the former inhabitants were stuck to the present. Perhaps he was one means by which future residents could continue the traditions, though he wasn't one to look to the future. He lived unto the day, with his eye on yesterday.

Pastoral admonitions and homilies stand side by side with rumbustious anecdotes: there is a thin dividing line between the sacred, the secular and even the profane as the months unfold. The Cup Final stands alongside Easter Day in 'An inspired answer' (p. 228).

Topics that might in other hands have been burdened with pious platitudes (p. 59, 'The transporting of the Evangelists') are spiced with an outlandish humour:

'Mr. Hyde-Parker, the evangelist … 76 … would as soon be without his car as Dick Turpin without Black Bess.'

He manages to make annual events enticing, even if they are unutterably mundane. Thus, the Easter Vestry of the church – its business meeting – is claimed to be 'nearly as interesting as the financial status of the people next door'. The rites of passage – christenings, confirmations, weddings and funerals – are sprinkled throughout the seasons. Occasionally there is a tired sense of the inevitability of such things (p. 240, 'The Black Angel has been at work this month'). Usually, there is a fresh way of describing the diurnal which links the natural world of Dorset with the human activities played out upon the landscape. Lambing is a counterpart of spring babies (p. 58) as autumn for swallows is like humans moving house.

Counter-balancing this tendency to embellish the routine is a boyish thrill at being able to record the most recent escapades at the eternal jumble-sales. Other significant moments like 21st birthdays or ruby weddings or 'being admitted to the noble army of grand-parents' (p. 66, Replenishing the earth) were given special prominence. The Vicar recorded very sensitively for those in sickness and in health.

Loders Fête in August and its reportage in the *Parish Notes* could be the subject of a separate book. I have been forced to exclude hundreds of words. I have concentrated on those which exude the sense of one big happy family having fun, old boys and girls and new side-by-side, and non-churchgoers and staunch congregation rubbing shoulders with visitors from the camp-sites. August is the silly season in journalism, and the *Parish Notes* are no exception. The Choir goes mackerel-fishing, and the Hut is invaded by Hawaiian dancers. There is a dearth of saints' days in August. Most spiritual inspiration at this time seems to come from inclusions in the Visitors' Book.

As the year closes in and we approach Christmas parties and carols and mince-pies, the enmeshment of the sacred and secular intensifies. All Saints' Day is caught up in Hallowe'en and Guy Fawkes. The Agricultural Discussion Club (p. 86, The Disgustion Club) vies with Lectures on Shakespeare for evening entertainment. Whilst the parish is exhorted to make items for the December Mission Sale, the children prepare to 'do a Nativity Play'. Remembrance Sunday was firmly implanted in the gloom and wildness of wet November days. It balanced the glorious autumnal gold of Harvest and made way for the numinous candlelight of the Christmas Midnight Communion.

It is difficult to know whether there was any particular element of English country life that the Vicar deliberately omitted. If so, it was that he just hadn't noticed, or no-one had told him. He knew very well what he knew, and quite well what he didn't, and kept quiet about that. He had the rhythm of the year. He had his eyes, his ears (though complaining of deafness on convenient occasions) and his wits about him.

With his commentary, you can feel the days passing from week to week, month to month and season to season. The village year was an intricate web of the religious, the agricultural, the social and the fiscal, with Nature always playing a dominant part. Voices off were the Rural District Council, the

Archdeacon, the present Government, the powers that be – but they were a long way off. The Clerk of the Weather held higher office in his scheme of things than the Prime Minister.

'Work' and 'labour' seldom appear because they assumed a natural place in life rather than being the antithesis of 'leisure'. The portrait of Mrs. Harry Legg making nets is a reminder that farmers had to farm, ditches had to be ditched, and hedges cut. Home-made wine and outsize carrots were as much 'work' as that which produced a wage packet. The Fête was hard work for all.

Mrs. Harry Legg

Lucky children

It is to be hoped that our children appreciate all that grown-ups do for them in the way of parties, and that they realise how much more petted they are than their parents were. It is also to be hoped that this appreciation may find expression in their becoming devoted and dutiful children. Grown-ups could not do more to make the children happy than ours do. Askerswell children have had two more parties since Christmas. The first was that organised by the Community Club, who gave them a sumptuous tea, followed by games and a film show operated by Mr. Barker. The second was the Cubs' and Brownies' party given by Miss Edwards (Brown Owl) with the help of Mrs. Barker. Eighteen Cubs and Brownies managed not only to get into Brown Owl's cottage, but to have there a delightfully rampageous afternoon of games and home-made pantomime, culminating in a tea, which a Cub told his mother afterwards was 'terrific'. The centre of interest at this tea was an iced cake in the form of a maypole, with jelly babies holding on to the ribbons. It had been made and given by Mrs. Adams. An unusual and most diverting feature of the afternoon was that the Shah of Persia and Old Mother Riley happened to call on Brown Owl. By a coincidence which turned out to be entirely happy, they arrived together, and departed intact, but minus the sweets and toys with which, by another coincidence, they happened to be rather flush. Brown Owl's ceiling successfully withstood the three cheers which brought the party to an end. For Loders children there was the party at Loders Court, instituted by Sir Edward and Lady Le Breton more years ago than we care to be reminded of, and firmly rooted in the affections of several generations of Loders schoolchildren. This party made its usual beginning with a conjuring show in the billiard room, but did not proceed as usual to Punch and Judy in view of the effect it was feared Punch's growing addiction to wife-beating might have on the potential husbands in the audience. The children were shewn George and the Dragon instead, and then adjourned to the great dining-room, which, in its party dress, might have been a fairy palace. An odd plate of bread and butter here and there was a sign that rationing had ended, but the guests fell to work at once on the mountains of meringues, and failed to demolish them all. Maurice Matterface, looking none the worse for his recent parting with his appendix, called for cheers for host and hostess, and the guests, on leaving, were presented with oranges, apples and half-crowns by Master Edward Laskey. Outside, a coach was waiting to take the distant ones home.

February 1955

Untraditional Christmas

A journalist writing a week before Christmas alleged that the snow and the icicles beloved of Christmas cards are not typical of the English scene, and that the English Christmas is much more often wet than snowy. History has proved him a true prophet of this Christmas. Not only was there a superfluity of rain; there was also a tempestuous wind which caused wet patches on the ceilings of supposedly weatherproof houses, and brought out the buckets in houses whose sponginess was well known. From Loders glebe, the mill stream and the River Asker could be seen in flood together – a rare spectacle – and in lanes with steep banks there were many landslips. Between them, the wind and the rain discovered all the weak spots in Askerswell Church. Enough rain got through the leads of the east window to soak the altar. At Dottery, which is still in the builder's hands, the congregation sat up when they heard Mr. George Gale tell the Vicar, in a colossal whisper, 'to mind the bath in the vestry'. The adverse effect which this weather was expected to have on congregations did not materialise. The crowd at the Loders midnight service was not quite as big as usual, but there were more at the eight o'clock service. The howling gale seemed to keep nobody away from matins, and it was a large flock of children that sang carols to their seniors from the chancel, and received chocolates put on the Christmas tree by the Mothers' Union. At Askerswell and Dottery, both of whose churches are much exposed to the elements, parishioners brought friends staying with them for Christmas, along the rain-swept roads to service, and service seemed the cosier because of the storm outside. The number of communicants again approached the 200 mark.

January 1957

Baby news

Mrs. Herbert, of Loders, proudly presented her husband and two small daughters with a baby boy for Christmas. She arranged things well, for she expected to be in hospital over Christmas, whereas she was at home, and with the boy on which all the family had set their hearts. The infant daughter of Mr. and Mrs. John Marsh, of Dottery, was christened Annette Bridget on the Sunday after Christmas. It will never be said of her that she let the family down by not 'crying out the devil'.

January 1957

Reaching into the stratosphere

Those who do not read the 'agony' columns of the *Daily Telegraph* were for the most part unaware that Mr. and Mrs. Whittle, of Loders, were celebrating their diamond wedding on December 17th. Mr. and Mrs. Whittle counted themselves lucky in being spared for this great event, for shortly before it Mr. Whittle, whose age is reaching into the stratosphere, had a nasty fall. However, he recovered in time to enjoy the anniversary and the company of his family.

January 1959

Where to live

In 1963 nobody died in Loders and there was no funeral. The winter of 1963 was the worst of the century. Rather a remarkable combination of facts! There was only one other year in this century in which nobody in Loders died, and that was 1911. The Askerswell register might produce many more instances of funeral-free years; there are many years in which Askerswell had no marriages – but curiously few in which it had no christenings. By way of contrast, Dottery is prolific in funerals for a place of its size. We trust that this information will not cause an exodus of the maturer ladies who are pillars of the church there.

January 1964

Brown Owl

The junior population of Askerswell, in the rôle of Cubs, Guides and Brownies, were given their annual party in the notably elastic cottage of their beloved Brown Owl, alias The Captain, alias Miss Edwards, and it is almost superfluous to say that a great time was had by all, especially in the tracing of presents on the ends of a network of threads which went all over the house. A handsome cake, made by Mrs. Adams, was the centrepiece of each of the two tea-tables, and the company rewarded Mrs. Barker and Miss Pam Fry with an impromptu play for doing the washing up. One of the Brownies summed it all up at the end thus:- 'Whatever we should do without Brown Owl I just don't know'.

February 1956

Shrove Tuesday

Thank goodness the almost universal English custom of 'threshing the hen' on Shrove Tuesday is quite dead. On Shrove Tuesday any hen that had not laid was liable to be chased round the farmyard by the men, blind-folded, with cudgels, and the one to kill her got her for his dinner. If the hens were all laying, then a cock would be the object of this sport. Sometimes he was suspended in an earthenware pot to be shied at, becoming the property of the first man to kill him after the pot had been broken. The custom of the Shrove Tuesday pancakes has not only survived, but is 'going strong'. A writer in 1634 might well be describing something that still goes on in some of our old schools today, and is echoed in every home, when he says:

> 'Every stomach is fritter-filled, as well as heart can wish,
> And every man and maid doe take their turne,
> And tosse their pancakes up for feare they burn,
> And all the kitchen doth with laughter sound
> To see the pancakes fall upon the ground'.

The pancakes may, and should, remind us of the Lenten fast that they precede, and the name Shrove Tuesday should remind us of the sins which need to be repented of and forgiven. Lent is nowadays more honoured in the breach than the observance, and at a time when the need for it is greater than ever. This is what a business man (not a clergyman, mark you), a loyal son of the English Church, wrote about Lent in the seventeenth century:- 'The Lenten fast is undertaken to restrain the looser appetites of the flesh, and to keep the body under; to give the mind liberty and ability to consider and reflect; to humble ourselves before God under a sense of our sins and the misery to which they expose us; to express revenge against ourselves for the abuse of those good things God alloweth us to enjoy and of which we have made ourselves unworthy by excesses; to raise in our minds a due valuation of the happiness of the other world when we despise the enjoyment of this. Above all, to make it acceptable to God, it should be accompanied with fervent prayer, and a charitable relief of the poor, whose miseries we may the better guess at when we are bearing some of the inconveniences of hunger'. If you are one of those who say, 'There are no poor nowadays', we would answer, 'Look at the refugees'.

February 1959

The bare face of Lent

The bare face of Lent is not pleasing to contemplate after the beauty of Salisbury (pp. 22–3, Focus on Salisbury), but self-discipline has its part to play, like beauty, in bringing us near to God, and Lent is upon us. Lent has little meaning for the generality of people today, but if our fathers found its quiet and its heart-searching so necessary in their slow-moving times, then our hectic ones have surely not outmoded it. Let the self-discipline be of the positive sort – shewing kindness in our own homes (where we least often shew it); sweetening our tongues when discussing our neighbours; using the privilege God has given us of getting straight through to him in prayer; reading our bibles, and taking part in the family worship of the church each Sunday.

February 1958

Quiet weddings

The strange theory is gaining currency that if you want a

wedding without pretty dresses, and bridesmaids, and choir, and organ, and bells, you cannot have it in church. The sooner this idea is scotched, the better. The picturesque wedding is quite in order for those who like such things, and usually gives pleasure to a large number of people, but the frills are not essential. Without them the wedding is equally valid, for the essence of Christian marriage is a man and a woman taking each other exclusively for life, in the presence of God, and certain human witnesses. If you want a 'quiet' wedding, only the priest, the bride and groom, and two witnesses, are needed, and the service may be at any time between 8 a.m. and 6 p.m. But stay – what the Army calls your 'security' needs to be absolutely leakproof. Otherwise, what happens to your 'quiet' wedding may resemble what happened to that shy but genial friend of Loders belfry, Mr. Charlie Lathey, when he lately essayed to marry a widow of Bridport. To avoid an affectionate demonstration by his workmates and half the town, he fixed the wedding for 8.45 at Loders on a Sunday morning, confident that the time and the day would fox them, if Loders Church did not. But his 'security' slipped up somewhere, and he and his bride found themselves plighting their troth either to other, before a sea of bright, early-morning faces, including the Mayor of Bridport's. Charlie found that having them all there was nicer than he had imagined. He, too, was happy, and he is no longer shy.

February 1958

Widow and widower wed

The other February wedding was in Loders Church on Shrove Tuesday, and had the distinction of being between a widow and a widower. The bride was Mrs. Amelia Jane Masters, of Matravers Farm, and the bridegroom, Mr. Harold Emund Lester, of Spring Gardens Farm, Frome-Selwood. It appears that the bride and the groom had been childhood sweethearts – as, by rare coincidence, had been their deceased partners – and they saw no reason why their conjunction should occur at eight in the morning, which is the preference of many in like circumstance. This wedding took place at mid-day, in a well filled church, with the prescribed matrimonial hymns led by the choir, and the wedding march on the organ. Outside the porch the happy couple faced a battery of cameras, both official and unofficial, as the bells in the tower above chimed over them, and the livelier guests prepared a fusillade of confetti.

March 1959

The clerk of the weather

The weather, which is normally a topic of conversation when one has nothing else to dwell on, has lately been worth talking about, because it has affected everybody for better or for worse. Milkmen, postmen, butchers and bakers who had to do their work on icebound roads, found the weather decidedly trying, as did also those country people who had to get to their daily work in Bridport. School children, on the contrary, found it a joy. A white morning held a possibility that the Askerswell teacher might not be able to get out from her lodgings in Bridport, or that the Loders teacher might be marooned in her home at Askerswell, or that the school bus which takes the senior children into Bridport might not appear. All these hopes, be it added, found some measure of fulfilment, and a sure way of becoming unpopular was to offer a group of waiting children a lift into Bridport. Which is a healthy sign, for when children like school there is something wrong with the school or the children. Some of the nice retired people from foreign parts, who have enriched our lives by coming to live among us, were shaken to find that it was possible for snow to fall in West Dorset. We trust that before they decide to leave, they will duly consider the twenty-foot snow-drifts, the fifty degrees of frost, and the frozen beer that have made life in other parts of the country more trying than ours.

March 1955

Sociable stitching

The spirit of Jane Austen visits Askerswell on Tuesday afternoons at Miss Edwards' thatched cottage beside the stream. There, such of the ladies of the parish as can ply a needle and, or, engage in pleasant conversation, come together to make saleable articles for the bell fund. The setting is perfect, and so is their handiwork. As one appraises the embroidery of a choice tablecloth, one feels the approving eye of Jane already on it. Her eye for certain other articles may be quizzical and puzzled even. 'And what might be those bags, so large in their Joseph coat of many colours?' 'O, those, dear Miss Austen – those are bags for the beach.' 'And what might these huge gloves be? They look like garden gloves, and yet they are so richly caparisoned that it would be a sin to cull dandelions in them. I feel that they should handle something that is precious, costly, worth its weight in gold.' 'Dear Miss Austen – how clever of you to guess. They are gloves for handling coals when you put them on the fire'.

A source of social history

As a document of social history the Askerswell March 1954 Log Book is on a par with the church registers and the churchwardens' accounts, and must be well looked after. Reading between the lines of Mistress Fry's crabbed hand, one can glimpse the whole background of village life in the third quarter of the 19th century. As one delves deeper and deeper into the diary, one's estimate of the trials that beset a teacher in those days gets higher, and Mistress Fry's head takes on a halo. To do her job properly, the teacher must have pupils attending regularly, and Mistress Fry did not have this. In her day, attendance was not compulsory: hay and harvest field competed with her for the children's time; sickness (or at any rate the excuse of sickness) was rife, and the poverty of the labouring classes made even the small weekly payments an effort. Here are typical entries in the log book – 'William and Sidney Walters withdrawn as they are going into the Union House'. 'William and Sidney Walters again put on the register their father having returned to the parish and taken them out of the Union'. 'Alfred Symes has been absent three weeks, not having any shoes to wear'. 'The three Bridges' names have been withdrawn as they cannot get across the fields from Loderland in winter'. 'The school was re-opened, but as usual a very poor attendance. This was to be expected, as the harvest is by no means ended'. 'There was no school today, it being Club Day at Litton, a great attraction to young and old in this parish'. 'Frances Gregory, aged six, died of fever last week.

This has caused several people to keep their children at home for fear of the infection'.

Every year Her Majesty's Inspector examined the children, and if they were not up to standard, the government grant could be withdrawn. This was once the lot of poor Mistress Fry. The Inspector's report of 1877 says, 'There seems to have been a great deal of sickness during the past six months, which probably accounts for the poor result of the examination. The discipline must improve. At present it is very inferior. H.M. Inspector is unable to recommend payment of the grant under Art. 19A. Better results generally will be expected next year, or the grant will be endangered'. But the report for 1878 was not much better. It reads, 'The discipline has improved, but in other respects the school is in much the same state as before. The grant is reduced by one tenth, for faults of instruction in arithmetic'.

After this, one is not surprised to read, 'In consequence of Miss Fry feeling so unwell, it was determined to begin the harvest holidays a little earlier than usual in order that she may get some rest' . . . nor this, 'Ellis Walden, a farmer's son at Sturt Hill, was re-entered yesterday, he having been at Shipton school meanwhile, but does not seem to have learned much there'.

February 1957

Askerswell Log Book: more extracts

Our last month's account of the Askerswell school log book aroused so much interest that we herewith dip into it further. Ex-pupils of the school now in middle or old age who are fearful of what the book might say about them, may rely on the Editor's discretion, provided their generous support of school and church continues. 'Alfred Mabey was taken away from this school, his parents intending to send him to school at Loders, where, it is to be hoped, he will be better behaved.' 'Miss J. Miller, the wife of a retired coast-guardsman, being in the parish, has engaged to attend in the afternoon school hours to instruct and superintend the girls in needlework at a salary of 2s. 6d. per week.' 'The children had their annual treat of tea and cake at the Rectory. Knives, needle-cases and thimbles were given to all who had completed 250 attendances in the past year.' 'Two little children, William and Mabel Vine, came for the first time this week from Nallers, but it is almost too far for such small ones to come.' 'The two Vines' names were omitted, as they only attended four times in as many weeks.' 'A new harmonium was placed in the schoolroom.' 'Owing to the lateness of the harvest, which has not yet commenced (Aug. 13th), the school will not break up for the holidays just yet.' 'Mrs. Fox (Rector's wife) gave the children their first singing lesson. As a rule, Thursday afternoon from 4.30 to 5 p.m. will be the time devoted to singing.' 'Harvest holidays will begin on Aug. 27th.' 'School was re-opened (Sep. 29th), but with a very small attendance, the leasing not being finished yet.' 'The children seem to take to the singing lessons, but the harmonium suffers from the damp and the changes of weather. The gentleman of whom it was bought promised to keep it in order for a year gratis, but hitherto he has not looked at it.' 'Two more boys from Luke White's family were entered on the books. In consequence of the number now attending from that family, the school managers have allowed the five children to come for 6d per week.'

March 1957

The clerk of the weather

Our organist at Loders believes in being topical. When the great cold gripped us, he switched the Sunday morning canticle from Te Deum to Benedicite, and we found ourselves beseeching frost and cold, ice and snow, fire and heat, to bless the Lord. Till then, we had been blessing it ourselves, especially those of us who are farmers. The rare beauty of the winter landscape, as seen from Boarsbarrow, Bell and Eggardon, did not compensate enough the grim business of having to hunt for water for the cattle while water from a burst pipe in the roof was seeping through the bedroom ceiling. Once again, those who live in old unpiped houses, drawing their water from well or spring, had the laugh over their progressive neighbours. The modern roadhouse on Asker Down, built not as our fathers would have built, in a sheltered hollow, but on the crest of a hill, exposed to all the elements, was easily the worst sufferer, but charity precludes us from reminding Mr. and Mrs. Duke of all they have been through. A good point about the cold was that it tested the loyalty of our Sunday congregations, and they came out with good marks. Parsons in this Deanery have been lamenting the effect of the weather on their congregations. Ours have turned out as usual, with the exception, perhaps, of the Askerswell evening congregation, but even Askerswell had its gallant few who clustered round the stove and politely ignored the clouds of their own exhalations. The attendance at Loders School was at one time depleted by sickness to ten children.

March 1956

Mothering without flowers

The frost has put paid to the prospect of Loders children taking flowers to the sick and aged of the parish on Mothering Sunday, March 11th. The children have decided to do this after a flower service to be held when there are flowers about. They hope to have all their mothers with them at the mothering service.

March 1956

Three bonny lambs

The lambing season is said to be somewhat late this year, but its human counterpart appears to be quite unretarded. We have to congratulate the parents of three bonny lambs – Mr. and Mrs. Derek Barnes, of Loders, who have a girl; Mr. and Mrs. Hatton, of Dottery, who have a boy; and Mr. and Mrs. Baggs, of Dottery, who also have a boy – a ten-pounder.

March 1956

Mothers' Union notes

Our correspondent writes:- 'In spite of relentless rain, and the enforced absence of seven of our most regular members, the February meeting mustered twenty hardy souls to learn (and unlearn) from Nurse Fooks what to do in many types of accidents. To round off her comprehensive and very worthwhile talk, she showed us how to give the 'kiss of life'.

March 1967

Transporting the Evangelists

The two village evangelists who visited us in connection with the Mission to Bridport have returned to their respective homes, Mr. Hyde Parker to Colchester and the Rev. P.A. Unwin to Figheldean, near Salisbury. They were as happy to be with us as we were to have them, and we appreciate their keenness in giving up their time and coming long distances to talk to us about the things that matter most. Mr. Unwin is a busy man. He has two parishes, is chaplain to the big R.A.F. camp at Netheravon, cultivates a large vicarage garden single handed, and runs a small poultry farm. Mr. Hyde Parker, being of the age of 76, and retired, makes up in valour what he lacks of business, for he did the journey from Essex in an ancient car, belching poisonous fumes from the gearbox, which made it imperative for all the windows to be open as he drove. Our readers will agree that the time for open windows is not yet. This car, however, was a real accessory to the work of an evangelist. Its ailing battery and temperamental lights were always throwing it on the mercy of good samaritans, and by the time these had done the necessary with their tow-ropes and screw-drivers, Mr. Hyde Parker had converted them. He would as soon be without his car as Dick Turpin without Black Bess. Both evangelists were reminded how small the world is. Mr. Hyde Parker found himself billetted under the roof of Mrs. Lenthall, whose husband had been bailiff to Nicholsons, who turned out to be first cousins of Mr. Hyde Park, and later he found himself the guest of Captain Aylmer, who had served in the Queen Elizabeth with Mr. Hyde Parker's admiral brother. Mr. Unwin, billetted at Loders Court, was delighted to find that his host, Sir Edward Le Breton, was the brother of the Colonel Le Breton with whose regiment Mr. Unwin had served in the Middle East, and whom he had met previous to that in Kenya.

April 1955

Shaking off the shrouds of winter

April the sixth is the day when we shall be raising the Easter shout to greet the spring of souls and the spring of the year.

With only a week to go, the question is whether nature will be able to shake off the shroud of winter soon enough to make the Easter hymns and lessons realistic. At present, the pastures are seared by Siberian winds, the daffodils beloved of Wordsworth are decimated by frost, and the primroses and violets that have plucked up courage to peep out are doing so very gingerly. But a day or two of the milder weather now coming in may work wonders, so that it will not be too strenuous an act of faith to sing on Easter morning, 'Now the Queen of Seasons, bright with the day of splendour, and the royal feast of feasts, comes its joy to render,' or to say on Easter evening, 'Lo, the winter is past, the rain is over and gone, the flowers appear on the earth, the time of the singing of birds is come, and the voice of the turtle is heard in our land.' When Easter falls in un-springlike weather, the tidy-minded people never fail to renew their plea that in the interest of holiday-makers the date of Easter should be fixed at a time when the weather would be fitting. And they never fail to ignore what is so apparent to the countryman, that the English weather defies domestication. It can put us in swim-suits in February and in fur coats in June. Even now we cannot recall what were meant to be Coronation frolics on Asker Down without a shudder. And that was June. We with untidy minds are content to let Easter continue to depend on the whims of the moon. The moon is as likely to be *au fait* with the weather as the planners. Also we like the centuries-old connection between Easter and the moon. It was in the light of the first full moon after the Spring equinox that Israel came out of Egypt; it was in the light of this same moon that Jesus prayed in the olive groves of Gethsemane; this same moon was looking down on Joseph of Arimathea's garden when life conquered death. As Mary Magdalene came early to the sepulchre, so, we hope, will all the faithful come on Easter morning to the Holy Communion to salute the risen Lord.

April 1958

Easter vestry

In Easter week, for longer than can be told, parishioners have met to receive church accounts and to appoint church officers for the ensuing year. The widespread impression is that this meeting is dull, and the impression is erroneous. To know what money the church has coming in, and exactly how it is spent, is nearly as interesting as the financial status of the people next door. It is also the meeting at which criticisms of the church (which are often aired in the bus) may be aired with more chance of righting the alleged wrongs. Every parishioner is entitled to attend, and will be welcome.

April 1958

Centenary celebrations

Three reporters, with their cameras, descended on the centenary celebrations of Askerswell School, and took enough photographs to fill the National Gallery. This is some indication of the interest that the event kindled over a big area. The great day fell on a Monday, and rain was falling too, but young pupils of five, and old pupils of eighty, with school managers, and friends from far and near, two former teachers in Miss Robinson and Miss Sellers, and a former manager in Miss Wilkinson, who had come all the way from Essex – these thronged Askerswell Church for a thanksgiving service. The lesson was read by the present mistress, Miss McCombie, whose discovery of the log book containing the history of the school and whose enthusiasm had enabled the centenary to be observed. In his sermon, the Rector pointed out that the people of Askerswell in 1857 saw the need of education and started their own school at a time when the State was doing next to nothing about education and had not provided a single school. He suggested that the lesson to be learnt from this was, when you see a thing wants doing, do it yourself, and do not wait for somebody else to do it. With the strains of 'Onward Christian soldiers' still in their ears, the congregation made from the church to the school, where there was country dancing by the present pupils, and the ceremonial cutting by the youngest and the oldest ex-pupil of a birthday cake, so beautifully made by Mrs. Adams that many thought the slaying of it a crime – until they tasted it. Mrs. Herbert Bartlett had sent over old photographs of the school and its pupils, and these gave the veterans something to talk about for hours.

Neither was the talk unfruitful: Mr. Fred Marsh got his old class-mate, Mr. Ernest Welch, so interested in the bells, of which they were once ringers together, that when Mr. Welch returned home to Weymouth he posted Mr. Marsh £3 towards the bell fund, expressing a hope that other old pupils would also do something.

April 1957

A halo goes abegging

One of the world's heroes is the unknown inventor of the jumble sale. He deserves a place in stained glass windows, if only for the amount of money he has raised painlessly, and even pleasantly, in good causes. The recent jumble sale at Askerswell, run by Miss McCombie for her school fund, is another feather in his cap, as can be seen by comparing it with the Agricultural Discussion Club whist drive. In the latter Mr. Charlie Gale bestowed a pleasant evening of whist, some £20 worth of turkey, whisky, and other delectable things, on his supporters, and made a profit of £11. Miss McCombie bestowed on her supporters an assortment of rummage, the whole of which one would think twice about giving ten shillings for, and made a profit of £25, with the added satisfaction of having fitted out some of the ladies of Uploders for Easter. The merit of a jumble sale is not to be measured in money terms only. There are its entertainment value, and its quite astonishing powers of healing. Parishioners who for any other purpose are in a perpetual state of ailment, are given the strength not only to walk to the sale, but to win honourable mention in the fight for bargains. The power of the jumble sale could be extolled still further, but this would not be politic, so we conclude by proposing its everlasting health.

April 1958

A Loders Mill wedding

When the banns of marriage of Mr. Douglas Rex Loveridge, of Buckland Ripers, and Miss Margaret Ann Barnes, of Loders Mill, were called, the people of Loders looked for a wedding on the grand scale to relieve the tedium of their existence, and the father of the bride, Mr. Hamilton Barnes, did not disappoint them. The sun shone, the bells pealed, and so greedy were the cameras of beauty still more beautifully attired that the bridal party took the best part of ten minutes to get from the church gate into the church, while the congregation stood and waited. The church, in all its Easter glory, was full of friends and clients, and the Vicar of Buckland Ripers was there in the chancel to assist the Vicar of Loders in hallowing the contract. To the strains of Mendelssohn's Wedding March, from 'The Midsummer Night's Dream,' the great company took carriage to the Greyhound Hotel, where bride and groom were toasted in champagne, and a waggish Master of Ceremonies told the father of the bride to cheer up – he still had two marriageable daughters.

May 1957

Discoveries at Well Plot

Loders is a very old place. Its church is old, its little hills are terraced by ancient lynchets, its principal hill is capped by an Iron Age barrow, and it stands on a Roman road. But, by an odd quirk of fate, it is the new council houses at Well Plot that are supplying the most convincing proof of Loders' antiquity. When the workmen were getting out the foundations, one of them did not agree that the broken pottery they were finding in some quantity was part of an unromantic rubbish dump, and he got in touch with our local archaeologist, Mr. Bill Butcher of Sturthill. Mr. Butcher, who has a well-stocked museum of his own, had no difficulty in identifying the pottery as Roman, Samian and mediaeval, and the coin that one of the men had found as belonging to the Empress Faustina (3rd Century). The perfectly preserved skull of an animal, with every tooth intact, defeats him. He thinks it might be that of a wild boar, but awaits the verdict of an expert. Mr. Butcher got in touch with other archaeologists, and the Ministry of Works were sufficiently interested to send down an inspector from the Archaeological department, who confirmed Mr. Butcher's opinions. Both he and Mr. Butcher are puzzled by the remains of the line of posts, and venture the suggestion that they are part of a stockade. We understand that the Ministry is too full of Works to excavate the site immediately, but as there is no present prospect of this part being built upon, the place has been officially noted for future attention. At Askerswell Mr. George Bryan's plough has turned up some Roman tiles and bits of Roman hot-air system, in a corn-field. What with this and Well Plot, it seems that when Mr. Butcher can no longer wrest an honest crust from farming, he will not be short of work.

May 1956

The prevailing mobility

Time was when it was usual for young people to marry within their own village, for the simple reasons that they rarely moved far enough from it to meet anybody else. Nowadays the tables are completely turned, and because of the prevailing mobility it is rare for the parties to a marriage to come from the same village. Of all places, the hamlet of Dottery has lately reverted to the old order of things by producing two sets of brides and grooms. On Easter Monday Mr. Adrian Scadden, of Dottery, married Miss Freda Harris, only lately moved from Dottery; on April 25th her brother, Mr. Clifford Harris, married Miss Phyllis Turner, also of Dottery. (Dottery people are obviously attentive to the dominical injunction to love one another.) The weddings were further alike in that they both picked on the wettest hour of two very wet days. But this did not extinguish their exuberance, nor impair their picturesque qualities. The bells chimed as merrily as ever while the camera men operated under cover of umbrellas, and the deluge was soon forgotten in the conviviality of the wedding feast. We are pleased that Mr. and Mrs. Harris are only going to the boundary of Dottery to make their new home, which will be in Mr. Powell's cottage at Seymour Farm.

May 1959

May fair

It must be many years since Loders School welcomed the month of May with traditional rites, as they did this year. The day was dry, and somewhat marred by an east wind, but the playground walls kept most of it out and there were the blossoming apple trees and a background of Boarsbarrow to compensate it. Linda Crabb had been elected Queen of the May. After Mrs. Willmott had declared the fair open, the Vicar crowned the Queen and did obeisance. The school then entertained the Queen and the assembly of parents and school managers, with a display of country dancing, after which the company moved indoors to the stalls and there spent £33 for the benefit of the school fund, which must be quite the most the school would have taken at a sale. A fancy dress parade into which much ingenuity had been put was judged by Miss Edwards and Miss Shimeld. Proceedings ended with the usual cup of tea and Mr. Price and Mrs. Niven feeling justly gratified.

June 1966

Some jumble sale

It is not often that Askerswell have a fête or a jumble sale, but when it does, that small community does not do things by halves. Its last fête made a profit of nearly £220, and its recent jumble sale has made a profit of £42.13s. Which means that when the church treasurer, Mr. Adams, goes to Lloyds Bank, he will no longer feel like the tramp who went into The Ritz and ordered one fish ball. He and the rest of us must be feeling mighty grateful to Mrs. Aylmer and her committee of ladies for putting the church in funds again. The Rector tempers all this gratitude with a wish that his flock could be as good at using their church as they are at raising money for it, especially on those lovely summer evenings when Mr. Spiller and he are left to bear the weight of evensong with little support. The beauty of the Askerswell jumble sale is that it always produces fun as well as money. For days after the universal swopping of clothes, it is a game to get right the identity of the people you meet in The Square, and even in Uploders (it is surprising to what extent familiar clothes and recognition tie up with each other). A nursery section of prams, pushchairs, high chairs and playpens made this jumble sale especially piquant. What ladies, it was asked, were getting rid of those serviceable articles with such abandon, and were they being altogether prudent? More to the point – who was buying them? No purchaser could openly face the eyes that sized up any lady who showed the slightest interest in the prams. Yet they were all sold. Mrs. Swaffield wishes it to be known that the high chair she bought was quite definitely on behalf of a shy neighbour. The only cool moment our reporter encountered in the heat of that afternoon was when he overheard the following conversation: Lady to neighbour near second-hand stall, 'Look at this lovely tweed coat I got for half a crown. It'll do me fine.' Neighbour: 'Yes, you'll look well in it, and the quality is good. It was mine.'

June 1956

Bus stork

In Dottery there were two births last month, a boy to Mrs. Bagg, and a boy to Mrs. Oxenbury. Mrs. Bagg is what Lady Macbeth ought to have been. This is her third boy. She would have liked a girl. Mrs. Ernest Crabb, of Uploders, was safely delivered of twin girls in Portwey Hospital, Weymouth. Their proud grandmother, Mrs. Harry Crabb, likes everybody to know what fine specimens they are, 'weight, five pounds thirteen ounces each, and nineteen inches long'. There was a strong element of surprise in their arrival, although the doctor says he knew it was twins all along.

June 1959

Replenishing the Earth

Mrs. Bolton, of Loders, has lately given birth to a son, and Mrs. Burrell, of Gribb, to a daughter. Mr. & Mrs. Barnes, of Bilshay, have been admitted to the noble army of grandparents, and Mr. & Mrs. Sanders of Loders, have been presented with another grandchild in Scotland.

June 1954

Whitsuntide

Two baby boys were christened in the presence of a large congregation at Dottery Church on Whit Sunday. They were

Philip Arthur, the son of Mr. and Mrs. R.J. Baggs, and Michael Peter, the son of Mr. and Mrs. P.S. Hattam (née Shirley Smith). Being males they know how to be quiet. Whit Sunday was an appropriate day for the Dottery approximation to a mass christening. Whit Sunday was so fashionable a day for christenings in the ancient church that it got its name from the white dresses worn by the candidates. Whit Sunday is also, of course, the birthday of the Christian Church.

June 1956

The gentlemen beat the pros

A discussion between Mr. Michael Foot, of the Travellers' Rest, and Mr. Stuart Crabb, of the Bridport football team, as to the latter's merits, led to a duel of a gentle nature. Mr. Foot got together a team of amateurs, which included Tom Foot, J. Foot, F. Lloyd, and K. Saunders, with Godfrey Elliott in goal, and one evening, on the Bridport ground, they played a team largely recruited from the Bridport Football Club by Mr. Stuart Crabb. Not only did Mr. Foot's team win 4–3; at half-time it was leading 3–1. With a much-reduced estimate of their status in the world of football, the Pros adjourned with the Gentlemen to the Travellers' Rest, where they were entertained to supper by the father of their challenger, Mr. Ron Foot.

June 1958

St. Aldhelm's day

The Young Communicants of Dottery, twelve in number, organised a party to join in the archdeaconry youth service at Sherborne Abbey on St. Aldhelm's day. They travelled in cars manned by Mr. Robert Barnes, Mr. Michael Gill and the Vicar, and on the way home they stopped in a forest glade for a picnic supper. The weather was much better than last year, and the light of a kindly moon was appreciated in dealing with the supper.

June 1955

The post of churchwarden

It may be news to some that mere election by the Easter Vestry does not make a person a churchwarden. He is not legally a churchwarden until he has been admitted by the Archdeacon's Court, which is usually held in May. All our churchwardens (excepting Mr. H Sanders, who was excused) attended the Archdeacon's Court in Bridport, and were duly sworn in. They were treated to an interesting account of the churchwarden's office by the Archdeacon, by which it appears that anciently the churchwarden was the chief officer of state in each parish. He was responsible not only for the fabric of the church, but for maintaining the roads and bridges of the parish, and relieving the poor. The churchwarden-in-vestry levied a rate for this purpose. He was also custodian of public morals, whose duty it was to present irregular persons to the proper authority for punishment. It is not to be wondered at that many good men and true declined this onerous office, but, if the parish elected them, they were compelled by law to serve. Times have changed, and the churchwarden's job, or most of it, has been distributed among parish, rural and county councils, public assistance officers, police and magistrates. But Archdeacon Chute reminded his churchwardens that they were still expected to be a 'tranquillising influence' in the parish. Your editor has recollections of a dear old churchwarden of his, a retired bacon curer, whose tranquillising influence was a subdued snore during sermons.

June 1955

Box pews

The late Mrs. Samways was buried in Loders cemetery after a service in Loders Church. She often talked of her girlhood, and of her sitting Sunday by Sunday in one of the old box pews of Loders Church, beneath the three-decker pulpit. Much of her life was spent in the farm near the school, now called Waddon.

June 1956

Gassed in the Great War

Mr. Henry Johnston of Ashe, who had been in failing health for some time, was found collapsed in his hen-run, and died shortly afterwards in Bridport Hospital. He had farmed Ashe for more than thirty years. In the Great War he had been badly gassed, and was never without the effects of this. Knapps Farm, Broadwindsor, was his birthplace, and his brother still farms there. Mr. Johnston was buried in his wife's grave at Dottery. The church was not large enough to hold those who came to pay their respects. It was packed close, and then there were some outside.

June 1959

Covered-in wagons

Newcomers to Shatcombe in Uploders are Mr. and Mrs. Spillman. Mr. Spillman has just retired from the postmastership of Wimborne, and completed forty-six years in the postal service which he began at the bottom of the ladder as a messenger boy. His wife is a sister of Mrs. Rogers, of Yondover. There is no question as to whether Mr. and Mrs. Spillman will like Loders, for they have known and loved it for years. Their memory goes back to when nobody in Loders – 'not even the gentry' – had a car, and when the road link with civilisation was a covered-in wagon, driven by Carrier Stephen Crabb, which left the Crown (one wonders how) and went to Weymouth.

July 1956

Folk-Dancing at Bovington

Loders and Askerswell schools were among the three thousand children who attended the County Folk-Dancing Festival at Bovington. The day was hot, and our young people to the number of forty-nine made the journey in a thirty-five seater bus, but they thoroughly enjoyed themselves.

July 1957

Women's Institute party

Loders Women's Institute suffered from no inhibitions in the celebration of their thirteenth birthday. Nothing went wrong: indeed many voted this the happiest of all their birthdays. The cynics hold that this thirteenth birthday was free of calamity because the birthdays of Loders W.I., like those of the women of Samaria's husbands are more than those confessed to, and that this, in fact, was not the thirteenth. The refreshments, including a cake made by Mrs. Rudd and Mrs. Christopher, were the envy of the guest institutes. A television addict remarked how refreshing were Mrs. Herbert's old time songs, and the very alive play, 'Ghosts of long ago.'

July 1960

The school pageant

It seemed that all the young people and all the young mothers of Loders were in the school playground to see the school's pageant on the eve of Loders' patron, St. Mary Magdalene. A half-holiday at Colfox School had enabled many ex-pupils of Loders to come as well. The parish should now be versed in its own history. The pageant began with the descent on the Boarsbarrow Britons of some highly altruistic Roman soldiers, who had come only to improve the Britons' houses, give them good roads, and stop them quarrelling (shades of Mr. Kruschev!). There followed a scene from Saxon life in Loders, and then the coming of a posse of Norman monks, under Prior Tommy Dennett, to take possession of the manor and church of Loders for the Abbey of Montbourg in Normandy. There was a glimpse of the hard times that followed the Black Death, and then the destruction of the stained glass and statuary of Loders Church by a villainous-looking mob from Powerstock. The next scene shewed the flight of King Charles II, the King spirited through Loders by royalist villagers very much afeared of being caught by the roundheaded lord of Loders Court (Sir Edward's face was a study in this episode). The pageant ended with scenes of contentment under the benevolent despotism of the lord of the manor in modern times, and with a universal shout, 'We are all proud that we belong to Loders.' (Here Sir Edward was positively beaming.) Lady Le Breton then presented prizes, and called for cheers for the actors and their teacher, Mrs. Hinde. Tea was served in the schoolroom by Mrs. Chard and Mrs. Miller, and so ended a pleasant and worthwhile afternoon.

August 1958

Of fêtes and umbrellas

The English summer is wet often enough to support those who argue that we should stop growing hay and corn and confine ourselves to silage. But hope springs eternal, and we go on trying to make hay when the sun doesn't shine. So it is with outdoor functions. We go on holding garden fêtes because of the lovely things they could be, turning our backs on the painful memories of what they often are. Our hearts went out to our neighbours in Bradpole over their recent experience of a garden fête. Much thought and work had been put into it. Sir Gerald Gladstone had brought his garden to the peak of perfection for the occasion. The morning of the fête was sunny, warm and cloudless, but in the afternoon when the jollity was about to begin a wetting drizzle descended, punctuated by sharp showers, and fog fell on the neighbouring hills. Stallholders had to put their wares under the counter if they had no covering of cellophane. But those who queued for tombola tickets could not be put off by the dripping down their necks of each other's umbrellas. Under the circumstances the fête did well to bring in £100. As might have been expected the Saturday following behaved itself and was gloriously fine, when it wasn't required to be. We hope that the long run of good luck enjoyed by Loders fête may hold this year, though we must not grumble if it does not.

August 1965

August the fourth

To the world at large, this is the date on which the 1914–18 war began; to the people of this neighbourhood, it is the date of Loders Fête. Once again Sir Edward and Lady Le Breton have invited us to Loders Court and, given a fine day, the setting for a fête could not be more congenial. Like all fêtes, this one will have a financial motive – to help pay for the excellent work that has been done on the organ, but we hope that it will also be a happy social event. Certain friends in Bridport are coming out to entertain us during the afternoon. Mr. Bernard Gale is bringing thirty dancers, and they will do a scarf dance, sailor's hornpipe, tarantella minuet, solo, Scottish sword dance, dance of the silver hoops and hunting dance. After tea, well-known masters of dance. After tea, well-known masters of mirth from Bridport Industries will give a variety show. As these artists wish to help the organ fund, we shall charge adults a shilling admission to the fête, which will cover the two shows but children will be free. The children are likely to provide us with entertainment of their own, for they are hard at work on a competition for the best decorated object on wheels – bicycles, tricycles, prams, scooters, motor cars, etc. In the evening there will be the usual social and dance in the Hut. The choir are running this, with the help of a few friends. We gather that there are to be gypsy songs, conjuring, and a visit from Dick Turpin, who will himself do the standing and delivering on this occasion. Dottery have a stake in this year's fête in the shape of a stall whose takings will go towards the renovation of Dottery Church, August 1956.

August 1956

Choral mackerel

Whilst Loders choir is in our thought it may be added that, on the spur of the moment, the choir recently took themselves to Beer for an evening on the sea, mackerel-fishing. Like most anglers they had not the remotest expectation of catching anything; indeed, if the ladies had considered close contact with a live fish at all possible they would have stayed on *terra firma*. Some naughty water sprite seemed to know this, and as the gossipping gondola idled round the bay in the setting sun, he lured it over a shoal of mackerel. Suddenly it seemed that mackerel were leaping on all the lines at once, and from the lines into the boat, on to the ladies' laps, and all over the gentlemen's Sunday suits. How the gentlemen coped with the situation they still cannot understand – the rush of mackerel, the shrieks of the ladies (which unnerve the bravest), and the danger that the agitation might upset the over-laden boat. But cope they did, and before they could really grasp what was happening, they had become possessed of a whole box of mackerel. At supper in a field, over good ale and strawberries and cream, they had much to talk about, and could not but be pleasantly conscious of their increased stature in the eyes of the ladies. It is a mercy that the Reverend Lionel Brown is unaware that the lamp outside the

Bridport Congregational Church was used for a division of mackerel towards midnight.

August 1955

Hawaiah comes to Loders

Loders Choir hope to give a programme of madrigals and drinking songs at the Social on the night of the fête, and members and the Women's Institute have spent hours at the home of the President practising a play for your delight. Your Editor has heard whispers that he doesn't altogether understand, about a girl called 'Hula', and leafy skirts, and Hawaiah, and he passes them on to you, in case you do understand. He heard them *à propos* of the Social.

August 1954

The best choir in England?

The Vicar of Grimsby, recently on holiday in Bridport, attended morning service at Loders Church. He stayed behind after service to congratulate the choir on their singing. 'I thought we at Grimsby had the best choir in England,' he said, 'but now I am not so sure.' Our choir certainly acquits itself well, and being at the west end of the church instead of the east, induces the congregation to sing with vigour.

August 1953

Loders fête

We hear from those who have relatives coming to stay with them for the August holiday that these relatives welcome the coincidence of their holiday with the fête. As the fête is really the parish-get-together of the year, it is the ideal place for renewing old acquaintances, and its home-made amusements are a welcome change from the usual dietary. Some fête-goers aver that when the weather is kindly, they are amply entertained simply to sit there on the lawn of the paternal manor house and browse over the pleasant scene. We are lucky to have had for many years a manorial lord and lady who make the parish so free of their home, and are old-fashioned enough to enjoy being like the old woman who lived in the shoe. If you notice any men of the parish looking pensive these days, you can be reasonably sure that they are figuring out where to find an old pram. The fête is to include a 'Pram Derby', in which devoted husbands, pushing their wives in a pram, will race each other. The school children are busy devising themselves as competing street vendors, and the good cooks are preparing for a musical procession of pies. Mr. Bernard Gale's dancers will no longer be wondering how they will get to the fête to entertain us, now that the bus strike is over. The charge that is made to adults for admission to the fête is to save the trouble of charging for the entertainment. Our good friends the performers like to feel they are making a tangible contribution to the financial object of the fête. Several of the July fêtes in this neighbourhood have had the misfortune to be damped down and extinguished by unfeeling showers, which has posed the question, What shall we do if it rains? When one has faith that it will be fine, one does not carry an umbrella, so we have no wet weather arrangements. If it rains, we shall carry on at the Court to the best of our ability.

August 1957

Overhead railway

Organisers of outdoor events have had little cause to worry about the weather this summer. Preparations for Loders fête went ahead in hot sunshine, and the day itself was all that could be desired. Some say that the attendance was not quite as large as last year. Others disagree. The question must be left open, because when there is no charge for admission there is no record of attendance. One fact that cannot be disputed is that the takings exceeded any previous year. They reached £185. 16s. 6d., which is rather remarkable, seeing that Loders is not a seaside place with a fleeceable population of holidaymakers. Expenses were £27. 7s. 9d., so the profit for the Organ Fund is £158. 8s. 9d. The children liked this year's fête above all others because of the overhead railway, which, incidentally, had cost Brigadier Hammond, Mr. Sanders, Mr. McDowall and Mr. David Crabb Junior hours of hard labour in the construction, and was to put them to still harder work in the operation. The 'railway' was the body of an old perambulator running on a steel wire high above the ground between two trees. Passengers boarded the train at one tree, and whizzed down the wire at high speed towards the other tree. The thrill was in the feeling that you were going to hit that other tree with a mighty bump, but you stopped within two feet of it. One small boy is alleged to have had seventeen trips at sixpence a time. The social in the evening, run by the choir, will also be remembered for the fun it gave to grown-ups as well as children, and was proof that sacred songs and solos are not the only string to the choir's bow. Colour films shewn by Wing-Commander Newall provided a restful interlude. Another pleasing feature of the fête was the contributions sent in by Old Loderians now living away from the parish.

September 1955

Their good turn

Girl Guides throughout the country have undertaken to do a good deed extraordinary to mark the Coronation year. Askerswell Guides asked if they might be allowed to keep the church clean. The church having no cleaner, the offer was accepted with pathetic eagerness. With a woman's wisdom, the captain saw that a start ought to be made on the tower. She had heard that the tower was a trifle unhygienic, and was somewhat unprepared for the Black Hole of Calcutta in which she and the Guides found themselves. The dirt of half a century included jackdaw's nests (a putload), bell wheels and stays eaten by worms to a powder, fallen plaster and motheaten bell ropes. This was pushed down the seventy odd steps of the spiral stairway, and out into the churchyard, where it was burnt. A thick coating of dust about their persons made some of the guides look like the Devil's assistants as they stoked the fire; the only human touch about them was the constant plaint of one, 'Oh dear, I had my bath last night.' This cleaning of the tower has revealed the shocking state of the roof and of the bell frame. It looks as if Askerswell's failure to put in a stitch in time is now going to cost nine. Bells are costly instruments, and they cannot be neglected for years for nothing.

September 1953

Running up the church path

The sun shone brightly and the bells rang for the wedding in Loders Church of Miss Carol Ann Harding, elder daughter of Mr. and Mrs. J.A. Harding of The Stores, Uploders. Her bridegroom was Mr. Alan James Weedon, who is a radar fitter at the Bawdsey R.A.F. Station, Woodbridge, Suffolk. To look at him, none would guess him to be the strong man he actually is. We have heard of a bridegroom lifting his bride over the threshold of the new home, but have never before seen one run up the path from Loders Church with her in his arms. This was to escape, not the parents, but the bombardment of confetti.

September 1956

Shakespeare in Loders

The annual course of lectures in Askerswell School will begin on Monday, Sept. 22nd, at 7.30 p.m. Mr. G.B. Smith will be the lecturer, on the subject of English drama, with particular reference to Shakespeare. It can be taken from us that the lectures are an agreeable institution which those who attend would not be without, and newcomers may be sure of a welcome.

September 1958

Holy Water

Water from the River Jordan was used for the christening at Dottery of Mrs. Wensley's grand-daughter, Bridget Annette, who was brought by her parents from their home at Symondsbury.

October 1953

Sunday School outing

The date chosen for Loders Sunday School outing was changed to suit the convenience of the organisers, and these thanked their lucky stars that they did change it. The date first proposed turned out to be a 'soaker'; the date finally settled upon was perhaps the best day of summer – an almost cloudless sky, and a really hot sun. In these conditions Weymouth is all that children can desire, and ours had a glorious time. They stuck the Loders flag in the sand, and settled to a solid eight hours of fun, which included donkey rides, round-a-bouts, Punch and Judy, floats and a motor boat trip to Portland. The motor-boat proprietor was offering trips at 3s. for adults, and children under eleven free. His face reflected the doubts he began to feel about the wisdom of this arrangement when Mrs. Willmott came aboard with eighteen under-elevens, half filling the boat, and he could only charge 3s. To his honour be it said that he didn't quibble. He only looked. The return from Portland was the signal for an *al fresco* tea on the sands. The children wish to thank the people of Loders for giving them this outing. The house-to-house collection produced just over £15, which was generous, coming so soon after the orgy of begging which is a concomitant of the annual fête. But Loders has a name for generous giving.

October 1954

The Coronation Procession from Uploders Chapel.

'For those in peril on the sea'

Mr. Anthony Wells, of the Merchant Navy, elder son of Mr. and Mrs. A.J. Wells, of Loders Post Office, was married at Bradpole to Miss Susan Margaret French, of Guildford, the Vicar of Loders assisting the Vicar of Bradpole. Mr. Wells' grandfather was sexton of Bradpole, and his family maintain their many connections with that parish. The reception was a jolly and sumptuous affair in the Loders Ex-Servicemen's Hut, and the marvel is that the bridal car ever negotiated the obstacles that fond uncles had interposed between it and the honeymoon. The uncles had not chosen the wedding hymns, but it was fitting that one should have been 'for those in peril on the sea'.

October 1957

Knights of the camera

Loders Church was beautifully festooned with flowers and reverberated to the bells for the wedding of Miss Christine Barnes, of Loders Mill, and Mr. Kenneth Edwards, of Almshouse Farm, Hermitage, Sherborne. The father of the bride, Mr. Hamilton Barnes, gets more and more accomplished in the art of weddings as he marries off his bevy of beautiful daughters. This time, as he came down the church path with the bride on his arm, he presented such a masterpiece that the photographers clean forgot themselves, and had the bridal party posing as if they were in the studio. The knights of the camera were oblivious of the dislocation they were causing in church, where the organist had played 'Here comes the bride', and the congregation were getting anxious as the minutes passed and no bride came. In the end the service had to begin without the bride, but the sound of the opening hymn loosed the photographers' clutches as nothing else could. If the photographers do not curb their zeal, vicar as well as bride may be missing next time.

October 1961

'Witches, darkies and spectres'

The Eve of All Saints is reckoned to be a spooky night. Weird things are supposed to happen in churchyards, and by the use of the proper spells, lovelorn maidens may discover the man they are to marry. These old superstitions are the theme of a parish party to be held in the Loders Hut on Tuesday November 3rd at 7.30 p.m. Mr. Nathaniel Pinkett, who made such a roaring success of the Coronation party, consented with alacrity to run this one, and is bringing from Bridport a troupe of dancing skeletons. No order, however unusual, defeats the resourceful Mr. Pinkett. We are not so certain, though, that Mrs. Harry Legg's refreshments will not defeat the skeletons. Charges for admission will be, adults 2s., children 6d. The Committee appointed by the parish meeting have asked – and been granted – to take advantage of this convivial occasion to make a presentation to Sir Edward and Lady Le Breton.

November 1953

The good seed

Our cycle of harvest thanksgiving is now completed, albeit reluctantly, leaving a memory of perfect autumn weather, with the morning sun lighting up the ancient arches of Loders Church, and a massive congregation raising the harvest hymns midst a plethora of autumn flowers, and a warm, fruity smell, as of a greengrocer's. It was the most vigorous harvest Loders Church has known for years. The church was filled for matins, and again for evensong by congregations who were highly appreciative of the work done by the small army of decorators, and of the choir's offering. Many people asked who had made the wheatsheaf of bread which graced the lectern. It was Mr. Gregory; and the enormous chrysanthemums on either side were grown by Mr. Baker. The Parish Clerk and the Vicar noted with satisfaction that Mr. George Randall had assumed the mantle of the late Mr. Eli Lenthall in sending two sacks of chicken corn to adorn the chancel, and these may have caused the extra fervour discernible in the Parish Clerk's 'Awmens'. At Dottery Church the space round the font had been converted into a display of flowers, fruit and vegetables of which a window-dresser might have been proud, and the chancel vied with it. The size of the congregation raised the temperature very considerably, and one farmer was heard to lament, after service, that he could not take his jacket off to 'We plough the fields and scatter'. Mrs. Wensley had sat inside the door counting the flock as they came in to service, but her health not being what it was, she gave up at 83, long before the little church was full. In spite of the scarcity of eggs, fourteen dozen were included in the decorations of the three churches. The old people to whom these were given wish to thank the donors. The Vicar is grateful to the Vicar of Bradpole for preaching both at Dottery and Loders. Church people are not famous (in a complimentary way, at any rate) for their response to the alms dish, but the harvest collections of the three churches totalled about £25 (Loders £13, Askerwell £6 and Dottery £6.)

November 1953

The Bishop's query

As the Lord Bishop of Sherborne [John Key] drove through Uploders to take the confirmation service in Loders Church he observed two notices by the roadside. The first, he said, was small and rather dilapidated, and warned motorists that here was a children's crossing; the second was large, magnifical and new, and warned motorists that here was a cattle crossing. 'Would a stranger be right in making the obvious inference as to your scale of values?' asked the Bishop. But he was too tactful to wait for a reply. As he appraised the newly confirmed in the Vicarage afterwards, he said he had a feeling that they were going to be a 'good batch.' If they turn out like the last 'batch' from Dottery they will be good indeed, for in four years not one of these has fallen away from the monthly Communion.

November 1956

Harvest Festival

Attractive posters painted by a member of the congregation, Mrs. F. Gill, summoned Loders to harvest festival on the second Sunday in October, and the summons was answered in no uncertain manner. The church was quite full for matins, and full again for evensong. The evening congregation included the oldest inhabitant of Loders, Mrs. ('Granny)') Hyde, who is in her ninetieth year, and one of her runners-up, Mrs. Martha Crabb, who is eighty-six. These grand old ladies did a thorough inspection of the decorations, and pronounced them as fine as any they had seen. The prevailing gold of bracken, chrysanthemums and masses of corn, was relieved by the purple of Michaelmas daisies and the yellow of giant dahlias, and the fruits ranged from the aristocratic fig to the common blackberry. This year the porch was decorated by children. Puckish groupings of acorns and chestnuts might suggest the hand of pixies, or even squirrels, but the conker in the corner was obviously the offering of a boy. Morning service was taken by the youthful Rector of Symondsbury, who is enamoured of Loders, and at both services the choir did an anthem in which the solo was sung by Mrs. W. Tiltman. Those who sent eggs, honey, jam and grapes are hereby thanked by the sick parishioners to whom they were distributed, and there is a special 'thank you' from an old lady to the grower of 'them turrible fine onions'.

November 1955

Saving up babies for christening

Mr. and Mrs. Sidney Fry are in no danger of losing their right to be regarded as the largest suppliers of grandchildren to the ancient font of Askerswell. On Oct. 27th their daughter Norma, of Nallers, brought her baby son to be named Ian Thomas, and their daughter Edna, of Grange Dairy, Dorchester, brought her baby daughter to be named Valerie Joy. As was fitting, they also brought a large congregation to witness the reception of the newcomers into the Church. The Rector much appreciates the kindly thought of Mr. Sidney's family in saving up two or three babies before beseeching a christening.

November 1957

Letting in the light

Mr. David Crabb and Mr. Horace Read have given their skilled assistance in removing a few of the many yew bushes in Loders churchyard. The effect of the clearance is to show up the remaining bushes and the church to better advantage, and to reduce the wearisome business of trimming the bushes, which wielders of seven-pound electric hedge-cutters will applaud. The removal of one bush restored to proper prominence the Victorian oil lamp near the top of the stone path. A slight hint to Mr. Spillman that the lamp would not mind a coat of paint, and he, with characteristic thoroughness, gave it a whole wardrobe of paint. He also had the oil part working for harvest evensong.

November 1962

Buxom babies

There were two christenings in Loders in October. On the 17th Mr. and Mrs. John Hyde and a large company of relations and friends came triumphantly with the first-born who had crowned disappointments and hopes. She was named Tessa. On the 24th Mr. & Mrs. Raymond Crabb came likewise with their daughter, who was named Rosalind Elizabeth. On each occasion the godmother had something to do to stand holding so buxom a baby for half an hour. Mr. Raymond Crabb confided in a bystander that his babe, at six months, was topping twenty-four pounds.

November 1964

A family affair

Both Mr. & Mrs. Reg Dennett, of Uploders, and their son Tommy, carried off some of the best prizes at Melplash and Dorchester Agricultural Shows against keen 'professional' competition. The certificates and rosettes make an impressive exhibition, and we like to think there might be a link between the fat prize money and the fat harvest church collections! At Melplash Mr. Dennett won two firsts for shorthorns and two reserve champions; at Dorchester he won a second for mangolds, a third for turnips and a reserve for kale. At Melplash Tommy won a first and third for pigs, a first and second for turnips and a third for Young Farmers valuation. Mr. Dennett won a second for apples and a third for cabbage and mangolds. At Dorchester Tommy won a third for porkers.

November 1964

November the fifth

Guy Fawkes Day was observed hereabouts with gusto. The children had bonfires on high points, at Boarsbarrow, Waddon and Shatcombe. At Askerswell House there was not only a bonfire, but a communal firework display, and the village children were outnumbered by adults. These were no ordinary adults either, but included admirals, captains, group-captains, colonels, knights, magistrates, a brace of divines, and the cream of the local aristocracy, who enjoyed themselves hugely, and were delighted with their hostess, Mrs. Aylmer, for thinking up such an agreeable entertainment. The roving photographer of *The Tatler* does not know what he missed. By universal consent the best bonfire was at Shatcombe. It had been assembled by young Tommy Dennett, Brian Hyde, David Gill and Co., with an industry which, if only it could be applied to lessons, would surely land them in the University. Ronald Tilley capped it with a few gallons of used motor oil, and the resulting blaze was colossal. Here again, it seems that the older people (and of these there are not a few in Uploders) enjoyed it most. Said 83-year-old Mrs. Wallbridge: 'When Ernest and I went to our beds that night, we didn't want the light on, t'were that bright. We opened our windows and let in the heat, and really, Mr. Willmott, t'were the first time our old bones have really bin warm this winter.' If the owners of Mrs. Wallbridge's cottage should read this, and subsequently detect a lot of blistered paint, they would, we trust, not lay it to the charge of the boys, but write it off as 'Act of God.'

December 1959

Wolf cubs on parade

Our Remembrance Sunday services left us with a pleasant feeling that we had paid our fallen their meed of homage. A good congregation at Askerswell included a parade of Brownies, and the congregation at Dottery was the largest for this service for some years. At Loders, the new Wolf Cub pack, led by Miss McCombie, held its first church parade. The Cubs were very smartly turned out, and the colour party, which presented the flag at the altar, would not have disgraced the Brigade of Guards. The choir gave a fine rendering of Stainer's All Saints anthem, and the organist (Mr. Tiltman) rounded off the solemn occasion with an impressive Dead March, in 'Saul'. Before and after the service the ringers rang half-muffled peals, and the flag on the tower was at half-mast.

December 1957

Remembrance Sunday

Remembrance Sunday falls on November 13th. As the memory of those who gave their lives for us in the world wars grows dim by natural process, it behoves us the more to brighten it up by attending their service on their commemoration day. All collections will be for Earl Haig's Fund.

November 1966

Obituary

November brought two additions to our abnormally long list of faithful departed. Mr. George Read, scion of an old Loders family, died at Damers House, Dorchester after a long illness, and was buried in the grave of his first wife in Loders churchyard. He had served in the First World War. He rose to be a foreman in the service of Dorset County Council, but ended his working career in North Mill. At Dottery another of the 'old brigade', Mr. George Legg, who seemed impervious to illness, was taken ill and gone within a fortnight. He will be greatly missed at Upper Pymore Farm; for between that and Washingpool he had done some forty years in the service of the Marsh family, who lament that they will never have his like again. He was an expert hedger and rickmaker, whose skills often won him awards at the Melplash Show.

December 1962

Unseasonal weather

It looks very much as if November is a reader of these *Notes*, and that our last month's waffle about the beauties of October goaded him into having a shot at the headlines on his own account. He certainly hit them. The few of us who manage to get up before Sunday is half spent found ourselves on that memorable

November the eighteenth looking out on a world thickly blanketed with snow. The known versatility of the English climate robbed the scene of some of its surprise, but the sight of trees in all the glory of their autumn leaves against a background of snow was something the oldest inhabitants could not remember. A further surprise was in store. Turning the switch did not produce the electric light. Examination of fuses, and the electric clock having stopped at 3.10 a.m., both pointed to a power cut, and the absence of the customary Sunday morning light from the window of the parish clerk seemed to confirm this. The cut lasted till after one o'clock. Dottery and Loders were affected, but most of Askerswell escaped. Chaos reigned in the cowsheds, except at the vicarage, where the undercarriage of Primrose, the house cow, does not know the luxury of electrical manipulation; and except at those farms which had not discarded their old oil engines. Upton Farm had to get down to milking ninety odd cows by hand. In Loders Church the electrical heating was out of action, but the several valiant worshippers were compensated by a co-related absence of sermon. The cooking of Sunday dinner posed a problem. In Uploders the distinguished ex-commander of the Sixteenth Paratroop Division was reduced to a frazzle by an unco-operative primus stove. In Loders Mrs. Frank Gill, the lucky possessor of a non-electric cooker, was kindly offering to cook anybody's goose; and at the Post Office the genial Mr. Albert Wells was dispensing hot stew to neighbours who were unable to cope with the strange world in which they had just woken up. But the medal must go to Miss Wallace of Dottery. Her broken leg is still in plaster, and she was due to return to London that day, by car, for further treatment. Fortified, in the absence of tea, by an 'inner warmth' we would like to know more about, she and her friend, Miss Hornsby, set forth bravely in the snow. At Askers Road House they met a scene to deter the strongest will – cars and buses across the road and a snow plough trying to clear a way. Most of us, even without the prompting of a broken leg, would have returned home to Dottery – but they took the advice of a bus driver, tried the Yeovil route, and after negotiating several trees across the road, reached London safely, where they laughed at their adventures.

December 1962

Wintry weather

This year it was November, and not March, that went out like a lion. We didn't receive the mauling that some parts of the country did, but we came near to tragedy, as when a huge elm near the gate of Loders court fell in front of Mr. Bill Ives (chairman of our Young Farmers), catching his bicycle but not him – and to comedy, as when Commander Lumby, garaging his car at Spyway, looked up expecting to see the roof overhead, and saw the night sky and the outlines of a neighbouring tree instead. He eventually found the roof, no more than twenty yards away. Mrs. Henderson points out that the wind was not entirely an ill one, for it left Loders High Street cleaner than she had ever known it.

December 1954

'The Disgustion Club'

Loders Agricultural Discussion Club, which is proposing to enliven the village with a grand Christmas whist drive on December 22nd, has, before now, been referred to, in all seriousness, by the natives of Loders, as 'The Disgustion Club'. The other day we heard a native of Askerswell call it – most reverently – 'The Concussion Club'. Which caused us to regard the hierarchy of the Club with new interest. Even though the chairman, Mr. Harold Saunders, hails from 'Rook'ems', so amiable a farmer cannot be the cause of the disgustion, but the poleaxe of Mr. Albert Wells, the secretary-cum-butcher, may have something to do with the concussion.

December 1958

Confounding the Jeremiahs

Christmas Eve in Loders was a lovely night of flying cloud and frosty light. As the clock neared twelve a stream of worshippers flowed down the long path to the church, and there, in the flickering candlelight and the glow of the Christmas tree, a congregation of harvest festival dimensions was soon singing 'It came upon a midnight clear'. At eleven on Christmas morning the church filled up again for matins, and the Sunday School, somewhat reduced by measles, sang four carols from the chancel step, and the Enroling Member of the Mothers' Union gave each child a present from the Christmas tree. The services at all our three churches were the more delightful because we were joined by old friends home for Christmas. Out of our combined population of 700, something like 500 attended Christmas services, and 200 made their communion. If this proportion were to prevail over the whole country, the Jeremiahs would have to find something else to wring their hands over.

January 1956

Dr. Edersheim's Census

Dr. Edersheim, Vicar of Loders, writing in the December magazine of 1881, said: 'As always, time has brought changes to our parish. Seventeen deaths have taken place, but I am thankful to say there has been no epidemic nor sudden accident. Twenty-eight baptisms have taken place during the year, and five marriages. At the same time the last census shows that our population, as in so many other agricultural parishes, has decreased – from 1,115 to 952.' At the 1951 census the population was 644, and at the last census it was probably less than that.

December 1961

Children's parties

After doing a nativity play which produced £3.4/- for the School fund and entranced the parents, Askerswell children devoted themselves to their own amusement – games, Christmas tree, presents and tea. Captain Mason brought them in a supply of pop for the games, and gave a prize for a competition. The children, and indeed all the parish, were grieved to know that on the day following their friend was in hospital, and very ill. Loders children also had a gay time, with tree, games, presents, and a sumptuous tea. Later, the parents made a presentation to Mrs. Hinde. For Loders children the dull days after Christmas were enlivened by Sir Edward and Lady Le Breton's party at Loders Court, which followed the time-honoured ritual of conjuring and Punch and Judy, followed by tea and crackers, and the presentation by Master Edward Laskey of an orange and a half-crown to each child. Cheers for host and hostess were raised by David Skeats. The 60 guests included five sets of twins!

January 1959

King George the Sixth

CHAPTER 3
Loders Court

The Court is at the west end of the straggling Saxon ribbon development from Loders through to Yondover, Uploders, Matravers, and thence to Spyway and Askerswell. It did have a regal, if jaded, feel about it. Whereas now it has been smartened up to handsome Georgian proportions, at the time this book covers it was rambling, with interminable corridors, and elegant stairways, and always the excitement of the attics, the cellars and the Billiard Room. Sir Edward Le Breton held court to all-comers, including the youth of far-distant Bradpole (one mile away) whom he permitted to convert his manor into a prototype Youth Club. Scouts filled the Park; tennis-players played on the front lawn, under the church tower; squash-players descended into the lower wood via wild garlic and bamboo; and Sir Edward usually won, even at the age of eighty. On ceremonial occasions Sir Edward was magnificent with his plumes and medallions as a former member of the Royal Bodyguard. At the lectern he had the capacity to make the warfaring antics of the Israelites hauntingly awesome, even if the congregation shared with him a sense of bemused incomprehension. Before the Second World War his lordly generosity at Christmas extended to sending every tenant a catalogue from Gamages with the invitation to make a modest selection. With rationing after the war this gesture had to be reduced to a half crown and an orange for all the children of the parish.

Lady Le Breton exuded a natural aristocracy. Her Miss Haversham face and demeanour were usually preceded by a wide-brimmed hat that made her features distant, but her ancient, warm laugh and her capacity for sly works of kindness meant she was held in affection by all. At teatime her speciality at the grand dining-table to delight young boys and girls was to chop off the top of a large orange and fill it with sugar lumps: a much coveted commodity. Then the cake was usually Battenberg, which other people call 'window cake'. She had an unusual custom of filling the silver teapot with fresh hot water and then pouring the contents on spots on the Persian carpet – 'to preserve the colour.'

The geography of the Court is such that the gardeners had to cross the churchyard to reach the spacious vegetable garden. In it were magical toolsheds, greenhouses and bonfires where turf was cooked on corrugated iron for cleansing in autumn, and mysterious places where leaves were left to dry and make a mulch. In spare moments 'Messr.' – a title of respect – David Crabb, the Head Gardener, would plant ageratum down the churchyard path to the accompaniment of a Woodbine cigarette, and a felt hat, and a dog called Sandy (of mixed origins). His daughter Jessie is continuing the tradition. In his pocket he would have a slab of Dairy Milk chocolate to sustain him and to reward the Vicarage boys if they saved him labour. The peaches behind the churchyard wall were always a source of temptation. At the bottom of the garden was a plantation of Kentish cobnuts which he would store in salt and water in a large stoneware jar.

If you know the *Go-Between* by L.P. Hartley, and have seen the film, then you know the atmosphere of this intensely English scene – but that novel was set in pre-First World War Edwardian England. The remarkable thing about Loders Court was that it was a way of life at its height just before the Second World War, with rich persons gallivanting between house-parties and bathing and tennis, and numerous servants. After the Second World War, the echo continued: the Court seemed trapped in a time warp. What was being enacted was a determination to ensure the continuity of a feudal way of life that was benign, generous and communal. Its detractors point to privilege, wealth, pomp and circumstance, and patronage: at the time, it seemed natural. The Vicar recited the words of the Baptism service off by heart for the great-grand-daughters of Sir Edward and Lady Le Breton when his eyesight was failing. He believed in continuity.

The shady nook

To lounge on the lawns of Loders Court in a baking hot sun, and watch the sellers of jumble sweating at their work, or Lady Le Breton coaxing customers to the remote and shady spot where she had parked the ice-cream, was in itself worth the admission fee to people who, the day previous, had been crouching over a fire lamenting that the rain driving against the windows marked the arrival of winter.

September 1953

Coronation brocade

A handsome piece of blue brocade from the Coronation furnishings of Westminster Abbey has been acquired for Loders Church by Sir Edward Le Breton. At his order Northover and Gilbert have framed it, and it now makes a seemly backing to the credence table in the chancel. A piece of brocade from the Coronation of King George VI, also presented by Sir Edward, makes an effective reredos to the Ladye Chapel altar.

January 1954

The palace of sweetmeats

'The Court Party', which is the local name for the annual children's party given by Sir Edward and Lady Le Breton, was a fitting finale to the round of Christmas feasting in Loders, and followed the pattern which has endeared itself to three or four generations of Loders children. A motor coach collected the children, and decanted them into the billiard room, where they found Punch and Judy ready to amuse them, and a magician from Crewkerne waiting to take over when Punch got tired. The children were trying hard to expose the knavery of the magician, and young Eddie Edrich was just getting into the way of being sorcerer's apprentice, when Lady Le Breton appeared, and swept them all into the Palace of Sweetmeats (which at ordinary times is the dining-room). There, such provision had been made that full and blown small boys turned from meringues remaining uneaten to a riot of cracker-pulling. Master Edward Laskey [Sir Edward's grandson] made a distribution of half-crowns and oranges, on the strict condition that he got his own first, and one of the little girls voiced the thanks of the company to the kind host and hostess in a speech admirably compressed. Sir Edward holds that nothing is worth saying if it cannot be said in ten minutes. This speech pleased him hugely. It took five seconds.

February 1954

Le Breton abroad

Mr. David Le Breton, nephew of Sir Edward, has gone to take up a post in Tanganyika, and is not likely to visit Loders in the next three years. The good wishes of the congregation will go with him. His occasional appearances at the lectern were much appreciated.

August 1954

Shot wires

The rook shooting at Loders Court fell on a day that was abominably wet, and in consequence few guns turned out. The bag amounted to some forty rooks and the telephone wires (as a result of the latter, Loders was out of touch with civilisation for many hours). Defaulting guns, having since learnt of the crates of refreshment lying about at Loders Court unopened, are cursing the rain. They should be repenting, for their generous host had provided mountains of food as well, which, in these days of peace and plenty, are not easily disposed of.

June 1955

A weekend in the country

Six officers of the Honourable Artillery Company came from London early in December to spend the weekend at Loders Vicarage (the Vicar being their chaplain). The weather and Sir Edward Le Breton co-operated in shewing these city gentlemen the Dorset countryside at its winter best. With Mr. David Crabb in the congenial rôle of head gamekeeper, the party did a shoot over Sir Edward's primeval forest on Powerstock Common. Mr. Crabb was worthier of the occasion than the guns, for he put up a creditable selection of the forest's denizens – pheasants, woodcock, deer, and even a fox – but the guns were too entranced by the beauty of the bracken and the forest glades to hit much. Perhaps they were a bit puffed, too, for wading waist-deep through bracken strains the sturdiest bellows. Although the officers had no exciting stories to tell at dinner that night, they enjoyed it all immensely, and are eager to come again. On the Sunday morning they lent a touch of colour to the church service by parading in full regimentals (their spurs being the admiration of the small boys), and one of them, Lieutenant Richard York, read the lesson.

January 1956

A pioneer of vaccination

After reference had been made in a Loders sermon to the alarming decrease in the rate of infant vaccination, which is worrying the Ministry of Health, Sir Edward Le Breton showed us an interesting old certificate. It was issued by the Royal Jennerian Society, a pioneer in the fight against smallpox, and this particular specimen records that 'The Governors by an unanimous vote did themselves the high gratification to elect the Reverend P. Le Breton an honorary member of their great royal establishment' on May 17th 1820, the anniversary of Doctor Jenner's birthday. The reverend gentleman whom the Society did themselves the high gratification to elect, was Sir Edward's great-grandfather.

June 1956

Sir Edward Le Breton

Anatomy of the fête

This year there was a fortnight of skittles, but it made only the same profit, £25, as a week of skittles had made the previous year. Which shows how much depends on the timing. The skittle alley had to be hired, and we could not have it at the usual holiday time. When we did have it, a belated haymaking season was in full swing, and a rival skittles was giving neighbouring Bradpole quite a night life. Our skittles chief, Mr. McDowall, therefore had no increase of profit to show for his labours. But Messrs. R. Dennett and B. Osborne netted the best part of another £7 for him with lawn skittles on the day. In a weak moment Sir Edward had allowed the skittles on his tennis court, and the balls were going straight to his heart until his head gardener, Mr. David Crabb, managed to convince him that there was nothing better for a damp tennis court than to be pressed by hundreds of boots and high-heeled shoes.

September 1956

A letter to the editor

'Dear Sir – I write as one who has a long and happy connection with Loders. I was married in Loders Church to the twin sister of Elston Paul. We always looked forward to our visits to see family and friends, but whilst in London one of the things we look forward to most is to receive our copy of your interesting and amusing *Parish Notes*. 'Today (Feb. 12th) I had an experience which I thought might make a story for a future edition. As a London taxi-driver I was hailed this morning to drive a lady and a gentleman and their son to Buckingham Palace for the Investiture. I recognised them as Mr. and Mrs. Laskey and Master Edward, but they did not know me. It was quite a coincidence that out of all the thousands of London taxi-drivers Mrs. Laskey should hail me, whose first visit to Loders in 1921 was made possible by her father, Sir Edward Le Breton.

Yours sincerely, Arthur Hosler, Clapham Common, London.'

March 1957

A double christening

The twin daughters born to Mrs. Denis Laskey at Summerlea Court, Dorchester, were christened at Loders Church on August 21st in the presence of a large family gathering. They were named Ellen Charlotte Le Breton and Audrey Nancy Le Breton. The hymns chosen for the occasion were 'O God, our help' and 'Who would true valour see,' with Mrs. Tiltman at the organ. Juliet Willmott read the Gospel. The twins assisted by being perfectly quiet, although they were both wide awake at the crucial moment.

September 1957

Missing the party

The Court party had to suffer change this year, for Sir Edward Le Breton was prevented by the death of his brother-in-law from joining his lady in the duties of host and hostess. This was probably the first time he had missed the party in thirty-seven years, and the degree to which the children missed him was suitably expressed in David Skeats' speech of thanks.

January 1957

The Misses Hinks

The middle cottage in the row of three known as Court Cottages, Loders, stands empty, and many a passenger regards it ruefully. For years it was the home of two of the best liked inhabitants of Loders, Miss Edith and Miss Elizabeth Hinks, and these have lately gone to live at Frome Vauchurch. Their father was coachman to Lady Nepean, at Loders Court, and they liked to recall old times, such as Primrose Day, when their father used to drive Lady Nepean through the village in a coach meticulously dressed with bunches of primroses. Miss Edith did domestic service in South Africa and Malta, and was with Lady Le Breton for twenty-three years. Miss Lizzie (as her friends called her) practically began her conscious life as a pupil at Loders School, and stayed on there as a teacher for forty years. She cannot properly be said ever to have left the parish. It was only the problems of advancing years, and not any dissatisfaction with the parish, that resolved them to leave. They are now sharing a bungalow with Mrs. Harvey, who was in service with Miss Edith Hinks at Loders Court. They said they would often be thinking of Loders, and we are sure they will be.

February 1958

Former butler at the rook shoot

This year's rook shooting at Loders Court was graced by the Jeeves-like presence or Mr. Frank Gillard, former butler at the Court, who was fetched from his retirement at West Bay by Sir Edward so that he might enjoy once more the function over which he used to preside with such dignity. Mr. Gillard sat enthroned on the step of the verandah, receiving the homage of old friends, while the marksmen applied themselves to cakes and ale on the lawn. Because of his failing sight, Mr. Gillard could not see how picturesque the scene was, but he must have sensed the surrounding affection, and the whiff of 'the dear dead days beyond recall'.

September 1959

Feeding the Panda

It will interest our children to know that Loders is helping to feed the giant Panda in the London Zoo. When an appeal was made for bamboo shoots, the nursery garden of Loders Court responded by despatching a few pounds, and has since been listed as a reserve supply.

January 1959

The court gardener

Mr. David Crabb has completed forty years at Loders Court. He is in his prime, and considers he has just embarked on the second forty years. His employer, Sir Edward Le Breton, has presented him with a handsome silver salver, inscribed 'To Mr. and Mrs. David Crabb, from Colonel Sir Edward and Lady Le Breton and Mrs. Denis Laskey, in memory of a friendship of forty years.' Mr. Crabb is very proud of this.

It is a rewarding proposition for anybody who feels the heat to ask to see it.

September 1959

The court butler

The funeral of the late Mr. George Gillard in St. Mary's, Bridport, was well attended by Loders people, and the Vicar was privileged to take part of the service. For years Mr. Gillard, as butler of Loders Court, then as a churchwarden and chorister, had been a Loders institution, and everybody felt that his passing, at a ripe age, had severed another of the few remaining links with the old order. Much sympathy was felt for Mrs. Gillard, who had been the stay and comfort of his years of blindness. The departure of a character as colourful as Mr. Gillard has produced a crop of reminiscences. To those of us who only knew him as the perfect Jeeves, never off his dignity, and with a knack of making the humblest guest at the Court feel like a peer of the realm, it was news to be told that he once sported a motor bike to do his lord's bidding the more expeditiously, but abandoned this form of locomotion after one tumble outside Loders School, and another at Chideock. When he made history in Loders Church by stumbling in the church-wardens' march to the altar and scattering the alms all over the floor, the Chancel noted with surprise that he could do with an almsdish what he had never done with the hottest dish of soup.

October 1959

The court party

The large tree which presided over the scene had been given, as usual, by Sir Edward Le Breton. For Loders children there was also the 'Court Party', with Sir Edward and his lady playing the rôle of host and hostess for about the fortieth year without a break. In the billiard room a conjurer found it no easy matter to bemuse an audience of adroit infants, who knew all the answers, and were not very forthcoming with pound notes for his experiments. Mr. Punch, however, had no difficulty, for he brought out of his armoury not only St. George and the dragon, but a new Beatrix Potter menagerie. A procession from the billiard-room to the dining-room put the children at the operational end of a tea which defeated even their seemingly insatiable appetites. On leaving, each child received an orange and a half-crown from a Santa Claus in whom the fanciful discerned a likeness to Master Edward Laskey. The vote of thanks was moved by Bernard Paul, who shewed promise of making a good after-dinner speaker.

January 1960

Edward Laskey in Rome

Loders Sunday School were pleased to receive a picture card from one of their members, Master Edward Laskey, who spent the Easter holiday with his parents, now stationed in Rome. The card reads as if he greatly admired St. Peter's and its thronging multitudes, but would not exchange Loders Church and Sunday School for it, even with a make-weight thrown in. There's loyalty for you!

May 1960

Ruby wedding

Sir Edward and Lady Le Breton celebrated their ruby wedding on June 19th. The news was a pleasant surprise to us. They both wear so well that we may be forgiven for not having anticipated it by inference. Had the ringers known, they would have pealed the bells. Dorset superstition rules that to do it after the day would bring the recipients certain bad luck, which God forbid.

July 1960

Baskerville Bible and Prayer-Book

Our attention has been drawn to a recent number of the *Illustrated London News*, which gives a picture of a group of boys in Scotch College, Melbourne, admiring a Baskerville Bible presented to the school by Sir Winston Churchill. Baskerville was printer to the University of Cambridge in the mid–18th century, and his workmanship is highly prized.

The big bible from which the lessons are read in Loders Church is a Baskerville, dated 1769. We also have a Baskerville Prayer-Book. Both were originally in the Le Breton family, and were presented by Sir Edward many years ago.

August 1960

The way to address a gentleman

Sir Edward Le Breton received a Christmas letter from his old batman in India. The superscription is 'Your Majesty Sir Sahib Bahadur Lord Le Breton – 'Salaam'. ('Sahib Bahadur' means 'The Lord, the Brave One'.) The letter continues, 'Your slave Jaghul urges that I am quite well here, with your grace. And I always pray God you may live long and keep sound health, Sahib Bahadur. I am still in the service, and I would have become retired after two years more service, and until I will live alive I would have been sent my best compliments in your service. I am full of confidence that you would have been replied of my letters. I would have become very grateful to you for ever. Pay my best respects to Lady Sahib. Pay my salaam many times to your Sahib and Miss Sahib. Salaam and best respects to all of you from my wife and son. I would be very grateful to you for reply soon. Your old humble servant Jaghul!' Sir Edward's amused comment on his slave's letter was, 'He is the only one who addresses me properly!'

January 1961

A hardy annual

Neither illness at Loders Court, nor the atrocious weather, not even the lack of school children, prevented the annual party given by Sir Edward and Lady Le Breton from pursuing the even tenor of its way. Indeed, the children with long experience of these parties voted it the best ever. Although there are at present not many more than a dozen children in Loders School, there is no lack of babes and toddlers. As these and their mothers were invited to the party, the sumptuous tea-tables were well furnished with guests and the cheers called for by David Skeats for the host and hostess rose lustily from sixty throats. Master Edward Laskey was not present this year to give out the half crowns and oranges as the guests departed, but they received them all the same, and the coach as usual was waiting at the gate to take the distant dwellers home. The children enjoyed the Punch and Judy show which is invariably part of the entertainment. So did Lady Le Breton. She tells us she noted with satisfaction that Mr. Punch's morals had improved. This year it was a crocodile he beat and not his wife. Obviously the civilising influence of Loders Court is beginning to be felt. But what a tough old boy is Mr. Punch. He resisted it successfully for forty years.

February 1961

Sir Edward's peaches

Those of us who are neighbours of Loders Court can lift up our heads again. Sir Edward grows peaches on his side of the south wall of the churchyard. Lately the peaches have been vanishing at an alarming rate. We catch a mutter of 'small boys' beneath Sir Edward's breath, and feel he is politely hinting at us, because the dearth of small boys is lamentable. But now we are cleared. Three grey squirrels live in the yew tree at the west end of the wall. They have been seen scampering along the wall to the peaches, and scampering back each with a peach in his paws. The peach itself is not the attraction, but the kernel inside the stone. Last Sunday at matins, the Vicar, high and lifted up in the pulpit, cast a preacher's ecstatic eye through the Ladye Chapel windows, and saw – one of the squirrels hopping along the wall to the peaches! This was the cause of the strange hiatus in the sermon, which he nearly forgot in his anxiety to draw the attention of the chancel to the spectacle. It seems, however, that the intelligence has now reached the chancel. It sounds, at this moment, as if the gardeners have opened fire on the thieves.

August 1961

Court deaths

Our Christmas was overshadowed by three deaths, all connected with Loders Court. Mr. Derek Barnes, the only son of Mr. & Mrs. H. K. Barnes, of Loders Mill, died at the untimely age of thirty, from leukaemia, curiously a disease in which he had taken a morbid interest months before he contracted it. He had been a man of great physical strength, with a huge capacity for sustained hard work. His sunny disposition, combined with a kind and obliging nature, made him popular over a wide neighbourhood. Loders Church could not accommodate all the people who attended his funeral. The sympathy felt for his widow and their three small children is tinged with admiration for the magnificent spirit in which she met this adversity. The flowers on Derek's grave were still fresh when the ashes of Sir Edward Le Breton were borne by his oldest retainer, Mr. David Crabb, to their resting place under the great yew tree near the south porch. Despite our sense of loss at the passing of the old order at Loders Court, the service was inspiring, thanks, perhaps, to the good singing by a congregation on whom the beauties of the old prayer book service were not lost. Under Sir Edward the temporal power of the manor of Loders was only a shadow of its former self, but the feudal spirit of centuries survived among the villagers, who continued to look to the squire as their natural leader, and their helper in times of need. They never looked in vain. Many stories could be told of secret acts of kindness that he did for one and another, especially before the coming of the welfare state. But it is the young people who will miss him most. Under his régime they needed neither youth organisations nor public playing field, for the Court was theirs for winter games, and its grounds for summer tennis. As the children grew up and went away, Sir Edward corresponded regularly with many of them, and a call on him was a 'must' when they came home on holiday. He was at his happiest at the Christmas Party he gave the village children every year in the dining room at the Court. In this he was aided by his lady wife, who always provided a feast which defeated the biggest appetite. (Here, may we say offstage, it is a heavy blow to us that she is to make her home elsewhere: her departure will leave a void quite as big as his, and nowhere will it be more keenly felt than at the 8 o'clock service, where she was the doyenne of the communicants). Sir Edward did not claim to be religious, but he had no doubt that the church was a good institution, and he set a fine example of regular attendance. It will take a long time for the picture of him striding down from the chancel to the lectern to read the lesson to fade from our memories. The third death was that of another prominent parishioner, Mr. Sidney Brown. He was a native of Loders, and spent all his long life here. He began work at Yondover Farm, and later became coachman to Major Beadnell at Loders Court. On the latter's death, he went into business as the village carrier, with a smallholding as well. He used to deliver string to the cottages for braiding. It was fitting that he should be buried in a family grave next to that of Major Beadnell. *Postscript*: One of the mourners at Sir Edward's funeral was Miss Wilkes, a former headmistress of Loders School, greatly beloved. She had had to be up at 6 a.m. to do the difficult train journey from Parkestone.

January 1962

Court Party

There were upwards of seventy children, from babes-in-arms to youths about to leave school, with a generous sprinkling of parents. It is the way of youth to gather rosebuds while it may, so the ghost of Sir Edward and the old Christmasses at the Court was not allowed to lower the temperature of the party (which his ghost would not have wanted to, anyway). The afternoon of games, organised by Misses Ruth Willmott and Pat Maddison, kept everybody on the move and boisterously happy until tea time, when appetites were ready for the feast of good things the hostess had provided. The company was bigger than anybody had forseen, but titbits enough remained to give some of the old parishioners a treat as well. As the children left the hall, each received the traditional half-crown and orange. Prudent parents hustled their charges out quickly after the cheers for Lady Le Breton. These were intended to reach her at Goring and they could imperil the structure of the Hut, without getting as far.

February 1962

Lady Le Breton

All her friends in Loders will like to know that she is now comfortably settled at the Grange, Goring-on-Thames, within easy reach of her sister, Miss Audrey Sawbridge, and not far from her ancestral home. She entertained the Vicar and Mrs. Willmott right royally the other day, and was avid for news of

Loders. She has since written in characteristic vein: 'Will you be so very kind as to put a notice in your famous paper? I shall then feel so much more *correct* towards my old friends of forty-five years' standing.' The notice is: 'Lady Le Breton would like to say how sorry she is not to have been able to say goodbye to all her friends and neighbours as she would have wished before leaving Dorset.'

July 1962

End of an epoch

The great event in Loders in June, and a rather sad one, was the sale of the surplus furnishings of Loders Court. To the 'foreigners' and dealers it was a sort of fête day. Some of the selling was in the open air; the Court was at its loveliest in the sunshine, and for those who had not brought sandwiches to eat on the lawn there was a refreshment van at the front door. To the villagers it was the end of an epoch, warranting a day off, and many bought mementoes of the old squire for their own homes. Like most sales it had its surprises. A small picture which the uninitiated would not have looked twice at was run up to £200 in a few seconds, and that we suspect was not the limit of its ascent. But the great mahogany dining table went for a song and suffered the indignity of having its legs sawn off and thrown in a corner. The purchaser only wanted the wood.

July 1962

In memory of Sir Edward Le Breton

Lady Le Breton who, we are pleased to say, is keeping well, and living with her sister, Miss Audrey Sawbridge, in the latter's home at Goring-on-Thames, has been corresponding with the Vicar about the form of the memorial she wishes to give to Loders Church to mark Sir Edward's long lay rectorship. He was Lay Rector of Loders for no less than forty-two years. This is an office which goes back for four hundred years, and one of the duties that used to be attached to it was the keeping of the chancel in repair. To compensate him for his outlay on the chancel, the Lay Rector received the rectorial tithe, which at Loders is the princely sum of five pounds per annum. So the Lay Rectors were never much in pocket. But ours never complained of their hard lot, as some in other parts of the country did, and there was never any need for Loders churchwardens to put Sir Edward in County Court, for he rather treasured his obligations to the chancel. In 1936 a benign government became aware of this small depressed class, the Lay Rectors of England, and came to their rescue. An Act of Parliament relieved all lay rectors of chancel repairs, and placed these squarely on the shoulders of the church councils. It also relieved the lay rectors of the rectorial tithes, and vested these in Diocesan Boards of Finance for the benefit of the chancel concerned. The Loders chancel fund now produces just about enough per annum to pay the chancel insurance. Although Sir Edward had been under no financial obligation to the chancel from 1936 till his death, Lady Le Breton felt that something connected with the chancel would be the most fitting memorial, and at first suggested the renewal of the chancel roof, which the architect's report says must be undertaken not many years hence. The snags in this scheme were that there is wear in the roof yet, and that prices when the job needs to be done are unpredictable now. The plan she has now adopted is this: she has vested the sum of £500 in the Salisbury Diocesan Board of Finance. It will be known as the Sir Edward Le Breton chancel fund. Loders Church Council may not touch the capital, but the profits arising therefrom will always be at their command for chancel repairs. The beauty of this scheme is that instead of the donation being put to one item of repair and exhausted, it is put to grow, and will assist all chancel repairs down through the centuries, with luck engendering thousands of pounds in the process. A small tablet recording Sir Edward's lay rectorship is to be put in the church. As the people of Loders read this, they will doubtless recollect that it was Lady Le Breton who gave them the electrical heating apparatus in the church. She might well have retired from the parish content with having more than 'done her bit'; now from Berkshire comes this further proof of her love of Loders Church, and her desire to help the parish bear the cost of its repair. Everybody will be deeply touched. This will be her memorial, too, for, come wind, come weather, at the eight o'clock she was rarely absent from the altar rail.

December 1963

Lady Le Breton

Our readers will be glad of news of another invalid in whom they are deeply interested, Lady Le Breton. She is in a pleasant nursing home beside the Thames at Goring, making light of a broken hip which refuses to mend. Friends descend on her with flowers to cheer her up, and make the odd discovery as they come away that it is she who has cheered them up. She is still greedy of scraps of news of Loders. Her heart is still here. She sends good wishes to everybody.

October 1964

The death of Lady Le Breton

The death of Lady Le Breton cast a shadow over Loders Harvest Festival. She died in the nursing home at Goring-on-Thames where she had long been confined to bed after falling and breaking her hip, which would not mend. The news came on the Saturday morning when the ladies were decorating the church for harvest. This was a task that she had joyfully performed on the chancel for over forty years. As the big bell tolled, the decorators could not help thinking how fitting it was that she should have died on that day of all days, for like most country people she liked harvest best of all the festivals. After the cremation at Reading, the ashes were brought to Loders by her daughter and son-in-law, Mr. and Mrs. Denis Laskey, for burial. The service, which drew a large congregation, was preceded by an hour of half-muffled peals of the bells, and the organist and full choir were in attendance. Mr. Laskey read the lesson, and Mr. David Crabb, head gardener at Loders Court, lowered the casket into the grave alongside the remains of the late Sir Edward Le Breton. The grave is under the yew tree opposite the south porch, the spot chosen by Lady Le Breton. There were masses of flowers. On either side of the casket on the chancel step was a pitcher of splendid chrysanthemums from the Mothers' Union (grown by

Lady Le Breton

Mr. Horace Read). There was also a large posy of autumn leaves and berries from the children of Loders School. Only a few of the flowers were put on the grave: the rest went to brighten the wards at Port Bredy and Bridport hospitals. Old parishioners who knew Lady Le Breton's whims noted with a satisfaction that the family wreath, into which Mrs. David Crabb had put all her considerable art, had a motif of her favourite belladonna lilies. As the funeral was only a few days after harvest festival the decorations were kept up, and the ladies watered and refurbished the flowers, so that her last service should be in all the glory of harvest. We haven't a shadow of doubt that she, on the other side of the veil, approved. She was not morbid about death and had discussed her funeral with the Vicar not long before. The sense of fun so characteristic of her was not absent even on this occasion. To her, death was but the natural way into livelier life. We in Loders, who found her so good a neighbour, and so loyal and generous a daughter of the church, feel that she is only a little removed from us. Her spirit lingers in the church and the walks she loved so well.

November 1966

Postscript

The Fund for repairing Loders Church roof continues to draw donations sizeable and small. Last month one came from Mr. Sidney Dunham and another from somebody signing as 'Self Denial'. Dr. and Mrs. Maxwell Jones (formerly of Bridport, now of London) kindly left a donation after their recent stay in Loders (where they were affectionately greeted by several patients). Miss Audrey Sawbridge, a sister of the late Lady Le Breton, also sent a donation. In her letter she says, 'I very gladly send a contribution towards the repairs needed, not only because Loders is such a lovely old church, but also because I have been to so many services there, including the Peace Day service of 1945 and Perronnelle's [Lady Laskey's] wedding. I remember the village and the church with the kindest feelings. It was quite part of my life during the forty years Sir Edward and Lady Le Breton were there and I am pleased to share a little in helping in this time of need.'

June 1967

Dottery Church

CHAPTER 4

From the font to the grave

The Court at Loders was one focal point for social life, as were the Vicarage, the school, the village hut, Askerswell School, and the pubs. In the Old Rectory at Askerswell lived an indomitable 'Cap'n' and Mrs. Aylmer. Their separate and joint exploits were side-splittingly eccentric and provided ample opportunity for the Vicar to create journalistic mirth. Mrs. Aylmer was a walking embodiment of the noble philosophy of jumble sales. Other characters got less coverage, but took their formidable cameo rôles in the village tableau. The village constable, P.C. Edrich, was a strong player, as was Granny Hyde.

What emerges is the Vicar's delight in characters as eccentric as himself. This was especially but not solely true if their actions and attitudes were fundamentally neighbourly and Christian. He revelled in characters if they added to the sense of fun with which he injected the humdrum rural realities. One person whom he admired was Dr. Morgan. This is what he wrote of him: 'Dr. and Mrs. Morgan have sailed for Australia to explore it from a caravan. The doctor has a store of experience in India and Tibet to ruminate upon, which he loves to do over a pot of ale with anybody who shows interest. The stories are all the better for this mordant humour, and for his free-lance temperament which is not too reverent for the conventions.' (February, 1962.)

That could well be one of the Vicar's own best epitaphs. His appreciation of human character made no distinction between a retiring widow and an ebullient bishop. He had a great knack of turning obituaries into celebrations. He delighted in people. Landlords get full coverage for obvious reasons, even if some of their enthusiasms receive dismissive treatment. (Mr. Jack Verrinder was keen on the gentle sport of bowls ... 'but is not bowls a kind of therapeutical occupation for the aged and decaying rather than a sport?' (pp. 137–138)

He knew everybody's address with no need for postcodes to direct him up every lane in the valley. At the end of the lane would be such households as the Frys at the far end of Eggardon in a winding crevice in the hills he called 'the fastness of Nallers' (p. 145). In Uploders was the eccentrically named 'Knight's Pightle' christened by Miss Armitage (p. 121). Further down the River Asker, and under the railway line, was a small cottage optimistically named 'Sunnyside', though it seldom saw the sun. Mrs. D'Alcorn succumbed to dreadful floods when the Asker was in spate (p. 141). Further west in Dottery were the Blue Ball, and the farm at Bilshay, where sons of Mr. Charles Barnes perpetrated inconceivable rural manoeuvres (p. 126).

Everybody had a place; everybody had a name; he lapped up the geography. He was the genius of the place.

The Aylmers of Askerswell

Reading from the New English Bible

The harvest sermon at Askerswell was preached to a full church by Dr. Maxwell Jones, of Bridport. Quite apart from the helpful things he said, it was good to have a doctor in the pulpit, shewing that religion and science are not mutually exclusive, as some people imagine they are. At Dr. Jones' wish, the second lesson was read from one of the latest versions of the Bible, and the reader, Captain Aylmer, operated in the unfamiliar element with commendable skill.

October 1955

Fête stings

It was a day on which beasts that sting had 'a down' on churchwardens. Mr. Cecil Marsh, churchwarden of Dottery, was so badly stung in the face by bees that he could not sit at the receipt of custom. Captain Aylmer, churchwarden of Askerswell, was caught by a wasp just as he was executing a delicate backing manoeuvre in the car park. Mrs. Telford's car, which was the one behind, had reason to be thankful that it was the Navy, and not some excitable lady-driver, that stopped the enemy dart, for it made the difference between a dented fog-lamp and a concertina'd engine.

September 1957

Flying the flag

A reference in the pulpit to flags flying from church towers on St. George's day jerked the officers of Askerswell Church into a reminder that their pole and rope were in no condition to fly a flag, so they got to work at once. Captain Aylmer, Mr. Adams and Mr. Donald Marsh ascended the tower, taking with them the Rector, not that there was work for more than two of them, but to save falling foul of the steeplejacks' union. Having reached the top with throbbing pulses and bulging blood pressures, they found that most of the tools needed were down at Captain Aylmer's, and great was the relief when the youngest of the four toilers, Mr. Marsh, volunteered to fetch them. The pole was lowered and the new rope attached, and then it was decided that it would be a crime to put the pole back up without a coat of paint. The paint, of course, was down at Captain Aylmer's, and this time it was he who volunteered to descend and fetch it. To everybody's relief, he eventually re-appeared on the tower roof with the paint and no burst arteries, and the job was completed. As the workers lounged about the battlements admiring their skill, gossiping, and presenting a fine study in still life, they were hailed by Mr. George Bryan from the yard of Court Farm, who wanted to know what the party up aloft was all about, he being a son of the soil and not understanding the urban notions of work. Next day he knew, for there, fluttering from the tower flagstaff, was the emblem of St. George. At Loders Mr. Harry Legg and Mr. McDowall found themselves in a similar tussle with their flagstaff, but over this we had better draw the veil.

May 1958

Getting out of the red

The reaction of Askerswell people to the news that their church is getting into debt was quick and characteristic. They called a general meeting, which decided to hold a Christmas Fair in the School, on the afternoon of Saturday, 12th November. The Fair is to include a stall for Christmas presents, another for cakes and groceries, and another for flowers and vegetables. There was a lively debate as to what the jumble stall should be called. Just as nowadays the undertaker likes to be called the mortician, the ratcatcher the rodent operative, and the chimney-sweep the fluonomist, so, it seems, the jumble sale likes to sound a bit more impressive. A shudder went through the meeting when somebody suggested 'second-hand stall'. This reeked of the back streets of Bermondsey. After much discussion, the jumble stall was put down as the 'bargain stall'. When the Rector began to argue that this title might imply, to the detriment of the entire Fair, that bargains were not to be had on the other stalls, the chairman, Mrs. Aylmer, put her foot down, and said there was to be no more argument. The jumble stall would be known as the bargain stall, and the Rector was to make it known through the *Parish Notes* that there would, of course, be bargains on the other stalls. Hence this paragraph. And so it came about that he thought discretion the better part of valour, and voiced no objection, when an area of fun and games for the children was designated 'children's corner', which can also mean a place of prayer. What's in a name, anyhow? Our village meetings would not be true to form if they ceased to make us laugh at ourselves. And all that really matters is that from now onwards the staunch churchfolk of Askerswell will be busy making and acquiring saleable goods for the Fair. *P.S.* – When it comes to raising money for the parish church, all are staunch churchfolk.

September 1960

Of carrots and cucumbers

The weather did not help the harvest celebration at Askerswell. It was murky for the morning service, and positively repelling for the evening, but nobody was willing to be put off by it. Congregations at both services were excellent. The profusion of flowers and garden produce within the church banished all thought of the fog and drizzle outside, and the lead of Loders Choir, who kindly came over for the purpose, soon had the most inarticulate members of the congregation making a happy noise. More and more the harvest festival seems to sublimate a local instinct for a flower show. The decorations become increasingly competitive. This year some monstrous new carrots from Captain Aylmer made Mr. Adams' pride and joy look like Pharaoh's lean kine. Mr. Sidney Fry was also in the field with a handsome cucumber whose length and weight had been widely published beforehand. At the sale next day Mrs. Aylmer, who presided, gathered in £9-odd for Church funds. How she does so well is easy to see. Mrs. Sidney Fry bought back her lord's cucumber for two shillings. When she heard the Rector asking for it she said he could have it for half-a-crown. Mrs. Aylmer agreed. Having already taken Mrs. Fry's florin, she took the Rector's half crown, and gave Mrs. Fry sixpence. The latter, minus her cucumber, and minus her two shillings, and with sixpence compensation, looked dubious, but was too well-bred to question the mechanics of any transaction in so good a cause. If the matter has since been sorted out, then our abject apologies to Mrs. Aylmer; if it has not, then congratulations on her salesmanship. After the harvest service there was a rival to the attractions of the decorations. When the congregation had finished inspecting the flowers and fruits, they gathered at the floor of the tower, and watched the young ringers ending the festival with a flourish.

November 1963

Mrs. Aylmer and Miss World

At their recent meeting in Askerswell House, Askerswell Church Council thanked the initiators and supporters of efforts for the organ fund, and reported that the organ firm's bill had been paid.

Capt. and Mrs. Aylmer

Church finances were healthy enough for the first stint of work ordered by the architect for the exterior of the church to be put in hand. After the meeting, which was guillotined to that end, Mrs. Aylmer invited the councillors into the drawing room, and filled their mouths with refreshments while their eyes feasted on the televised choosing of Miss World. If the councillors arrived home cross-eyed, it was because one eye had been fixed on the screen, and the other on the Rector.

December 1963

Granny Hyde

Rogationtide service

As the congregation left church to the music of the bells, we found to our delight, that it had included the Grand Old Lady of Uploders, 'Granny' Hyde, who is now in her 89thπ year. She had been brought by a nephew who lives at Salwayash. Mrs. Hyde is now somewhat deaf, but she said she had heard and joined in the singing, and had enjoyed it all.

June 1954

A survival of Victorian independence

Mrs. Granny Hyde, who keeps the little shop in Uploders, became a household word overnight by reaching the age of ninety in the service of the public. In these days, when everybody leans on the welfare state, Granny Hyde is a survival of rugged Victorian independence and self-help. With her old dog and her cat, she sleeps alone over the shop at night. Nationalisation held more terrors for her than burglars, and now that this is in cold storage for four years, she sleeps soundly. By day, besides dispensing lollipops to small boys, and Woodbines to naughty wives, she helps the balance of payments by keeping thirty hens to supply the packing station with eggs. She has a lingering suspicion that there is some connection between the troubles of the Chancellor and the fact that her hens have stopped laying. Strange to say, she has a good opinion of modern youth. She cannot speak too highly of her grand-daughter-in-law, Mrs. George Hyde, who, she says, tidies her up every day and waits on her hand and foot. Another of Granny Hyde's peculiarities is that she adores medicine. Most ancient people attribute their longevity to never having seen a doctor, but she ascribes hers to plenty of physic. The ordinary medicine bottle she disdains, and insists on a magnum, holding near half a pint. It pleased her highly that two doctors called on her birthday, and naturally they did not call empty-handed on so fine an advertisement. Whatever may be the cause of her longevity, we are sure that the parish hopes it will continue to operate for many years. Uploders without Granny Hyde is unthinkable.

December 1955

Towards their century

Our two oldest inhabitants celebrated their birthday last month. Mrs. Gibbs, of Dottery, was 92, and Mrs. Hyde, of Uploders, was 91. Mrs. Gibbs marked the day by dining out in Beaminster, making the journey in Miss Mackensie-Edwards' chariot, but 'Granny' Hyde's business instinct would not allow a trifle like a ninety-first birthday to take her away from the counter of her shop. Both ladies enjoy remarkably good health, though we regret that at the time of writing Granny Hyde is not quite her usual self.

December 1956

The passing of Granny Hyde

Uploders can never be the same without Granny Hyde and the little corner shop she presided over for fifty years. She was the village's oldest inhabitant, having reached 94. The will to live, which had brought her through many illnesses, seemed to forsake her shortly after Christmas. She took to her bed over the shop, and never fully came to life again, while her friends did their braiding in the parlour below, and kept ward. Mrs. Hyde was born in South Street, Bridport, the second of the seven children of Mr. and Mrs. John Gurd, who kept a fruit and fish shop there. She began work at the age of nine, and had to sell a box of bloaters each morning before she could go to school. On leaving school she worked at Pymore Mill, her day being from 6 a.m. to 6 p.m.! She married Mr. George

Granny Hyde at the Coronation

Hyde at St. Mary's, Bridport, in 1886. There was no honeymoon. She went straight to the cottage opposite Askerswell Church, her new home. She worked in the fields picking stone, and at harvest time she gleaned. On top of this she did the Rectory washing – often ten blankets at a time – and she made butter for 'the Marshes' at a shilling a day. Nor was it often that her place in Askerswell Church was vacant on Sunday. Later she moved to 'the cottage up in the garden on the right-hand side going into Askerswell', and started a shop, and began to keep her beloved hens. In 1906 she moved to Loders to the house at the top of New Street Lane now occupied by Mrs. Steve Newberry, and opened shop there. She used to go reed-drawing in the nearby barn. In 1910 she bought the shop in Uploders, and there enjoyed many happy hours with her hens in the orchard. She celebrated her golden wedding in 1936, and lost her husband in 1941. She had one son, and a daughter who died at the age of two. It is thanks to her grandson, Mr. George Hyde, his wife Dora, and their son Brian, that Granny Hyde was able to maintain till the end the independence she so greatly treasured. Although they lived many yards up the road from her, they waited on her hand and foot for nineteen years, Mrs. Hyde junior often having her own mother to care for as well. They set a fine example of duty to the aged – as did her kind neighbours.

April 1960

In memory of Granny Hyde

Mr. and Mrs. George Hyde offered, and the Easter Vestry promptly accepted, a flower stand of wrought iron to go in the blocked-up north doorway of Loders Church. A stand regularly borrowed from Mrs. R. Pitcher at festivals has proved the effectiveness of this spot as a background for flowers. The new stand will be in memory of the late Granny Hyde.

May 1960

* * * * * *

A worthy deputy

Mr. Harold Spiller, the Askerswell organist, finds it difficult to attend choir practice in the haymaking season, and his place at the organ is being filled by a versatile member of the congregation, Mr. John Barker, who plays five instruments of music. Mr. Barker is the answer to those who question whether the scientific and artistic temperaments can co-exist in the same person, for until his retirement Mr. Barker was pharmacist of a big London Hospital, and a university lecturer in that subject. With Miss Wilkinson giving the choir the benefit of her knowledge of voice production, it should go from strength to strength. When Mr. Spiller resumes the organ stool at the end of haymaking (which should be about Christmas at the present rate of progress) he will think he has come to the wrong church.

August 1953

Postscript to the fête

The only person for whom the fête was a disappointment was our local soothsayer, Miss Minnie Crabb, who had promised to do the fortunes, as usual, but on the fête day found herself in Portway Hospital for a serious operation. Loders fête usually finds her in a dim mysterious tent, beneath the sign of the witch and broom, waited on by a queue of clients. So pleased are we to have her safely home again that we will not ask how she managed to be in Portway Hospital on fête day without predicting it.

September 1953

'Knights' Pightle'

Reading in last month's *Notes* that this is the name given by Miss Armitage to her cottage in Uploders, some people are asking what 'Pightle' means. Miss Armitage's brother-in-law, who teaches classics at Dartmouth college, says it is a Saxon word, meaning 'a small plot'.

January 1954

Flattering Askerswell

Loders has betrayed the admiration it has for Askerswell's skill at running fêtes by imitating some of its methods. First, there is to be no admission fee; second, there is to be a week of skittling for a pig in the plot behind the Loders Arms prior to the fête; and third, a darts competition with a bottle of whisky as prize, is already in progress at the Crown. The pig has been presented by Mr. A.J. Wells. This will be the third pig he has presented to good causes in Loders in recent years. He thereby earns the title of champion pig donor, but he can scarcely boast that he won it in a fierce competition. In the matter of insurance against rain, Loders prefers not to imitate Askerswell. The latter did not heed their Secretary, or study the terms of the policy, and found that after paying a premium of £1.15s., they could not have claimed had the rain come down in bucketsful. The company had undertaken to pay the difference between the gross takings and £20 provided the rainfall equalled 1′10″. But it would be a poor fête that would not take £20 on a wet day. The experience of both Askerswell and Loders has been that there is nothing like a wet day for opening the bowels of compassion.

July 1954

Age cannot wither her

Miss Holmes and Miss Butterworth, who were the pivot of Loders social life when they lived here four years ago, paid a return visit in September, and called on many of their friends. They look as young as ever, and are still full of good works. What Shakespeare said of Cleopatra is equally true of each of them – 'Age cannot wither her, nor custom stale her infinite variety'. Loders' loss has been the gain of Ashton Keynes, in Wiltshire, where they are more than pulling their weight.

October 1954

The deserted smithy

The Forge is generally the busiest spot in Uploders. The clang of metal upon metal and the hiss of the bellows reach you before you turn the corner and behold homely cart-horses waiting to be shod, or impatient farmers clamouring to have a vital bit of machinery mended. Now the door is shut, and silence reigns. The reason being that the smith, Mr. Charlie

Gale, has damaged his ribs. He did it on a Saturday night, but we hasten to add that it could have been done as well on any other night. We are glad to report that Mr. Gale is making a good recovery, and finds laughing easier than he did. But while the Forge remains silent, we shall continue to be reminded of an epitaph on a stone in Loders churchyard, now decayed and lost. It was to a Loders blacksmith named George Cox, who died in 1823, and it ran:

My sledge and hammer lie reclined,
My bellows, too, have lost their wind,
My fire's extinct, my forge decayed,
And in the dust my vice is laid.
My coal is spent, my iron gone,
My nails are drove, My work is done.

October 1954

The late Mr. G.F. Gale

Our last number had just gone to the printers when we heard of the sudden death of Mr. Gale, of Bell, and so our sympathy with his daughter, Mrs. Good, is belated. Mrs. Good had to endure not only the shock of finding her father dead in bed, but the disturbing formalities of the Law which it observes when a person in robust health dies unaccountably. However, the findings of the post mortem examination saved her the further ordeal of an inquest. Bell, standing aloof from civilisation under the brow of a lonely hill, is rather romantic. It is said to have once been an inn, deprived of its licence on suspicion of being a poachers' rendezvous. Mr. Gale, wearing a heavy beard, carrying his eighty-four years lightly, and not minding how dark it was when he went by the cemetery enjoyed living at Bell and rather relished the awe in which the village children held him. The aura of a byegone century hung around him, and aesthetically it was entirely fitting that he should live at Bell.

February 1955

A loss to Loders

Mr. Percy Darby, whose brave fight against heavy odds was referred to in our last issue, died in Wimbledon hospital, and after lying a night in Loders Church, was buried in Loders cemetery. Speaking of him in church on the Sunday after the funeral, the Vicar said Mr. Darby had been a fine example of cheerfulness in adversity, and of neighbourliness. He was the village handyman, and would tackle the mending of anything from a child's doll to a tractor. His charges were so small that those who did not know his desire to be of service, and the satisfaction he got out of his varied jobs, wondered why he did it. His greatest hobby was the mending of clocks, and Mrs. Darby recalls how his household could always tell when the job in hand was 'ticklish', for then he would hum the hymn 'Christian seek not yet repose' *sotto voce*, and woe betide anyone else who made a sound. This hymn was sung at his funeral.

April 1955

Gent by name, gent by nature

The main topic of commiseration in Uploders is not the continuing cold winds but the departure to live with his sister of Mr. Roland Gent. The influence of this cultured and kindly hermit vastly exceeded his sociability. He laid claim to none of the latter, for he successfully parried all 'invitations out', and lived the remote life of a Diogenes in a hut, opposite the Forge, cultivating colds in winter, and strawberries in summer. His seeming aloofness did not deceive the people of Uploders, for they knew his lively interest in local affairs, and his generous support of good causes. His only public activity that we know of was to occupy the chair of philosophy at The Crown daily, from 11.40 a.m. to 12.40 p.m. We are glad he was able to vacate the said chair alive, which none of his illustrious predecessors did, and we are certain that the fortunate people to whom he has retired will before long be describing him in the terse formula of a former landlady of The Crown, 'Gent by name and gent by nature'.

April 1955

Household names

Mr. George Hansford, of Cuckolds' Corner, lately home from a major operation and a long session in Dorchester Hospital, is, at 75 years, as full of life as ever, and was busy clipping the garden path when his father in God called on him. It is not surprising that Mr. Hansford's sociable nature made him many friends among the other patients. He now gets calls from them, and of letters not a few. His address, like Loders Vicarage (which often becomes 'Lodgers Vicarage' on an envelope) is subject to rationalisation, and he finds he is now living at 'Cuckoos' Corner'.

July 1955

'Them were the days'

The thinning ranks of the 'old original' inhabitants of Askerswell have been further depleted by the death, at the age of 83, of Mr. Mark Fooks. His widow with whom much sympathy will be felt and he had been married for fifty-four years. Mr. Fooks had been a bellringer, and a member of the choir when the choir was over thirty strong. Like most ancient men, he lived much in the past, and never tired of comparing former times with the present, unfavourably to the present. He remembered when, of an early morning, no less than fifteen men passed through the Square to their work on Court Farm, and did not doubt but what 'them were the days'.

July 1955

Land worker

Old Mrs. Eastment, who lived in the thatched cottages opposite the Loders Arms, so rarely went out that some of her newer neighbours did not know of her existence. Yet she had a lively interest in the village and its church, and indeed in national occasions, for on Coronation Day the Vicar found her dressed in her Sunday best, hat and all, in honour of the Queen's Majesty, with her ear glued to a wheezy old wireless set. After the Coronation she nailed a poster of the Queen to the wall near her fireplace, and sat under it in her old armchair. It was still there when she died. Her passing was in keeping with her life, serene and unobtrusive. She had a slight stroke on Christmas morning. It was arranged to take her to Bridport hospital in the afternoon, but she ate her Christmas dinner first, then went to the hospital and slept peacefully away. She was buried at Loders cemetery in the grave of her husband, who had long predeceased her. From the age of nine she had worked on the land, and she loved it.

January 1956

Helping the newsmongers

With his usual thoughtfulness for others, Mr. McDowall, of Loders, allayed the seasonal shortage of news in February by having a fire which, incidentally, destroyed his garage and car. It was not his fault that there was a complete absence of wind, for a little co-operation on the wind's part might have made an inferno of all the neighbouring thatched roofs, and produced a news story bigger, brighter, and better still. The frost did what it could, but that was only to freeze the firemen's hose to the road – when the fire had been put out. The credit for starting the fire must go, it seems, to one of those fire-proof lamps that cautious people put under their cars to keep Jack Frost out of the cylinders, and the credit for calling the fire brigade so promptly belongs to Mrs. Chard, who sent her husband to the telephone kiosk while she fetched Mr. McDowall from the Archers (those Archers will have much to answer for one day). We fear that Mr. McDowall's kindness in filling the hungry columns of these *Notes* put him to great inconvenience, but the effects of his kindness were greater than he could have foreseen. For instance, all the sick of Loders were healed at a stroke: the rare excitement of a big fire got them out of bed and down the street in no time. And again, the fire and the talk about it were so warming that the inns did their best trade since the inception of television. Anybody who might be encouraged by Mr. McDowall's new car to think that a nice little fire, well away from the house, isn't a bad thing, is hereby warned to beware of insurance company logic. For it seems that if you lose a car when cars are appreciating, the company insist on paying the sum insured. But when cars are depreciating they insist on paying the market value of the car, and not the sum insured. It is to be feared that our hero's cheerful countenance masks a less cheerful heart.

February 1956

Personal

Mr. and Mrs. Malcolm McDowall acknowledge with grateful thanks the information that they are leaving Loders. Would any kind friend who knows when please communicate at once with Mrs. Malcolm McDowall at 'Raikes,' Loders? (Advert).

[Mr. McDowall lived in Loders until 1998 when he moved to a nursing home in Bradpole.]

June 1956

Excitement at Bilshay

After sticking to the work of their father's farm at Dottery with years of quiet efficiency of which the busy world took no notice, the sons of Mr. Charles Barnes have hit the headlines, one by taking a horse to drill mangold in a field and letting it bolt with the drill as far as Bridport Post Office; the other by letting a tractor run away with him into a stream. In neither case was the son very much at fault; Robert's horse had a thorough-bred hunter as its mother, and took fright because Robert had not shaved. Charlie's tractor was a bit porky because a drop of the famous Bilshay cider had got into the fuel tank by mistake. We are happy to report that Robert's ankle is out of plaster, and that no chances are being taken with the thoroughbred – Charlie leads him with chin newly reaped, while a man holds on to the drill.

June 1956

Farewell to the ladies

In 1950 Mr. and Mrs. Paddison left their nice old house in The Square, Askerswell, and the house then acquired the unusual distinction of becoming the home of four retired school teachers – Miss Webb, Miss Wilkinson and the Miss Croxsons. Dorset people are good judges of character. They promptly christened the newcomers 'The Ladies'. To call them anything else has never occurred to anybody, and this after six years, says more for them than a *Times* obituary. Their strenuous life in London would have been some excuse for their turning Askers House into a sort of enclosed nunnery, insulated from all village activities, with the senior Miss Croxson as Mother Superior, but, true to the form of ladies, they chose instead to pull their not inconsiderable weight in village affairs. Now that their departure is at hand, everybody is sad, and painfully aware that their place in the social life of the village will take much filling. They were the heart and soul of the Women's Institute, pillars of the Community Club, the mainspring of the winter lectures, and the guardian angels of the village school. In the days when there was no church caretaker they took their turn at church cleaning; they also helped with the altar flowers. They put their zest and their endearing sense of humour into church bazaars and jumble sales, and Miss Wilkinson, the musician among them, gave up her Friday evenings to train the church choir. When she returned from a long spell in hospital, suffering still from the effects of a tragic accident, she again took up her work for the choir. This notice of The Ladies may sound like an excerpt from 'Cranford' but it is no fiction, neither is it circumscribed by the law *De mortuis nil nisi bonum* because 'The Ladies' are anything but dead. Miss Wilkinson goes to live with a sister at Great Bromley, and Miss Webb and the Croxsons have taken a bungalow in North Allington.

November 1956

P.C. Edrich

An old soldier

Mr. Charles Edrich, grandfather of the Loders police constable, came on a holiday to Loders on a Wednesday and died of a heart attack in the small hours of the following Sunday. Like our Capt. Welstead, he had served in the Boer War. He had also served on the Indian frontier, and had been in Kitchener's Army, 'The Old Contemptibles'. His funeral was in his home town of Dorchester. When the clergyman and the mourners had departed, an ancient man came to the foot of the grave, with an effort drew himself to attention, and saluted. He was also an Old Contemptible.

June 1954

Baby for the constable

Two babies have been born since our last *Notes*. One was to Constable and Mrs. Edrich, of Loders, and although it weighed only three pounds at birth, and touched a low point of two and a half pounds, it is now doing well. It is a girl, and was baptised Heather Valerie at Portwey Hospital, Weymouth.

December 1955

Doubling its weight

Constable and Mrs. Edrich, of Loders, now have the custody of their premature baby, born at Portwey Hospital, Weymouth, in November. It has more than doubled its weight, and is doing well.

February 1956

Dick Turpin drops in

The choir's contribution to the fête was a social which added £15 to the funds and passed the evening most pleasantly. They took the stage as a gang of gipsies, interlarding the frying of sausages at a camp fire with song and dance. The song that was intensely local in its application was highly popular, and so was the dropping in on them of Dick Turpin, who recited The Highwayman so feelingly that it was felt he had just missed his vocation in being the village policeman. A lady visitor with a good voice insisted on embellishing the programme with some half dozen songs, and a child conjuror from Bridport received rapt attention. But the act that brought the house down was unrehearsed. Our organist was playing the part of the itching tramp on the park seat, and was trying to rid himself of fleas, when Tessa the Vicarage dog who was supposed to be at home and in bed, but was the principal spectator, sat up and begged for one with all the guile that she brings to bear on cakes and chocolates.

September 1956

Village bobby to Cyprus

Loders has a special interest in Cyprus now that its policeman, P.C. Edrich, has gone there in response to an appeal for volunteers for the re-organisation of the Cyprus police force. His term of duty lasts for twenty-one months, and he is likely to become a sergeant, having passed the examination some time ago. The ambitions of Master Maurice Matterface have also turned in a military direction. His smallness of stature and good health have gained him acceptance as a drummer boy. He will be sorely missed at Cloverleaf Farm, where he was shewing promise of making a good farmer. The thoughts of Master Frank Good, but not his ambitions, are also on the Services. He has had to register for national service, and will be going before long. This will create problems for his mother in her isolated cottage at Bell, and for Loders ringers, whose small company can ill afford to lose so regular a member as Frank. He will also be missed in choir and Sunday School.

September 1956

An intelligent appraisal

Sergeant Edrich, erstwhile our parish constable, is home on leave from Cyprus, and his many friends in this locality have seized the opportunity of getting an intelligent appraisal of the present situation in that troubled island. Sergeant Edrich joined the Sunday School outing to Weymouth, and gave a welcome hand in piloting the tea through the teeming traffic to the beach – nearly as tricky a job as handling terrorists. He was interested to be told by the Governor of Cyprus, Sir John Harding, at an inspection of the Cyprus police force, that Sir John as a boy learnt to swim at West Bay.

September 1957

Bastion of the law

P.C. Elliott, lately of Bridport, has taken up residence in the magnifical new police station at Welplot. Our former policeman, Sergt. Edrich, is in Cyprus. After a year of exemplary behaviour without a policeman, when we thought Authority was beginning to trust us, it is somewhat deflationary to have this bastion of the Law established in a dominating position in our midst. Strangers, seeing it, might jump to the wrong conclusion about our characters. But Mr. and Mrs. Elliott shew promise of becoming very acceptable neighbours, and if we persist in our good behaviour he may tell us why the south door of his mansion should be painted Mediterranean blue, and the east door canary yellow. We are sure there must be some deep reason for it.

January 1958

A proper endowment of mischief

Police-Sergeant Edrich and his family have left Loders for a new appointment, carrying with it a new house, at Weymouth. They were eight years in Loders. Two of the children, Eddie and Hazel, had grown up here, and were tearful at leaving their friends in Loders School. Eddie had a healthy boy's proper endowment of mischief, which found an outlet in Choir, Sunday School, and Cubs. All his friends in these organisations felt a pang at his departure, and are hoping to meet him on trips to Weymouth.

July 1958

* * * * * *

The laughing landlord

To the sorrow of the hospital staff, Mr. William Graves, landlord of the Crown and sidesman of Loders Church, is home again after a successful operation. His scintillating humour, and essays in Dorset dialect, transformed the hospital into a kind of Lido, and made some of the patients better before they meant to be. From his sick bed he sent a letter which made even the Easter Vestry laugh. Long may he make people laugh.

May 1957

An Askerswell worthy

Mr. John Granger Farwell ('Old Jack' to his friends) died at the home of his daughter Rose at The Fisherman's Arms, Chickerell, and was buried at Askerswell in the grave of his wife, who predeceased him in July, 1954. Mr. Farwell began his working life at Court Farm at the age of nine, and carried it on for fifty-seven years, until his retirement in 1939. With the exception of a spell at Loscombe, he was employed for the whole of this time at Court Farm as a carter and ploughman. When he began at Court Farm, it was a bigger holding than it is now, for it also included Stancombe, Nallers and East Hembury. Mr. Farwell made a substantial contribution to the Sunday worship of Askerswell Church, for he was a keen ringer, who rarely missed his place at the rope's end; his son blew the organ, and his four daughters sang in the choir. Although the final score of his eighty-five years were, as he put it, 'tarmented be them there rheumatics', he never lost his powerful sense of humour. It is a pity that his stories of an order of things now past were not written down as he told them. They would have made delicious reading.

March 1958

Martyr to asthma

By the death of Miss Lucy Isabella Scott (at the age of 77) in Uploders, the parish has lost one of its finest characters. She was a retired nurse, a native of St. Kew in Cornwall, and with her companion, Miss Friend, had been living in Uploders since 1934. It was her misfortune to be a martyr, in the full meaning of the word, to asthma, and night and day, for several years, she was under its constant attack. The doctors who attended her had the highest opinion of her fortitude. Although confined to her room, she took a lively interest in the church and the parish, and was a generous supporter of good causes. Her suffering never got the better of her sense of humour, nor made her self-centred, and she deeply appreciated the devoted care bestowed upon her by Miss Friend. Like the late Lady Pinney, she bequeathed her body to assist medical research, and after a funeral service in Loders Church, it was taken to the anatomical department of Bristol University.

March 1958

Mr. Billy Baggs

That authentic son of Dorset, Mr. Billy Bags, has lately been forced by indifferent health and advancing years to reduce his farming in Uploders to the keeping of a few chickens and pigs. Most of the land of the farm has lately been sold, and the stock also, but he will stay on in the house. The decision to stay on will give general satisfaction, for his twenty-five years of farming in Uploders and his rugged individuality have made him part and parcel of the local scene. When our reporter called on Mr. Baggs he was sitting on a barrel, bending over his stick and, of course, wearing the ancient hat that Uploders thinks he must wear to bed because they have never seen him without it. Mr. Baggs was chuckling at having scored a point off the doctor. 'It were like this,' he said – 'the doctor fixed a thing like a milking machine on me arm, and pumped, and looked at a little clock. Then he looks at me an' sez, "Baggs," he sez, "your pressure can be up a bit. You must stop takin' salt." I looks straight at 'im, an' I sez, "Can you tell me 'ow I can stop takin' salt? I don't touch the stuff – an' never 'ave." That put the doc in a flummox, I can tell 'ee,' concluded Mr. Baggs, with a fruity chuckle. 'Did the doctor tell you to stop taking this?' asked our reporter, with a nod towards the hogsheads ranged round the cider press. 'That's just where I 'ad 'im again,' said Mr. Baggs, 'I stopped meself, months ago, because I found a glass of Guinness at Mr. Graves's agreed with me tubes better.' We cannot think how this defection of the master cider-maker of Loders will be taken by the older drinkers.

October 1956

A grave departure

Loders is sad at the prospect of losing Mr. and Mrs. William Graves, who will shortly be leaving the Crown Inn, and taking up residence at Frampton, near Dorchester. His philosophy and wit were above the level of bucolic landlords in general, and went down exceptionally well with a glass of ale. Now that he is going, we regret that we did not imbibe more frequently of that fountain, which, in defiance of St. James, put forth the sweet and the bitter simultaneously. By instinct, if not so much by practice, a great Church of England man, he served as a sidesman of Loders Church, and was ever the genius of the sideshows at the fête. Like all good churchmen, he saw that the spiritual and the material are complementary rather than antagonistic, and it was entirely in character that his first present to the church should have been a set of prayer books, and his last a bottle of whiskey for the fête skittles. We wish him all the best and trust that his prophecy that we may still occasionally see him and his lady wife over from Frampton to church, may come true.

July 1959

Goings and comings

We are nearing the time of year when the swallows get together and go off to the sunny south, and pigeons come down from the north to take their place. This autumnal movement of birds seems to have its counterpart among humans. We have noted time and again that when parishioners leave for new homes, and others take their place, they tend to do it *en masse*, and in autumn. This adds to the melancholy which is one of the beauties of autumn, because those who leave us are not always birds of passage, but old friends, embedded in our affections, with whom we have shared the ups and downs, the joys and sorrows of years. Among this year's swallows are Captain and Mrs. Welstead, and their daughter Rosemary, of Uploders. Within a few days they will be gone to Wales to a new home. For 24 years they had been one of the delights of life in Loders, full of old-world courtesy and good works. The Sunday morning congregation will sorely miss 'The Captain'. Swallows come back, but he will not.

October 1955

A letter from Captain Welstead

So many enquiries have been made after the health of our old friend, Captain Welstead, late of Uploders, and now of Dolgellau, N. Wales, that we feel the following extracts from a recent letter of his will be of general interest: 'We are nearly recovered from the 'flu, but it leaves an old image like me in a battered condition. Our Bungalow is in a very rough little field, and we have been trying to start a garden, which may take many years. I have stripped the weedy turf off a 66' square, and dug over some, but 'tis very slow work after 'flu. Dolgellau is the quaintest town I know of. Many streets are no more than 9' wide, and never go straight for more than a few yards. I still get lost in it. Years ago a prisoner escaped from the jail, tried all night to find his way out of the town, and then in the morning gave himself up. The church is not beautiful, but large, and instead of stone pillars in the aisles, it has huge oak posts. Although the population is only 2,500, we have fifteen chapels of various sorts. A few Quakers still exist here. Not one of them quaked as much as I did in the cold of February ... It is a wonderful bit of country to view – little grass fields with stone walls, plenty of trees, and some sheep which live almost wild and can jump six foot walls. How they live this time of year puzzles me. The townsfolk are wonderfully polite, but I shall never understand their language, nor the weird spelling of their place names ... I must end now. Greetings to all the nice folk around you – and who is not nice in Loders?'

April 1956

'The Captain' passes on

News of the death of Captain George Welstead spread quickly in Loders, and was received with deep regret by all who knew him. He died of heart failure at his home near Dolgelley, North Wales, on May 19th. The manner of his passing suited his energetic, outdoor nature, for he was only in bed a week. The cremation was at Birkenhead. In deference to his wishes there were no flowers; he could no better bear to see flowers cut than he could to see trees felled, or a predatory pigeon shot. One wonders how so tender-hearted a man contrived to be so excellent a professional soldier. A special prayer for him was offered in Loders Church, where the memory of him will long be treasured. Winter or summer, rain or shine, he was usually in his pew on Sunday morning, having walked all the way from New Road, and he always arrived in good time, even when he was past his eightieth birthday. The choir liked his word of thanks for the singing as he came out of church, and the congregation liked his enquiry after their affairs as they went up the long path. 'The Captain' was a sermon in himself, for he shewed how attractive Christianity can be when it is lived.

June 1958

Gravelling at 81

The Sexton of Askerswell, Mr. Samways, has done excellent work in levelling the path up to the main entrance of the church, and putting down gravel on all the church paths. The path to the main entrance had become slippery, and one member of the congregation is known to have had a fall on it, so the gravelling will be welcomed for more than aesthetic reasons, although it has certainly smartened up the approach to the church. The pulling of a heavy roller on a slope might have taken the stuffing out of a man half Mr. Samways' age (he is 81). He makes light of it, however, and says that the paths are in for another rolling when the gravel has settled.

December 1958

Mrs. Hilda Jones

Mrs. Jones, wife of Dr. Maxwell Jones, has given Loders Church a fine lace super-frontal, which belonged to her late mother, who liked worshipping in Loders when she stayed in these parts. The super-frontal looks well on the very ancient chest which serves the Ladye Chapel as an altar, and hides the lock, which proclaimed rather too loudly that the chest was not an altar.

April 1954

Doctor in the pulpit

A notable feature of the Askerswell decorations was its exceptionally fine potatoes, carrots and gourds, which, as a rule, do not find a dry season congenial. The harvest sermon at Askerswell was preached to a full church by Dr. Maxwell Jones, of Bridport. Quite apart from the helpful things he said, it was good to have a doctor in the pulpit, shewing that religion and science are not mutually exclusive, as some people imagine they are.

October 1955

A thought for Easter

The appeal for a quarter of a million pounds for the restoration of Salisbury Cathedral has now almost reached its target. Loders Church, in about a year, has raised two thousand pounds for the repair of the Ladye Chapel roof, which leaves four hundred pounds still to be found. Our friends, Dr. and Mrs. Maxwell Jones, have just gone off to Africa to exercise a healing ministry in the name of Jesus Christ, for no material reward. And St. Paul says that this and everything like it, is futile, if Christ be not raised from the dead. The Resurrection is the corner stone of the Christian faith. No Resurrection and there would be no cathedrals or parish churches, no church people and no medical missionaries like the Joneses.

April 1968

Old boys of Loders School

Mr. and Mrs. Bartlett, of Matravers have staying with them until January Mr. Bartlett's elder brother Willoughby, who is on holiday from New Zealand, to which he emigrated forty-eight years ago, and where he is now a successful farmer of fifteen hundred acres. The brothers are both thoughtful men, and your reporter counted it a privilege to be present the other day when they awoke from a post-prandial siesta and began to exchange ideas. They are unanimous in ascribing any success they might have achieved in life to the strict discipline imposed on them by their old master at Loders School, Mr. Fooks. Looking at the local countryside with the eye of a comparative stranger, Mr. Willoughby is impressed by the quality of the thatching, and the tidiness of the hedges. Mr. Herbert agrees, but alleges that while the hedges may be tidier, thanks to hedge cutting machines, the men who can lay a hedge are getting fewer and fewer. Mr. Willoughby attended harvest services at Loders Church, and stoutly maintains against all that is said in praise of the golden-age of church-going, that he never saw the church more crowded, or better decorated, or heard heartier singing. Mr. Herbert concurs. Mr. Willoughby cannot think, when England is so splendid in its natural scenery and old buildings, why anybody should ever want to go holidaying on the continent. Mr. Herbert is entirely with him there, and insists that there is no need for anybody to go further than Loders. A problem that puzzles Mr. Willoughby is why New Zealand, with ten times fewer cars than England, should shew ten times more battered mudguards. Thereupon Mr. Herbert archly enquires the price of whiskey in New Zealand, and is assured it is lower than here. Mr. Willoughby sees the light, and says, 'Oh no! That ain't the reason.' Mr. Willoughby is convinced that people in England are happier than New Zealanders: they are more contented, and not so prone to over-reach themselves. Not having lived in New Zealand himself, Mr. Herbert prefers to reserve judgment. Mr. Willoughby alleges that any young man who wants to get out of the rut and make his pile can do it here without bothering to go to New Zealand. Mr. Herbert nods sagely. Mr. Willoughby contends that the British farmer is the most pampered farmer on earth. At this stage brotherly love shews the first sign of discontinuing, and our reporter deems it the proper moment to withdraw.

November 1959

Mr. Jack Verrinder

The new landlord at The Crown, Uploders, is Mr. Jack Verrinder, of Southall, Middlesex. A glowing testimonial from his workmates on his retirement shews that he was manager of the shipping and auxiliary services department of Quaker Oats, having worked his way up from the bottom. An unmistakeable military bearing that one does not naturally associate with Quaker Oats is explained by his having been in the Royal Marines for eight years, which included the Great War. (He and Mr. Owen senior, of Matravers, have discovered that they were on the '*Resolution*' together.) Mr. Verrinder is a man of parts. That he played for Southall soccer club merits his wife's description of him as 'a keen sportsman', and well accords with his lively, cheerful nature, but to be told in the same breath that he is a champion player of bowls is disconcerting, for is not bowls a kind of therapeutical occupation for the aged and decaying rather than a sport? Be that as it may, Mr. Verrinder has played for Middlesex, and has a sizeable box of medals of the kind commemorating the engagements in which bowlers take part. In fact, it was coming to Lyme Regis for holidays and bowls which minded Mr. Verrinder to retire to these parts. He is no stranger to licensed houses; his daughter keeps an inn at Richmond. Both his sons work for the Associated Equipment Company, and the elder is commercial marine manager. Mrs. Verrinder was a church worker at Southall. We hope she and her husband will be happy and take root here.

August 1959

Mine host's bowls

Mine host of the Crown, fresh with the glory of winning with Mr. Critchard the open pairs bowling championship at Weymouth, and beating an international in the process, is laying on some spicy competition in bowls. The number of new babies in the parish and their mothers' pride in them has made a baby show inevitable. It seems therefore that if the sun will but beam on us, we should be in for a jolly afternoon.

July 1960

Long service

Reporters of the local newspapers find Loders a gold mine of interesting news items. The other day they dug out our esteemed parish clerk, Mr. David Thomas, and gave his thirty years of service to Loders Church a good write-up, and also published with it a photograph of him which we all liked. The only fault to be found with the article was that it called him the sexton, which, of course, he is not. The sexton attends to the churchyard and the digging of graves, which Mr. Thomas does not. He is the verger, because he keeps the church clean, but what we prize him most for is that he must be one of the few remaining parish clerks, whose chief business was to lead the responses. We have a photograph of the interior of Loders Church, taken shortly before the restoration. Midway down the north wall of the nave is a three-decker pulpit. The bottom deck was for the parish clerk, to lead the responses; the middle and upper decks were for the parson to pray in and preach in respectively. Were the old three-decker still functioning, Mr. Thomas would be saying his 'awmens' and responses from the lower deck. As things are now, he officiates from the region of the choir. We hope he may be spared to lead us for many years yet. Without him the service is horribly lacking, and we feel all at sea. Another record of still longer service to Loders Church is held by Mr. Harry Sanders. For the last thirty-four years he has been either sidesman or churchwarden, and a practising one at that. He has lately retired from his job with Bridport Industries, and has given the church the benefit of his leisure by roughing up some of the paving stones that tend to be slippery near the south porch. This will earn him the thanks of not a few ladies who have measured their lengths there.

March 1960

A good farmer is a bad talker?

Loders Agricultural Discussion Club did themselves a good turn when they got Mr. Willoughby Bartlett, formerly of Loders, now of New Zealand, to give them a talk on farming in New Zealand. He produced out of his forty-odd years of experience one of the best and most entertaining talks the Club has had, belying – we hope – the saying that a good farmer is a bad talker. Mr. Bartlett noted that having been born in The Crown, it had taken him forty years 'down under' to qualify as a speaker in the Uploders Room, next door to The Crown. He returns to New Zealand this month.

January 1960

Changes at Loders police station

With the swiftness and silence characteristic of the operations of the Law, our Police-Constable and Mrs. Elliott vanished overnight, and in their place were P.C. and Mrs. George

Miller and their four children, who have already taken to Loders like the proverbial duck to water. We owe the loss of P.C. Elliott to his being so good at exams. He has been promoted to the C.I.D. at Dorchester. We regret his (and his wife's) departure, because they suited us, and villages are not every policeman's cup of tea. They have our best wishes. It will be a relief to the parish to know that the Vicar's first impressions of the new constable and his family are very favourable. In view of the Vicar's contacts with the police – which, unfortunately, are increasing – these impressions may be relied upon, especially as they are confirmed by the next door neighbour to the police station, Mrs. Darby. The two elder children, Julie (aged 11) and Kenneth (9) are already established in day school and Sunday school; and Jacqueline (3) and Caroline (18 months) are having a taste of Loders measles. Here a friendly word to potential disturbers of the Queen's peace – with P.C. Miller it will always be wise to 'come quietly'. He was the star turn of the judo club at Parkstone, his last station, and is a holder of the Green Belt in judo. Incidentally, Mr. and Mrs. Miller were stationed at Broadwindsor for four years before Parkstone, so they are not strangers to West Dorset.

February 1960

Obituary

Last month saw the decease of an old inhabitant of New Road, Uploders. Mr. Adolphus Brake died, rather unexpectedly, at the age of 85. He was born in Bridport, and grew up to be a mason. He did a lot of work on the prison at Portland, and was for a time in South Wales, where he was badly gassed in helping rescue operations in a mine disaster. He also served in the Great War. For the past twenty-one years he had been in retirement in Uploders. He was buried in his first wife's grave in Bridport cemetery, the Curate of Bridport officiating on behalf of the Vicar of Loders.

March 1960

Dottery churchyard

Mr. George Legg has been obliged by bad health to give up his work on Mr. Cecil Marsh's farm, where his skill as a rick-maker and hedge-maker was highly prized. He also, to our regret, had to surrender the care of the churchyard. It is fortunate that this has passed to a young man of rather startling energy, Mr. Reginald Bagg, who works hard on the farm at Ash, and then finds time to tend half the gardens and sweep all the chimneys in Dottery. 'I scarcely see him in the summer,' was his lady wife's rueful comment at her press conference on the appointment.

June 1960

Bad and good luck

Mr. Graham Roper, of Dottery, has been in the news for having turned his car over one day and passed his driving test a couple of days later. This compensates the disappointment he suffered on his twenty-first birthday. The celebration had to be postponed because the Portwey Hospital at Weymouth chose that day of all days to call in his mother who had been waiting for months for an operation. We are glad to say that Mrs. Roper is home again and recovering from a rather grim experience.

June 1960

Mrs. D'Alcorn

A measure of the severity of recent rains is that for the first time in our memory (which admittedly is not as long as some), Mrs. D'Alcorn's cottage near the railway bridge at Yondover was badly flooded. The cottage is called 'Sunnyside', but it looked anything from that when the lawn vanished under water, and the furniture floated on the ground floor. A great quantity of mud brought down by the water had choked the drains. Mrs. D'Alcorn is a widow, and on the sick list. She cannot speak too highly of her neighbours, who rescued her, and did not put her back until they had cleaned and dried the cottage.

October 1960

The irrepressible Mr. Graves

A pleasant experience befell the Vicar as the congregation was filing out of church one Sunday morning in January. The irrepressible Mr. William Graves (who with his lady wife is still a regular worshipper at Loders) waylaid the Vicar and craved leave of absence until Easter. Not that their room would be more welcome than their company. On the contrary. But it was so nice – and rare – to be made feel like a headmaster *vis-à-vis* a pupil who knew his place. Had leave not been granted, certain worthy youngsters in Taunton who are being tended by Mr. & Mrs. Graves would have been denied that unforgettable experience and the parents gravely incommoded, so really the Vicar had no choice. But everybody will be glad to have William's cheerful presence back at Easter; to be without it during Lent will be an appropriate mortification.

February 1962

Visitors from Canada

It was good to have our old friends Mr. & Mrs. Fred Vacher, of Toronto, in the Loders congregation last month, if only for the air of distinction he imparted (some say he is the late Aga Khan's double, and others that he is the image of the late John Foster Dulles, neither of which gratifies Mr. Vacher, for he is allergic to race horses and the U.S.A.). Preaching to Mr. Vacher gives the preacher the feeling of being the victim in a *viva voce* examination. He was brought up on the Bible, and knows all the difficulties, and, fortunately, all the answers. On this occasion the Vicar's heart sank when, in the midst of the sermon, Mr. Vacher rose and reached for his coat. Before the Vicar could begin to think what he had said wrong, Mr. Vacher sat down again, and all was well. He had only wanted to get a little warmer. It is not only humble country parsons who have to watch their step with Mr. Vacher, but Billy Graham and Winston Churchill, and all the public humbugs of Toronto, where Mr. Vacher's name is a household word as a deflator of over-extended balloons. He has lately published a book, full of good sense, and those who would disagree with its contentions could not but admire the English in which it was written. The book speaks volumes for the education he received (and not beyond his thirteenth year) in Whitchurch

Fred Vacher

Canonicorum school, and for the influence of the King James Bible on his language. It is not by word alone that Mr. Vacher propagates his ideas. He sometimes does good by stealth, as, for instance, when he made the blind children of Toronto happy, and his bank balance exceedingly miserable. It is seven years since he was last in Loders. That is too long a time to leave us without the stimulation of his lively mind.

April 1962

The voice of the parish clerk

The feature most lacking in the January services at Loders Church was the voice of Mr. David Thomas leading the responses and capping the prayers with his honest 'awmens'. Loders is aware of its good fortune in having a parish clerk in the ancient tradition, and scarcely knows itself when illness keeps him away. We are happy to say that he looks to have pulled through another illness, and hopes to be back at his duties as soon as his legs, which were the trouble, will carry him.

February 1963

Mutual feeling [Bishop of Sherborne, Victor Pike]

When the Bishop got back to Salisbury from preaching at Loders he told one of the cathedral clergy that he had set out hoping to do Loders good, and instead Loders had done him good. What we did to the Bishop only he knows: what he did to us is affirmed by everybody who heard him. The only adverse criticism raised against him is that he did not speak longer. People say they could have listened for hours. The Bishop is Irish, and when the Irish get talking they are irresistible. It was a service that will be long remembered. The church was packed, and the chancel seats had to be used. The last hymn was 'Onward Christian soldiers'. When the congregation took this old favourite into their own hands, and found it running away with them, Mr. Tiltman brought them under control with all the power of the organ, and the resulting volume of music was something the Bishop had never heard in a village church before. On leaving the chancel the Bishop went straight to the south porch, where he stood, a fine figure in full canonicals, shaking hands with the people as they filed out.

July 1963

London taxi-cabs

Mr. and Mrs. Ted Richards (née Alice Rogers), plus their daughter Wendy and her husband, arrived in Yondover in a London taxi to celebrate the silver wedding of Mr. & Mrs.

Richards. The two men are London taxi-drivers, and for a week their cab was parked outside Mrs. Rogers', where the celebration took place. It was rare excitement for local motorists to miss a collision with a London taxi-cab on a Loders corner. It was also a secret comfort to the said motorists to discover that London taxi-cabs are not so different from other cars after all, in that they sometimes have to be pushed, and parked on a hill for starting.

October 1963

The fastnesses of Nallers

Mr. and Mrs. Sam Fry have moved from the fastnesses of Nallers to the cottage next door to Mr. Sidney Fry, off the Square, Askerswell. Mrs. Samuel, rather surprisingly, finds the hub of Askerswell 'too quiet' after Nallers. She hears a passing car, and before she can look, it is gone. At Nallers she was never out of sound of the animals and the children.

November 1963

Mrs. Thomas' ancestry

Bad weather persuaded our Mothers' Union to begin their outing to Abbotsbury with a tea at The Flower Pot and not a perambulation of the gardens, as planned. The tea was a present from the Enroling member, Mrs. Garrard, who was warmly thanked by Mrs. Willmott. The company then adjourned to the church for a service, in which they were joined by the Abbotsbury M.U. whose Vicar told them some of the history of the parish. In some respects it was the great day of Mrs. Thomas, wife of the Parish Clerk of Loders. She had been christened at Abbotsbury. The Vicar got out the register, and settled what had been a problem of years for Mrs. Thomas, whether she had been christened Caroline Ella or Ella Caroline. To celebrate the end of a debate which everybody had come to regard as eternal, Mr. Garrard took a photograph of the Vicar of Abbotsbury and Mrs. Thomas, with the register.

July 1968

CHAPTER 5

Outside world

The writings of Rev. Oliver Willmott were anything but 'parochial', even if by his own admission they were 'intensely local'. He himself referred favourably in the *Notes* to a radio programme which was 'intensely local, but of national significance'. He kept abreast of current affairs with the assiduity of a Dimbleby. He passed comment on some momentous world events. In his account of the last days of Dr. Ralph Vaughan Williams, he even had the temerity to take on a Dimbleby himself. Richard Dimbleby's Rolls at the Askers Roadhouse was compared disparagingly with the Vaughan Williams' Dormobile, as a sign of the imbalance of value accorded to the world of music and the media in English life. He liked to regale distinguished visitors with stylish dinners, which cost the rest of his family dear in terms of preparation and washing up. It was one of his means of keeping up with world affairs. In this respect he was the opposite of his ascetic hero Savonarola (p. xii, illustration), hanged in 1498 for daring to criticise the Papacy and the politicians. Savonarola criticised the great from a monkish distance. The Vicar preferred to gather his 'evidence' first hand, over a good meal.

He had a habit of comparing the people and the affairs of the *beau-monde* with Loders' microcosm since, for him, his parishes were the centre of the universe. Almost without exception Loders fared better in the comparison. Thus he contended that Loders' financial arrangements were handled much more successfully than Rab Butler's national budget (p. 149). Always Loders Fête 'beat' the rest of the county. Loders' Earl Haig Fund collections often exceeded Bridport's. Loders' writers and musicians were of national quality; the church choir was 'the best in the country'. Loders-born Fred Vacher of the Budden family was claimed to have a knowledge of the Bible far exceeding that of Billy Graham. Even the Clerk of the Weather was assumed to bestow special favours upon Loders, especially on Fête Day. As with the owner of a bookshop in Hay-on-Wye there was always a slight danger that the Vicar might declare Loders an independent republic, a veiled way of declaring himself a patriarch.

But it was his wider perspective that led to a dimension of national and international interest in the *Parish Notes*, as indeed to his sermons. For example, in the December 1956 edition more than half the 30 items have an international frame of reference, perhaps counterbalancing other editions where turnips, rabbits and jumble sales prevail. He steers a straight course between revering Dr. Martin Niemoller as a hero of Christianity versus Nazism (p. 20), whilst a few months later giving a warm welcome to a German couple bringing their expatriate baby to Loders font within twelve years of the war in which he had been a British Army chaplain. Then he shows sympathy for Walter Hansford in September 1958 who may have had a premature death caused by a piece of shrapnel from a bomb dropped on Waddon Hill. (One wonders what can have been the point of off-loading bombs in the heart of deepest Dorset, unless the Germans mistook Waddon for Portland Bill on a foggy night?)

In such moments, he lost his reverent little Don Camillo hat, and propounded with the force of an Enoch Powell on the impotence of the United Nations, or the echoes of Nazidom in South Africa. He was a fearless pronouncer, and he seldom slipped up. His pronouncements always raised eyebrows. He liked to stir up debate.

A first glimpse of England

Mr. and Mrs. Hilton, of Gribb Farm, Uploders, have had a Christmas they will remember. Their son Ernest, his wife and son (the Hilton's only grandchild) paid their first visit to England from the U.S.A. Mr. and Mrs. Hilton senior migrated to the U.S.A. when Ernest was two years old, and were there for twenty-five years before they learned that there is no place like home, and came back. By this time Ernest was growing up, and doing well on the railroad. He elected to stay in America, and this first visit to England did not quite succeed in weaning him from the land of his adoption. The three things in England that fascinated him most were the small fields with their hedges, the great age of churches like Loders, and the Guards in Whitehall. As for Master Hilton, he thought Loders Sunday School, which he attended during his brief stay, was better than anything in America.

February 1954

Distinguished visitors

The clergyman and his wife who, on a recent Sunday, attended Holy Communion and Matins at Loders, and Evensong at Askerswell, were the Rev. Sir Reginald and Lady Champion. They were staying the weekend with Capt. and Mrs. Aylmer, at Askerswell. In Capt. Aylmer's naval days he was used to addressing Sir Reginald as 'Your Excellency', for the latter was then Governor of Aden. On his retirement, Sir Reginald came forward to help the man-power of the Church by taking Holy Orders. He was ordained by the Archbishop of Canterbury [Geoffrey Fisher] and is now Vicar of Chilham, in Kent.

October 1954

King Abdullah of Transjordan

Four sets of banns were called at one service in Loders recently. This happened last year as well, and is a rare occurrence in a small village. One of the couples is Mr. Roy Wheeler and Miss M.P. Symes, who are shortly to be married at Hainault, Essex. Roy lately completed his national service with the R.A.F. Regiment. He was lucky enough to spend much of his time in the Holy Land, and he confirms what he learnt in Loders Sunday School, that a bather in the Dead Sea cannot sink. Roy tried it for himself. A souvenir which he brought back from the Middle East and thinks much of is a photograph of King Abdullah of Transjordan and himself in a jeep. It records an occasion when it was his job to drive the King.

March 1955

Mr. Butler's budget

This year's Easter Offering amounted to £31. 16s. 7d. (Loders £28. 13s. 7d. and Dottery £3. 3s.). For the first time since the Church Commissioners introduced minimum stipends they will not count this as part of the benefice income – it will be an extra – and although it is still liable for income tax, Mr. Butler's budget has put it well beyond the grasp of our friend in Top o' Town, Dorchester. Wives seem to have a greater interest than their husbands in the latters' pay increases so, at the Easter vestry, the Vicar thanked the parish on his wife's behalf. Those who would question the seemliness of this have only to peep into the Vicarage kitchen, preferably on wash-days.

May 1955

Other parishes please note

The public spiritedness of aspirants to public office in this parish has spared Loders the indignity of too many candidates scrabbling for too few seats on the parish council. No unnecessary polls and consequent inflation of the rates here! When four candidates were nominated for the three places resigned by Messrs. Pitcher, Bishop and Brown, the would-be councillors conferred as to how democracy could be served without the expense of an election. The upshot was that the chairman, Mr. C. Gale, who topped the poll at the last election, surrendered his seat to the new blood of Brigadier Hammond, Messrs. D. Crabb, A. Wells & G. Hyde, and these, with

Messrs. W. Crabb, H. Bartlett & C. Harris, constitute the new council, which has it within its power to reward virtue by co-opting Mr. Gale as chairman. When the public spirit of the nation rises to the level of Loders, we shall be spared the indignity and expense of general elections. Then, it will be 'Over to you, Tony', or, 'After you, Clem old boy'.

June 1955

When ends do not meet

Mr. Adams, chancellor of the Askerswell exchequer, had bad news – like that other Chancellor [Rab Butler] – for the autumn assembly of the church council. He predicted that expenditure this year would exceed income by about £30.

December 1955

A thought for others

The children of Loders School are putting extra effort into this year's mission sale because the proceeds will go to help fellow Christians in the West Indies (the most loyal of British colonies) who have lost their homes and schools and churches in two hurricanes. With the help of Miss Swain and Mrs. Lennox, their teachers, the children are putting on a Nativity play, which will follow their sale. The whole school is taking part in this play.

December 1955

Dutch ancestry

A young man stood in the porch of Loders Church till the children's service was over, then came in, bought a guidebook, and with its help inspected the things of interest. He said it had been his life's ambition to come to Loders, and he had now achieved it. His name, he said, was Lother, he was Dutch, and his Dutch ancestors had come to live in Loders in the early sixteenth century. When there is time for an investigation, it will be interesting to see whether the parish registers corroborate this story.

July 1956

'Doctor Livingstone, I presume?'

Mr. Alfred Gale, whose home is in Uploders, and who works for the Bristol Aircraft Company, has flown out to Salisbury, Australia, where he is attached to the guided missiles range at Woomera. He is not likely to be home for two years. When Alfred's plane touched Singapore, he arranged to meet his naval cousin, Mr. Oscar Symes (also of Uploders) whose ship happened to be in dry dock there. When the cousins met, they were not at all certain that they were embracing the right person, for Alfred was not a little foxed by the beard of tropical luxuriance that Oscar was wearing, and Oscar was rather dazzled by what he called Alfred's 'middle-age spread'. We hope Alfred got the sympathy he deserves, for according to Falstaff it is not middle-age, but grief and sighing that blows a man out.

July 1956

Secretary to Selwyn Lloyd

It could not have been inferred from Mr. Denis Laskey's delightful reading of the lesson in Loders Church the other Sunday that he was in the thick of the London Conference on Suez. He is now secretary to Mr. Selwyn Lloyd, the Foreign Secretary.

September 1956

Praise indeed

Major Ian Scott, late of the Old Mill, was a welcome visitor to Loders Church the other Sunday morning. He is now a doctor in the Royal Army Medical Corps as was his esteemed father before him, and has just ended a tour of duty as senior medical officer to the British Gurkhas in India. The Gurkhas are reputed to be the world's best fighters, but the testimonial they gave Major Scott throws a gentler light on their fierce natures. With apologies to Major Scott for having burgled the testimonial from his home at Netherbury, we submit the following extract: 'During the period each one of us have had the pleasure of serving under your kind command, you have treated us most kindly, and we wish to convey wholeheartedly the following message: It has been an enjoyable experience to have worked under you, and we thank you, not only for having received so many benefits, but also for your justice and parental interest that you took in us all. We thank you for all that you have taught us, and assure you that it will be used to the best of our abilities. In conclusion, permit us, Sir, once more to give our heartfelt assurance that we love you and are proud of you. It is with the deepest feeling of sorrow that we say goodbye to you, and wish you a very happy and safe voyage, Godspeed and His choicest blessings wherever you are.' The testimonial was accompanied by a choice specimen of the Gurkha knife, the kukri, in a magnificent silver scabbard.

September 1956

Hungarian refugees

The congregation of Loders Church responded well to the Rural District Council's appeal for help for the Hungarian refugees. A Sunday's collections were given to the appeal, and these amounted to £16. 12s. A collection among members of the Mothers' Union raised a further £8. 5s. The appeal is still open. Cash contributions should be sent to the chief financial officer at Mountfield, and clothing to Ward's shop, in East Street, Bridport. The refugees coming into England have a powerful claim on our compassion. Most of them have lost everything except their lives.

December 1956

With Rommel in Africa

Mr. & Mrs. Edward Randall and their son Mark have left Uploders for Wincanton for a post on a poultry farm. This is not the first time Mr. Randall has left home. On his war service in North Africa he had the distinction of being captured by Rommel's Afrika Korps and escaping to fight again.

December 1956

Football with Prince Charles

Local readers of the *Daily Express* noted, in a picture of boys playing football with Prince Charles, one boy who looked very like Edward Laskey, the grandson of Sir Edward and Lady Le Breton. And so it was. The young prince sometimes joins the games at Edward's school. About another picture on the front page of the *Sunday Times* there is division of opinion. This picture shewed a gentleman in consultation with the English Foreign Secretary at the United Nations conference. He looked very like Mr. Denis Laskey, Edward's father, who is private secretary to the Foreign Secretary.

December 1956

General Burns

In Askerswell the happy partnership of Mr. & Mrs. Squires in making a beautiful home and garden of Court Orchard was brought to an abrupt end by a seizure, which led within a few days to Mrs. Squires' death in a Weymouth Hospital. She was buried at Broadwindsor. Mr. Squires, by the way, was a gunner officer in the Great War, and was a messmate of the General Burns who is now commanding the United Nations Force in Egypt.

December 1956

Television artist

Loders people flocked to their own or their neighbour's television sets to see Mr. Roy Taylor, of Uploders, give an account of his five thousand mile cycle ride to the Sahara and back. The television appearance must have been more of an ordeal than the ride, but Roy came through it well. He now thinks highly of the B.B.C., who housed and fed him well, conveyed him to the studio, and gave him three guineas to boot – all for two or three minutes on the screen.

March 1957

False alarm

When the wireless gave repeated warnings that England was about to be struck by the hurricane that had destroyed the sailing ship *Pamir*, the parish paid attention. The parish was a bit sceptical, because no warning twinges had come from the lumbageous backs and the radioactive corns that the parish finds every bit as reliable as the meteorological office. Then the *Dorset Echo* came out with a front-page headline that the hurricane was imminent, and the parish believed, for everything that the *Echo* says is gospel. Apples were hurriedly scrabbled in from the trees, fowlhouse roofs were battened down, tarpaulins were tied tight, chrysanthemums were culled in armfuls, and beds under shaky chimneys were moved to the safer end of the room. The parish lay awake, waiting for the fury to burst, but there was a great calm. The morning sun rose brightly, and the parish eyed the wireless suspiciously. The announcer still spoke of the imminent arrival of the hurricane, which had got christened en route, but discerning ears detected that he did not sound convinced of what he was saying. A night passed and another beautiful day dawned. The wireless was now talking of anti-cyclones as if it had never heard of a hurricane. The parish shrugged it off as being yet one more instance of the futility of the meteorological office. But as for the *Echo*, that could not be shrugged off.

October 1957

Northcliffe and *The Times*

The departure of Mr. and Mrs. Parker from Loders was so quiet that many of us were unaware they had gone. We have since learned that this was because Mrs. Parker is allergic to farewells. She and her husband are staying for the time being near Orpington. They will be greatly missed from Loders Church, and the children passing to and from school already know that they have lost the kindly interest of Mrs. Parker and the occasional sweet. Few people were aware that her venerable husband, who greatly enjoyed his country walks, had been on the reporting staff of *The Times*, and when the all-too-rare opportunity occurred, could talk most entertainingly about Northcliffe, under whom he served. Some of his reminiscences are written in a beautiful copper-plate hand, and are deposited at the Vicarage. When the *Notes* are short of news, we shall be tempted to draw on them.

October 1957

A German baby at Loders font

Mr. and Mrs. Alfred Feist, of Fir Tree Cottage, Dorchester Road, whose home is in Eastern Germany, brought their infant son to the children's service at Loders to be christened Stephen Wolfgang. German friends of theirs accompanied them, and it was remarked that their English was more readily recognisable than that of the congregation! Mr. Feist has been working for some years at Chilcombe, where he is highly esteemed. Both he and his wife have become attached to the land of their adoption.

December 1957

Land of their fathers

This is the season when Americans, Australians and South Africans visit their ancestral homes in England. It is not unusual these days to see expensive cars drawn up outside Loders Church, to hear rich Yankee voices issuing from behind the churchyard yews, or to find the sons of Uncle Sam on the tops of altar tombs, taking snapshots of the church, and declaring it to be a 'vurry cute li'll ole place'. If you happen to be the parson, you heed these warning noises and take cover; if you do not, you will find yourself picking your way through a jungle of family relationships in the parish registers with an excited American who would gladly keep you at it for a week. Nevertheless, you are glad to see him at church on Sunday, to hear of his enjoyment of the service, and you can safely show him round when you know you will be at Dottery at three. Our overseas visitors have included cousins of Mr. George Randall, namely Professor and Mrs. Satterly, of Toronto, and Mrs. Babcock, of Los Angeles. The former come to England every two years, and one wonders whether that is often enough, seeing that a haircut in Toronto costs 7s. 6d. Mrs. Babcock is not so frequent a visitor – she was last in England when she was two. The party was brought over to Loders by another cousin, Mr. Roland Gent, the memory of whom is still green in Loders. One of the Americans taking photographs in the churchyard was Mrs. Barrick, of Stillman Valley, Illinois. She is a descendant of the John and Jane Bishop who flourished in Loders c. 1800. Her zest for photographs and for discovering the history of the church had, she confessed, an ulterior motive. When she gets back to Stillman Valley she would not be allowed to stay there unless she gave the local Women's Bright Hour an illustrated lecture on her English tour, to be repeated to the other eleven societies to which she belongs. Mr. Fred Taylor has had a sister from Canada, Mrs. Teague, staying with him in Uploders. She comes to England every ten years, and this time she came in a plane specially chartered for their staff by the Toronto store for which she works.

July 1957

Débutante

Our local links with the Royal family have been in evidence in the past month. Miss Susan Newell, of South Eggardon, was one of the four hundred débutantes at what is thought to be the last of the presentation parties at Buckingham Palace; and Mr. Denis Laskey, son-in-law of Sir Edward and Lady Le Breton, was in attendance on the Queen's state visit to Holland, in his capacity as private secretary to the Foreign Secretary. Mrs. Laskey flew to Holland to join him, and Loders Court were much exercised to detect them in the television of the proceedings.

April 1958

The *San Flaviano*

When the newspapers announced the bombing and wrecking of the Shell tanker *San Flaviano*, off Borneo, those of us who knew that our friends Mr. and Mrs. Dick Waley, of Askerswell, were passengers of hers on their world tour, were distinctly alarmed, especially on reading that the bombing occurred at 7.20 a.m., when all godly passengers would be sound asleep in bed. To our surprise and relief, we learnt from

Capt. Mason that he had received a cable from them that they were alive and well. Following the cable came a letter, giving details of their marvellous escape. 'Our particular miracle', says Mr. Waley, 'was that only at the last minute, due to delay in the ship's unloading, we decided, fatefully as it turned out, that we would spend one more night ashore at Shell's guest house in Palik Papan, because our bedroom there was air-conditioned, and our cabin aboard was not. Had we elected, as we very nearly did, to sleep aboard, we should undoubtedly have 'had it', as the full force of the explosion hit precisely on our cabin, which instantly became a raging inferno of fire from which there was no escape, and at 7.20 we would certainly have been in our cabin. This is the unanimous verdict of all who were amidships. We and the entire ship's company were extremely fortunate. Indeed it was a miracle that every single one escaped unscathed. At the moment we are staying in Raffles Hotel (Singapore) for about three weeks, and our first objective is to re-kit, as of course we lost everything except what we had with us. Those on board fared still worse. Our captain, for instance, got ashore with one pair of under-pants and his wrist watch. ... We hope all goes well with you and our other friends in Askerswell and Spyway, to whom, as and when you see them, please remember us very kindly, including the Rector, lacking whose weekly sermon, I feel sure, our moral outlook is sadly deteriorating'. The Rector has since had a card from them saying they are on their way to Japan and China, and hope to be back in mid-July.

June 1958

Distinguished visitors

The late Dr. Ralph Vaughan Williams, O.M., England's greatest contemporary musician, whose ashes are to be honoured by burial in Westminster Abbey, spent a night in Loders two weeks before his death. He, his wife, and his niece, were on a motor tour in these parts, and they called at the Three Horse Shoes, Powerstock (with which they were not unfamiliar) for a bed. From the Three Horse Shoes, which was in the throes of alterations, they were recommended by various stages to the Farmers Arms, Loders. While the hostess, Mrs. Maddison, was getting supper, the ladies went for a five-minute look at the village, and the great composer settled himself with a pot of beer to a book in the parlour. The book must have been dull, or his ladies true to form – possibly both – for he swore that their five minutes had been forty, and they had kept supper waiting. Mr. and Mrs. Maddison were as yet unaware of the identity of their visitors, not being addicted to music of the Vaughan Williams sort, but their daughter Pat had her suspicions, strengthened by seeing the name in a panama hat in the porch. When these suspicions were confirmed next morning, Mr. Maddison saw that the party signed his visitors' book. Mrs. Vaughan-Williams wrote, 'Thank you for welcoming us so warmly so late.' They were going over Eggardon to see the Cerne Giant, and left the Farmers Arms very appreciative of its hospitality. All great Englishmen seem to be fond of the country's most typical institution, the village inn. Round about the time when Loders was entertaining Dr. Vaughan Williams, the Road House at Askerswell was entertaining the radio and television celebrity, Richard Dimbleby, who stopped there for tea. The difference in the value set by the great British public on good music and the amiable chatter of the television star was apparent in the different modes of transport. Vaughan Williams was travelling in a van which he called his Dormobile: Dimbleby was sporting a magnificent Rolls.

September 1958

Cause to be thankful

September is upon us, with a hope of better weather. The old people say there were never such wet summers as this, in their young days, and blame the nuclear explosions, forgetting that as far back as the sixteenth century Shakespeare wrote, 'The rain, it raineth every day.' As we look at the corn still waiting to be taken in, we realise how lucky we were in getting a tolerably good day for Loders fête, although it had its bad moments.

September 1958

Bombs on Waddon [pp. vi & vii, maps]

The body of the late Mrs. Mary Jane Hansford, who died in Herrison at the age of seventy-seven, was brought to Loders for burial in the grave of her husband. She and her family had lived in the cottage now occupied by Mr. Thomas, and previous to that at Welplot. They were well liked here. She was one of those rare birds, a good laundress, and she did the church linen. Her son George was a gardener at the Court for seventeen years. Her husband, Walter, an enthusiastic Territorial and Home Guard, had the distinction of being slightly cut by a flying stone from a stick of small bombs dropped on Waddon. His death shortly after this was widely attributed to the bombing, but the pensions people 'weren't having any'.

September 1958

Roses from among the thorns

Major and Mrs. Robin Chater, daughter and son-in-law of our trusty friend Colonel Scott, are back in England after a two-year appointment in the United States, and have appeared at service in Loders Church, where they received a warm welcome. At Fort Knox, where Major Chater was Liaison Officer, they were the only English among forty-three thousand Americans, but the great lump of American ignorance about England at Fort Knox is now so leavened that the Americans no longer ask if there is room for any fields among the dark satanic mills of England. Mrs. Chater's brother, Dr. Ian Scott, is on the staff of the General Hospital at Louisville, but he works so hard that he scarcely saw her. Major and Mrs. Chater now have a posting to the British Army of the Rhine in Munster, where her brother, Lieut. Donald Scott, of the Scots Greys, will be stationed. So Mrs. Chater goes from one brother in America to another in Germany. Her sister, Miss Joan Scott, a nurse in the Red Cross, is in Hong Kong. The family are hoping for a reunion at Netherbury next year.

November 1958

Changes at Uploders Place

After fourteen years residence at Uploders Place, Mrs. Lane has gone to live at Medway Farm, Rotherfield, Sussex. Her companion, Mrs. Adams, has gone with her, and also Mrs. Adams' husband, Colonel Adams, and her mother, Mrs. Gordon. It was through Mrs. Gordon that we came near to having Sir Anthony

Eden as a parishioner when he was house-hunting some months ago. Mrs. Gordon's late husband was champion steeplechaser of Europe, and a friend of Sir Winston Churchill. When Uploders Place was in the market, Mrs. Gordon suggested to Sir Winston that it might suit Sir Anthony. Sir Winston passed the tip, with the result that Sir Anthony and Lady Eden arrived in Loders one Saturday afternoon. Mr. Derek Barnes saw them looking over a wall at Loders Court and at the Church before they went on to Uploders, where they had tea with Mrs. Lane and Mrs. Gordon. It will surprise our readers that the only fault Sir Anthony could find with the house was that it was not big enough. And so we lost a most desirable parishioner, who would certainly have put Loders on the map. Uploders Place was purchased eventually by a Mr. Dodderell, of Blandford. He and his family have not moved in yet.

December 1958

International Deck Quoits Champion

Loders Vicarage had a visit the other day from an old Loders boy who had made good, and was desirous once again of seeing his ancestral haunts. He was Mr. Robert Maynard Crabb, of Sidney, Australia. His father was Robert Crabb, and he remembers his grandfather as one who dressed flax for ropes, and operated teams of waggons. This Robert Crabb moved from Loders to Guernsey, and eventually to Liverpool, where he died. Our visitor learnt to be an engineer in Liverpool, and took a post with the Orient Line in Australia. There he prospered and rose to be a director of the Jersey Oil Company. To our surprise (for nobody could have guessed it) Mr. Crabb announced that he was ninety, and at eighty-nine had won the International Deck Quoits championship on the way over. He has been on holiday in Bournemouth for a year, and will be returning to Australia next month. Mr. Crabb had his wife with him. He wanted to know if by any rare chance there were a Crabb left in Loders!!! We, of course, had to put our thinking cap on. After much cogitation, we were able to direct him to Mrs. Martha Crabb, of Uploders, assuring him that if anybody knew the whereabouts of any other Crabb, it would be she.

April 1959

Major-General and Mrs. Rome

At long last Uploders Place, which is now divided into two residences, is inhabited again, and by people who we are sure will soon be made to feel at home here. They are Major-General and Mrs. Rome, who have come from Berkshire, where Mrs. Rome was a friend of Lady Le Breton's family. Up to his retirement, General Rome had been for three years British Commandant of Berlin. Previous to that he had commanded the Sixteenth Airborne Division. He has that part of Uploders Place overlooking the long lawn, towards Askerswell. We gather that the lady who bought the other part had the misfortune to die before she could take up residence.

October 1959

Bishop Key to Truro

Newspapers, wireless and television have left nobody with an excuse for not knowing that the suffragan bishop of this diocese, the Bishop of Sherborne, has been nominated by the Queen as the new Bishop of Truro. For some unaccountable reason, suffragan bishops do not often become diocesans, which makes this a surprisingly happy choice. In his twelve years in this large diocese the Bishop has succeeded in getting to know the clergy, their families, and the parishes. He has a good memory for names, a huge capacity for friendship, and is universally liked. The Cornish people are fortunate indeed to have him as their new father in God. We shall miss him very much. He did the confirming of most of those who have been confirmed in these parishes in the last twelve years, and is more than a name here. As recently as October he took our confirmation. It was characteristic of him then that he did not confine his chatting to the company on the lawn, but sought out the back-room girls doing the work in the kitchen, and thanked them.

January 1960

Discovery at South Eggardon

Further evidence that we in these parts live, and move, and have our being, over a gold mine of archaeological remains, has been furnished by Group-Captain Newall. A contractor, working in one of Mr. Newall's fields near Loderland, unearthed a disc of Kimmeridge shale, worked with a design, and some Roman roof tiles. The Dorset County Museum, with whom the disc now resides, acclaim it as a find of importance, although they cannot be sure of its original function. They suggest that it may be the wheel of a model chariot, of the kind which used to be put in very ancient tombs. The curator's letter to Mr. Newall says: 'Mr. R.A.H. Farrar, of the Royal Commission on Historical Monuments, has now seen the shale disc, and in his opinion it is an example of Celtic art, uninfluenced by Roman civilisation. Dating is at present difficult . . . In Mr. Farrar's opinion it is the best example of such a thing that he has seen. May we send it either to the Institute of Archaeology or else the Bristol Museum for treatment and restoration? Because of its probable importance, we are most anxious to add it to our collection.'

February 1960

Birth of a prince

Loders bells were chimed in honour of the birth of the new prince [Prince Andrew]. Sufficient ringers could not be mustered to ring on the day itself, because their number is depleted by sickness and by care of the sick. Sunday ringing has been maintained, however, and we owe this to the good offices of our new young ringers.

March 1960

Rio Pongas

Our readers will have noted that Dr. Victor Pike, Chaplain-General of the Forces, is to be the new Bishop of Sherborne. This is an appointment which will please General Rome, of Uploders Place, who has seen much of the Chaplain-General, and greatly admires him; and also the Vicar, who served under him in Greece. He is one of a remarkable family of five brothers, who have all made their mark. When Dr. Pike is consecrated, his mother will have the rare distinction of being the mother of three bishops – the Bishop of Sherborne, the Bishop of Meath, and the Bishop of Gambia and Rio Pongas.

When the last named came to England for the Lambeth Conference, the reporters, who are not quite at their best in reporting things ecclesiastical, put him down as 'the Bishop of Gambia and Miss Rio Pongas'. When his wife saw this in the paper, the Bishop had to do some quick thinking.

March 1960

The Suez crisis

Mr. Denis Laskey, son-in-law of Sir Edward and Lady Le Breton, who is in the Diplomatic Service, has been made a Counsellor to the British Embassy in Rome. He, his wife, and the younger members of his family, go into residence there at the beginning of this month. He was private secretary to the Foreign Secretary during the Suez crisis. Some of us feel that if only he could publish his memoirs, they would make Sir Anthony Eden's very small beer indeed.

March 1960

Exodus

The absence of General F.D. Rome, of Uploders Place, from his well-worn seat in church, is due to an honour bestowed on him by the War Office. He was appointed military adviser to film producer Otto Beminger, who is making a film of the book 'Exodus', in Thrace and Cyprus. 'Exodus' is not the Biblical one, but tells the story of the large-scale Jewish return to Palestine after the war, and their underground fight against the British to establish the state of Israel contrary to the rules and quotas drawn up by the United Nations. The book itself is violently anti-British, but the film, while remaining pro-Jewish, presents the British in a much fairer light.

May 1960

A reminder

The collections in all three churches on Sunday, May 8th, will be for the Refugees. Their name makes a pleading of their plight unnecessary.

May 1960

Mr. Heathcoat Amory

The treasurer of Askerswell Church has put up in the porch an appeal for help to meet the running expenses of the church, which we herewith commend to all parishioners of Askerswell. While its tiny population has been engaged so successfully on the special task of raising £1,200 for its bells, ordinary expenses, and items such as fallen slates and the repair of the stove, have been quietly dissipating the credit balance on the current account, with the result that the bank has respectfully pointed out that Askerswell is in the red. Now is the time for one of those 'agonising re-appraisals' with which Mr. Heathcoat Amory has made us acquainted. It behoves us to examine our consciences to see whether infrequent or non-attendance at church has been reducing our share of its upkeep; or whether, if we are regular, our giving is in proportion to our income. Our mother Church of England makes no levies: she relies on our sense of fair play. In the present prosperity it is a scandal for any house of God to be in the red.

July 1960

Chauffeur to the Governor General of New Zealand

Mr. Clive Crabb's bride was Miss Susan Scourey, of Sunningdale, Berks, who had formerly lived in Bridport and worked for Bridport Industries. Her father went to New Zealand as chauffeur to the Governor General, Lord Cobham. Mr. Crabb went with him as footman, and in that capacity waited on many eminent persons, including the Queen Mother and the present Prime Minister. Clive likes New Zealand, and hopes to get back there eventually. For the honeymoon he and his wife are staying with a friend near Paris.

July 1960

The other Vic Oliver

Mr. Vic Oliver, who is now appearing at the Alexandra Gardens, Weymouth, has graciously agreed to open the fête, at 2.30 p.m. He and his co-star, Miss Vanda Vale, will judge a competition for the best preserved grandmother, and dispense

The two Vic Olivers

autographs for the fête fund. Vic Oliver is by birth an Austrian. He became a British citizen in 1945. 'The Old Vic', as he likes to call himself, has successfully combined middle-brow comedy with highbrow music. He conducts the hundred piece British Concert Orchestra, and yet delights the multitude with 'pop' songs and slap-stick comedy on stage, radio and television. His greatest venture in recent years was to take his West End Revue to the principal towns of South Africa in 1958. He has just returned from a second visit. His popular weekly radio show, 'Variety Playhouse', will begin its ninth year in September.

August 1961

Mr. Alan Rice-Oxley

The parish was grieved to learn of the untimely death at Moffatt House, Weymouth, of Mr. Alan Rice-Oxley, of Knowle Farm, Uploders. They knew that he was carrying on his farm at great odds of ill health, and were hoping that he would be spared to enjoy a quiet retirement after all his hard work and what he had endured as a prisoner of the Japanese. Those who sometimes have to foot it between Loders and Bridport will miss his offers of lifts, made so gallantly as to give the impression that it was he receiving the favour. He shewed us that farming can be a gentlemanly and civilised business. We offer our deepest sympathy to his widow.

August 1961

Glamorous grandmothers

In the present unsettled weather, Loders can look back on its recent fête with satisfaction. The morning of the fête day was as unpromising as it could be – leaden skies and steady rain, with the wintry sound of the wind whining on the housetops. The postman brought a ray of sunshine to the Vicarage in the shape of a letter of good wishes and a donation from a former fêteworker, Miss Marjorie Randall, now in sunny Tanganyika. Thereafter the morning lightened, and preparations went ahead in faith. In the early afternoon the ringers, acting unconsciously on some urge of ancient folklore, pealed the bells and cleared the air. The weather became all that could be wished, the sun beamed on a large assemblage, and the band, strategically parked near the tea and ice-cream booths, were soon perspiring. The highlight of the afternoon was the adjudication by the stage and television star, Vic Oliver, of a competition for glamorous grandmothers. Nobody envied the judge his job. Never before has mutton looked so lamb-like. His choice was Mrs. Thomas, the wife of our worthy sacristan, whom he gallantly kissed. Asked next day how she was feeling, Mrs. Thomas said she had had to take a sleeping tablet at 2 a.m.

September 1961

Summer birds of passage

The summer which is now ending has brought many welcome old faces back to services in Loders Church. These are too numerous for all to be mentioned, but they have included Miss Joan & Mr. & Mrs. Edgar Bishop, formerly of Yondover. The Scott family who are well and truly scattered, have had a complete reunion at Colonel Scott's home in Netherbury, and have all been over to Loders Church – Major & Mrs. Robin Chater from Cyprus, Dr. Ian Scott from the U.S.A., Miss Joan Scott from Aldershot, Captain Donald Scott from Blandford and his fiancée, and the former nanny, whose merit as such precludes us from knowing her by any other name. On one Sunday we had the headmaster of Winchester in our congregation, and another the Bishop of Southwark. We have also had a visit from Mrs. Stirling, widow of the colourful colonel of that name who is the hero of the book 'Safety Last'.

October 1961

Rev. Beardmore

Many of his old friends in Loders and Dottery were sorry to hear of the death at Worthing, on Jan. 8th, of the Rev. Leslie Beardmore, Vicar of Loders 1935–38. He was 83. Most of Mr. Beardmore's ministry was spent as a chaplain, either in the Army, or in hospitals, or in Continental stations. He was a regular chaplain to the Forces from 1908–29, Chaplain at

Knocke-sur-Mer 1929–31, chaplain at Rapallo 1931–32, assistant Chaplain at St. Thomas' Hospital, London, 1932–35 and chaplain at Worthing General Hospital 1948–54. His heart and thoughts were often in Loders after he left here. He used to send his good wishes on the feast of St. Mary Magdalene.

February 1962

His Excellency the Governor of Gibraltar

We hear from Miss Joan Scott (who, with her sister, Mrs. Robin Chater, was recently in England – and at Loders – for their brother Donald's wedding) that these *Notes* now include among their readers His Excellency the Governor of Gibraltar, who has voiced his opinion that Loders would be a delightful place to retire to, and its Vicar an agreeable parson to live with. We humbly advise His Excellency to consult Askerswell before committing himself.

March 1962

Flying doctor

Dr. and Mrs. Morgan, of Uploders, seem to be enjoying their tour of Australia, according to their latest letter. Their caravan has already covered more than ten thousand miles. As doctors are in short supply in Australia, Dr. Morgan has found himself doing more *locum tenencies* than he bargained for, but is rather enjoying the experience. Once he had to officiate for the famous Flying Doctor at Charters Towers, the gold mining town. They sail for England on Jan. 20th. A warm welcome awaits them from the many friends they have made in this neighbourhood.

November 1962

Mr. Macmillan and the Easter offering

Public interest fixes on the Easter Day collections because from time immemorial they have been a kind of parson's benefit. The Easter Offering is a thoroughly English institution, affording parishioners an opportunity of giving parson a smack in the eye or a pat on the back, and saving him from the sin of pride by putting his services to annual valuation. This year's Easter collections were a record, £68. 10s. (Loders £50. 10s.; Askerswell £13. 2s. 6d. & Dottery £4. 17s.6d.) Which can mean either that parson has been behaving himself for once, or that new parishioners have not yet 'found him out', or that there is gratitude to Mr. Macmillan in at least one quarter for relieving the Easter collections of income tax, which was always a sore point with congregations in general. In the Prime Minister's defence it should be said that he is not favouring the clergy of the C. of E., but merely extending to them a privilege always enjoyed by priests and ministers of other denominations. At rock bottom the privilege is really no privilege at all, for expenses of office or business are allowed against income tax in every walk of life, and parson incurs many expenses of office such as visiting of distant hospitals – which are not covered by his stipend. So here the Vicar, or Rector as the case may be, would like warmly to thank all the kind people who made this contribution to his expenses of office.

May 1963

Viscount Hood at the British Embassy in Washington

Viscount Hood, elder brother of the new owner of Loders Court (the Hon. Alexander Hood) had his first look the other day at Loders Court, which is still very much in builders' splints. The weather was good, Loders looked at its best, and the viscount was well pleased. He also had his first taste of a service in Loders Church, and that was to his liking. Which is well, for he has been assigned a niche in Loders Court, and will be a frequent visitor. Until a few months ago he was second in command of the British Embassy in Washington. He is now back at the Foreign Office. He is a bachelor. The Hon. Alexander Hood is his heir presumptive.

June 1963

The Bishop of Salisbury

The enthronement of Dr. Joseph Fison (no connection with fertilisers) as Bishop of Salisbury was up to the best English tradition in ceremonies of this sort. As our new bishop looked down from the pulpit on the sea of three thousand faces he seemed very tiny, yet his thirty-five minute sermon on the duty of everybody to look up to everybody else shewed that he had the mastery of the multitude, and occasional rumbles of laughter shewed that he and the multitude were in tune. When, after the service, he entered the chapter house for a private word of greeting to his clergy, they clapped him in and clapped him out. Rarely does Barchester expose its feelings so.

June 1963

The marriage of his Excellency the Governor of Gibraltar

The other wedding at Loders on Michaelmas Eve was an event of national interest. It drew a swarm of cameramen to the south porch of the church, and made Tommy Dennett and David Gill rush up the tower to hoist the flag. The bridegroom was none other than the Queen's representative in one of Britain's oldest colonies, His Excellency the Governor of Gibraltar, General Sir Dudley Ward and the bride was Miss Joan Scott, eldest child of Colonel and the late Mrs. Scott, whose family set down roots here in 1948, roots which seem to go deeper as the family gets further away from Loders. We were pleased and proud to have this great event celebrated here, for few people have done more than the Scotts, by way of gymkhanas and fêtes and socials, to restore the church to its present state.

October 1963

State funeral of Sir Winston Churchill

Sir Winston Churchill, and the debt the world owes him, was remembered at services in our three churches the day after the state funeral at St. Paul's. In spite of the cold, the occasion brought out sizeable congregations. It even brought out that old warrior, Mr. Norman Adams, whom the Askerswell congregation were delighted to have among them again after his long illness. At Dottery the service was preceded by a tribute to the late Mrs. George Gale, who died on the same day as Sir Winston. She had been church caretaker for several years. The flag on Loders tower had hung half-mast all week, and muffled peals rang out before and after service. The hymns sung were those chosen by Sir Winston for the church parade on the battleship *Prince of Wales* at his meeting with President Roosevelt in 1941. The service ended with the Dead March from 'Saul', played as only our Mr. Tiltman does on an organ which no other village church can have the like of. It was being said on the way up from church afterwards that he had beaten Dr. Dykes-Bower of St. Paul's in feigning the roll of drums, and in his terrific contrast of the soulful with the majestic.

February 1965

A loss for Loders

Alas, there is no need for your editor to ask himself what to begin the *Notes* with this month. Major-General and Mrs. Rome are leaving Uploders Place at the end of the month, and returning to the neighbourhood of their old home in Berkshire. It is not that their love for Loders and its church has grown cold, but that the domestic conditions under which they took Uploders Place have changed, and become more than they can cope with. And so Loders loses two of the nicest and best parishioners it can ever have had. By Christian precept we should be thanking the providence that brought them here for four years, but actually we are feeling mighty sorry for ourselves. As wife of the officer commanding a paratroop division and later governor of the British sector of Berlin, Mrs. Rome had that care for the men's families which has been a tradition with the wives of British Commanding Officers. In Loders she carried on with her public service, helping to operate the 'meals on wheels' for old people, opening her home to Mother's Union and Women's Institute, and doing her bit in local institutions like the Floral Society, the Musical Society and the Askerswell Lectures. She had a genius for making her neighbours and newcomers to the parish feel at home with her. 'Do-gooders' are not always easy to get on with, but she was everybody's darling. The fact that the General used to hide himself or get out with the dogs when his house was full of Mother's Union did not imply disapproval. In the sphere proper to a gentleman he emulated his lady's good works. The local Scouts Association found him more than a figurehead, and

Service Associations were always trying to bag him as an after-dinner speaker. Like St. Paul, he condescended to people of low estate – with the condescension conspicuously lacking. At least one small boy will be eternally grateful to have graduated from worm to fly-fishing under the General's tutelage. But it is at Loders Church, where he was one of the church wardens, and a lesson reader, that he will be most missed. There will be an aching void in the church council, too. Perhaps without knowing it, he was there a great time-saver. He would ask the chairman to give briefly, in English, what perhaps two or three pages of official letter from Salisbury meant, and would then say he was 'for' it, or 'agin' it, and usually the councillors would have the wisdom quickly to follow suit. So ends this obituary notice, and your editor relishes the sweat the General will be in when he reads it. For one of his virtues – great and rare in a holder of high office – is that he hates publicity.

February 1964

An episcopal astronaut

We are all agog at the spectacle of a Russian astronaut attached to an airship by a kind of umbilical cord, floating high above the world in space. But let it be recognised that religion, in the person of the Bishop of Woolwich, anticipated this achievement of science by several months when he published his book '*Honest to God*'. The idea that Jesus did not rise from the dead is as old as Christianity itself. Every generation has thrown up the odd heretic ready to pit his puny theorising against the mighty experience of the apostles, who saw, touched, and died for the risen Christ. What hit the headlines this time was not the old heresy, but the startling incongruity of a bishop being the exponent of it. A bishop in search of God! A bishop writing in the *Sunday Times* 'God is dead'. A bishop asking, 'Can a truly contemporary person avoid being an atheist?' 'If God be dead, and Christ be not risen', why bishops? If Woolwich be right, he has annihilated the ground of his own existence as a bishop. But he continues as a bishop, which suggests he is not quite convinced that he is right. Whom will you believe, the apostles, who saw the risen Christ, who said 'If Christ be not risen then is our preaching vain', and who died for their Easter faith? Or the Bishop of Woolwich, who collects fat cheques from the *Sunday Times*, the Student Christian Missionary Press, and television fees for undermining the Easter faith? The Methodist Church has already shewn that a church cannot expect to be taken seriously if it tolerates such contradiction against itself. It relieved of his office a minister who thought like the Bishop of Woolwich. All honour to the minister, he accepted this as reasonable and just. Perhaps it is time for the C. of E. to sever the umbilical cord, come down to earth, and leave the Bishop floating in space. Country men who can think see so much evidence of resurrection in nature that they have no difficulty in accepting the apostolic faith about Jesus. Let them crowd the churches at Easter and wipe out the dishonour done to the risen Christ.

April 1965

To Buckingham Palace

We wonder whether Askerswell and Loders are generally aware that on May 21st they were represented at Her Majesty's garden party at Buckingham Palace? The party was given by the Queen in honour of the golden jubilee of the Women's Institute. Each branch was invited to send a representative. Our branches wisely did their choosing not by voting, but by names in a hat. The owners of the lucky names were Mrs. Horace Read, Loders, and Miss Shimeld, Askerswell. These ladies have been tighter than oysters as to what they would wear at the Palace. But what they are wearing at Whitsun should give us a clue. We trust that the ladies confided in each other beforehand. Their appearing in similar outfits could open a breach between Loders and Askerswell that would take centuries to close.

June 1965

Weather commentary

'It's all very well these men going up and meeting in space, but they don't do our weather any good.' (Mrs. Lenthall, welcoming the carollers to sausages and coffee at Upton Peep on a very wet night.)

January 1966

Episcopal visitation

The Bishop of Salisbury [Joseph Fison] spent four hours of his Deanery visitation in Loders. He visited the school, with his pastoral staff of ramshorn and hazelwood, where he chatted to the children, and had lunch afterwards at the vicarage. On a public platform the Bishop is rather formidable, but in the privacy of the home his engaging qualities of father-in-God come to the surface, and Loders, in company with the other parsonages, was very drawn to him. He was most effective at an any-questions session in Church House, Bridport. But where is Bridport's hospitality? Somebody had put a collection plate beside the poor Bishop as he stood in the doorway shaking hands with people as they left, the idea being, presumably to recover the expenditure on the cups of coffee. He deserved better than to be made a beggar of.

April 1966

Olympic awards

Miss Bridget Newall has put Askerswell in the place of honour on the front page of the *Bridport News*, where the parish doesn't find itself often. She has capped an impressive list of skiing awards by winning the Golden Lion, the second highest award in the Olympic Games. Still more impressive from the mere male point of view is that she combines this athletic prowess with a Cordon Bleu in cookery, and a stoicism that regards as a mere nothing a leg broken in five places and a resulting six weeks of traction in hospital.

September 1966

Death watch beatle [*sic*] in Loders Church

It was too much to hope that when the Ladye Chapel roof was stripped the timbers beneath would be found intact and capable of carrying the new lead roof. Thirteen joists had almost been eaten away by the death watch beatle and it was at first feared that one of the beams spanning the ceiling had suffered a like fate. Fortunately only one end was badly affected and this has been repaired by a metal shoe. All the woodwork has now been treated by Rentokil. At present the

Ladye Chapel is sealed off by a polythene screen and is full of scaffolding. In the nave of the church one may get an uncommon view of the sky through the Ladye Chapel roof. The builders had got it well covered by tarpaulins before the recent storms, so no water came in. The repair of the defective woodwork will add appreciably to the original cost, but some of our old people will count it a good omen for finding the money that the bees had left honeycomb between the roof and the ceiling . . .

July 1967

Of Beatles and beetles

Donations for Loders Church roof continue to trickle in, and are hereby gratefully acknowledged. Last month brought offerings from Mr. Arthur Budden (formerly of Loders, now of Montacute), the Newberry family, Mrs. Forbes and 'Self Denial'. A specially kind gesture was made by Lord Northbourne (brother-in-law of the Hon. Alexander Hood), who is heavily engaged in repairs to his own parish church in Kent, and yet so enjoyed a recent service in Loders that he sent a donation. Unfortunately the cost of the work rises faster than the offerings. The death-watch beetle has ensured that it will not be much under £2,000. We apologise to the other Beatles for having accused them, and thank our learned friend, Miss McKenzie Edwards, for helping us to distinguish the species.

August 1967

The King Edward's Horse Artillery

That abiding pillar of Askerswell Church, Mr. Norman Adams, forgot his eighty years and went to Whitehall for the fiftieth re-union of his old regiment, the King Edward's Horse Artillery. We went to print before he got back. We hope he did, because we ourselves are not altogether ignorant of what old soldiers do when they get together. It will be interesting to know whether Bishop Anderson, formerly of Salisbury, was also there, because he was in the same regiment with Mr. Adams. When Bishop Anderson was new to this diocese, and was lost looking for Powerstock he called at Folly (when Mr. Adams was living there) to ask the way and Mr. Adams answered the door. The meeting of Stanley and Livingstone had nothing on this one.

June 1968

CHAPTER 6

Of birds, bees, beasts and flowers

In earlier days the Vicar claimed he was allergic to dogs. That was in *Yours Reverently* when on page 107 he refers to an attack by seagull on his verger Mr. Thomas in 1951. He praised Tessa the Vicarage dog for attending a service for the churching of women, even when there weren't any puppies to be found (p. 101, *Yours Reverently*). However, he ended his life insisting that his ashes be divided between the graveyard at Loders, next to Sir Edward Le Breton, and a bank at Bell Cottage, next to Beano, his yellow labrador. Having shot rabbits and pigeon for supper for his family in early life, he got softer in old age. His bird-table became a major focus during retirement with his wife.

Always he had a countryman's eye for what nature was doing, whether a squirrel snitching Sir Edward's peaches during the sermon, (p. 101) or a primrose blooming in December (p. 179). He was not a naturalist, nor vastly interested in flowers, since they can't be eaten. He left it to his wife to provide him with names. But he had an eye for the gossipy business passed on by magpies, bees and moles, and he noted what happened in hedgerows. In retirement, at Bell, he admired his neighbour farmer, and gentleman, Raymond Crabb, who would never lift a hand against an animal, and who conserved the right of way from Loders to Nettlecombe for his pigs. He had been saddened when his own pig, called originally 'Pig', was struck down by rat poison on the bank of the mill-stream. 'Pig' was a runt provided by the Rudds from Corfe Farm who couldn't cope with his upbringing while they were getting married.

His head, whilst occupied preponderantly with celestial matters, was also earthbound. His love of cats, and eventually dogs, was closely allied with a respect for the exterminating powers of arsenic, especially for moles. When given some cherry brandy for an Easter Offering from a lady, he acknowledged the gift in the *Parish Notes*, thanking the anonymous lady for the fruit, and the spirit in which it was given.

A time for stirring

There is a close correspondence between nature and the bible, which is appropriate seeing that the God of nature and the God of the bible are one and the same. Christmas, the birth of the Light of the world, comes at the turn of the year, when the days are just beginning to get longer. Easter, the triumph of Christ over sin and death, comes when spring is rising out of winter deadness. Lent, the stirring of the soul towards God, comes between Christmas and Easter, when nature is busy beneath the surface preparing for spring.

February 1956

Of superstition

The spell of mild weather just ended has produced a spate of stories of prodigious happenings in field, farm and forest. Mr. Gillard had a pear tree in blossom at West Bay; Miss Marsh picked primroses in the hedge at Askerswell; a blackbird laid an egg somewhere beyond Eggardon, and Loders churchyard had to be mown – all in December. A puzzling feature of these unseasonal events is the moral drawn from them by the locals, whose verdict, one and all, is, 'Mark my words if we don't suffer for this.' It is understandable that Julius Caesar would draw gloomy conclusions when the owls came out by day, and the king of the jungle night blinked in the sunlight of the Capitol, but why should the appearance of sweet Spring in the depth of Winter be a sign of ill? When winter comes at mid-summer, as it often does, why don't people say then, 'Mark my words, we shall suffer for this'? We write boldly, and preen ourselves as debunkers of superstition, yet we cannot eliminate from the bottom of our own heart a suspicion that we may live to break off our candle flame at night because it is frozen and cannot be blown out, and to hear the locals say, 'Now what did I tell 'ee?'.

January 1954

Target practice

The weather vane at Askerswell is not a cockbird but an arrow. It has been so cobbled in the course of centuries that little of the original metal remains. When it was taken to Mr. Charlie Gale to be fitted with a new pivot, he was able to explain the three small holes in the tail. If memory serves him right, they are bullet holes. Mr. Gale recollects a day when one of the Bryans just missed a rabbit with a .303 rifle, and fired it at the church weather vane to prove to his pals that that rabbit had been amazingly lucky.

April 1954

Bees on the altar

The bees which for years have preserved a mysterious connection with Askerswell Church, chose the hour before a Sunday evensong to swarm, and the place they swarmed at was none other than the altar. Mr. Spiller arrived (fortunately well before the service) to find the altar teeming with bees. Mr. Dan Nantes answered Mr. Spiller's frantic S.O.S. and cleared the bees before the congregation assembled. To the superstitious this swarming augurs huge good fortune for Askerswell Church.

August 1954

Of rabbits and nets

The corpses of rabbits that we see on the roads, and the hundreds that farmers see in the fields, are constant reminders that myxomatosis is here, and here in strength. Although on balance Brer Rabbit is more of an enemy than a friend, nobody rejoices at the sudden destruction that has come upon this hero of the Beatrix Potter books. He who chases Brer Rabbit with ferrets, nets and guns, finds no satisfaction in being able now to walk up to him and take him as he sits blind, deaf and swollen, nibbling grass. Indeed, he feels only pity, and a hope that Brer Rabbit is not feeling as bad as he looks. It is some consolation that he may not be. Knowledgeable people hold that the rabbit's senses are so paralysed by the disease that he knows very little about it, and the fact that he goes on eating to the end rather supports the theory. This destruction of the rabbit is not an unmixed blessing. The loss of his meat and fur will mean a considerable sum of money, and the Bridport Net people reckon that the loss to them in the sale of rabbit nets may approach £20,000.

January 1955

Reynard

Foxes are getting bold. Mr. Arthur Crabb, of Yondover, had a fox come up to the back door and seize one of his cats. The cat, however, gave a good account of himself, for he came home next day, albeit the worse for wear. At Askerswell a fox chased Mrs. Holland's cat into a tree.

March 1955

First foxes – then badgers

Last month we were remarking on the boldness of local foxes, who, deprived of rabbits, were turning their attention to cats. It seems that the repercussions of myxomatosis have now reached our badgers who, living up to their nickname of 'The English bear', have visited several local hen-houses, and finding them shut up, have clawed holes in them to get at the hens. To date, the casualty list runs something like this: Askerswell, Mr. Down, 8 hens killed; Yondover, Mr. Newberry, an unspecified but considerable number of hens killed; Loders, Mr. Ford, 8 hens killed and 10 so mauled that they had to be slaughtered; Loders, Mr. F. Osborne, 2 hens killed; and Loders, the Vicar, 3 ducks and 2 hens killed. Three badgers have been accounted for, two by Mr. Arthur Crabb, of Yondover, and one by the Vicar. One badger that had got into Mr. Newberry's hen-house and could not get out was despatched by Mr. Arthur Crabb, who also caught a second in a wire. The third badger caused some liveliness at the Vicarage towards one o'clock on a black cold night when Christians expect to be snug and asleep. A commotion in the hen-run brought out the vicar in his night attire with a gun in one hand and a torch in the other. The torch wasn't one of the best, but it revealed a hen-house with the egg-box broken open, and a badger with a hen at its feet. The badger made off, and a hunt joined by Mr. David Crabb failed to locate it. The hunters retired to bed, but a suspicious sound in the hen-run brought the Vicar out again, and his torch caught the badger as it was re-entering the run. A lucky shot got it in the head. Some days later a somewhat apprehensive vicarage household got roast badger for lunch, and the Parish Clerk got badger-dripping to rub into his rheumatics. He says it is a sovereign remedy. When roast, the badger-meat looked and tasted exactly like venison. Michael had two helpings, but nobody followed suit.

April 1955

Badgers have the last laugh

The habit of our great contemporary, the *Bridport News*, of filling its columns with extracts from these *Notes*, has put Loders on the map. This is the kind of thing you are now likely to hear: 'Where did you say you lived?' 'Loders.' 'Oh, I know. Haven't you a Vicar there who shoots badgers in his nightshirt?' And in the cake shop a saucer-eyed girl behind the counter says, with bated breath, 'I'm not wrong in thinking you are the Vicar of Loders, am I?' 'No,' says he, and her eyes get bigger and she gives his change to the next customer. With a supreme gesture of faith in the *Bridport News* not to destroy the reputation it has built up for the Vicar, we record a fact well known in Loders – that the badgers got the last laugh. While the Vicar was at Farmer Eade's, in the dead of night, keeping watch with him for a badger that had visited his hen roost the previous night, what seemed to be the excited ghost of a lady in night attire appeared to the two watchers scaring them stiff and telling them that badgers were busy in the Vicar's hen-roost. So, it transpired, they had been, but by the time of the reverend gentleman's arrival they had withdrawn, leaving a dead hen in their haste. Obviously, they too were readers of the *Bridport News*.

May 1955

A live rabbit

It is reported that a live rabbit was seen in the vicinity of Knowle Lane one day last month. Is this a record?

May 1955

Poetic justice

Conversation overheard in Loders: A. 'Poor old Burton Bradstock has caught it again – first, floods, now thunderbolts and fires.' B. 'I'm not a bit surprised. Wasn't it they who brought myxomatosis to these parts?'

September 1955

Why he stayed at home

Mrs. Wallbridge, one of the octagenarians of Uploders, has been for some weeks at Montacute with relations who have nursed her back to health. The relations offered to have her lodger, old Mr. Hawkins, as well, but he declined to leave the parrot which is the ornament of the Wallbridge ménage. This parrot occupies a very big cage in the middle of the kitchen, and the cage is now heavily draped with sacks against the cold. Mrs. Wallbridge inherited the parrot, together with a hundred-weight of seed, from an old neighbour in Burton Bradstock thirty years ago, and the parrot was no chicken then. It has a large vocabulary, and does not mince words. When the Vicar called the other day Mr. Hawkins was a-tremble lest the parrot should mention the weather. There was no knowing what a product of Burton Bradstock might say.

March 1956

Unholy words

Our oldest inhabitant is Mrs. Wallbridge's parrot, who can be proved to be at least 100. Mrs. Wallbridge has to confess, with sorrow, that as the parrot gets older she does not grow in grace (she was always reckoned a he until she produced a few eggs in her late nineties). Long years ago, when the parrot lived at Burton, the men who carted sand from Burton beach tried their hardest to teach her a few nautical terms of dubious taste. She resisted, and instead learnt the Lord's Prayer, which she *could* say right through to the end. But nowadays, when she attempts the Lord's Prayer, which is not as often as it might be, she does not get very far, and it is a bit less every time. But what distresses Mrs. Wallbridge beyond words is that when the parrot sees a titbit on Mrs. Wallbridge's plate, and asks for it, and does not get it, she screams, 'Go to hell, Mother'. As Mrs. Wallbridge is sure the neighbours must have heard, there is no harm in our mentioning it here.

December 1959

The century-old parrot

The cottage in Shatcombe occupied for so long by Mrs. Wallbridge, Mr. Hawkins and their century-old parrot is at present empty. Passers-by miss the chats they used to have with Mrs. Wallbridge as she and the parrot sat sunning themselves at the front door. They miss, too, their colloquies with Mr. Hawkins on the cursed ways of late frosts and the villainies of pigeons. (He was a great gardener.) Mr. Hawkins is now in the infirmary at Stoke Abbot, and Mrs. Wallbridge is with relations at Montacute.

June 1960

Hail and farewell

After being empty for many months, the cottage at Shatcombe, formerly the home of Mrs. Wallbridge, is now a hive of activity as its new owners, Mr. & Mrs. Radley, and their two boys, settle in. Mrs. Radley greeted the Vicar as he made his first pastoral call with: 'I suppose you are the one who went through Mrs. Wallbridge's floor?' Which was correct, and reminded him of that afternoon when he accepted Mrs. Wallbridge's invitation to step into her sitting-room, which she called – rather prophetically – 'The Lunge'. He put his foot in the middle of a region of dry rot, and clutching at the geraniums in the window did not save him.

June 1961

Return of the wild rabbit

A wild rabbit full grown and energetic, was seen in the road at Yonder the other night. Some were also seen on Waddon a few weeks ago. Mr. Bennett told the Agricultural Discussion

Mrs. Wallbridge's Parrot

Club that rabbits are on their way back to this part of Dorset. He said that Portland had never been touched by myxomatosis, and is full of rabbits.

April 1956

Oysters in the wall

A writer to the *Dorset Echo* reports that he was surprised to find the spaces between the stones in an old wall at Chesil Cove packed with oyster shells, because he had never heard of oyster shells being found on the beach. He learnt later that there used to be an old oyster bed off Portland, which flourished for two hundred years, but of which no trace remains. Mr. Harry Sanders has pointed out to us that there are oyster shells in the mortar of the west doorway of Loders tower. We wonder whether if these also came from the extinct oyster bed off Portland?

May 1956

Bulls of Basan

It was delightful to have Loders Church full again for the annual Rogationtide service, and for the parson to be looking down from the pulpit on the faces of so many young farmers. The lessons were well read by Mr. R. Dennett, of the Farm Workers; Miss Caryl Davies, of the Askerswell Young Farmers; and Mr. C. Gale, chairman of the Loders Agricultural Discussion Club. It was Mr. Gale's first appearance at the lectern and his deep voice, coming slowly and distinctly, made everybody hope that it would not be the last. The proper drill for Rogation Sunday is to say the prayers for the growing crops while going in procession through the fields. We may find it possible to do this with the morning congregation next year. But praying in the open fields can at any moment call for steady nerves. We read that when the singing started at a Rogationtide service in a meadow at Ross-on-Wye, a herd of Hereford bulls rushed across the meadow and joined the choir. Fortunately for the dignity of divine worship, the ladies did not stampede, and the bulls left the singing to the choir. When the procession moved on, the bulls fell to the rear, and took a reverent part in the service till it ended.

June 1956

Fidelity

In Uploders Shepherd Steele, late of Upton Farm, died as he was on the point of moving into one of the new Council houses at Well Plot, and three generations of a family of shepherds came to an end. At his death he was still pining for his old sheepdog, Nell, whom the vet had had to put to sleep.

December 1956

In Indian file

When we have time, we must try to elucidate why Askers House, standing demurely off The Square, is especially attractive to communities of ladies. The four ladies who left it last month are followed by three ladies who have come from the new town of Bracknell, in Berkshire. They are Mrs. Orago, and her companions Miss Kelly and Miss Thwaites. Those in Askerswell who are given to 'seeing things' need not pinch themselves if they see one of the new Askers community proceeding to the post office, followed by six cats in Indian file, for the ladies are breeders and great lovers of cats, and this was a not unusual sight in Bracknell. Another of their hobbies is a marionette show, which we may have the good fortune to see when the ladies have recovered from their work.

December 1956

Flying ornaments

Mrs. Parsons, of Vinney Cross, went into her front room to do some cleaning and noticed on the mantelpiece a new ornament that neither she nor anybody else had put there. She was about to dust it (albeit rather gingerly, because it was so lifelike) when it flew across the room. It was a baby owl, that had, presumably come down the chimney.

February 1957

Worms to catch moles

The long stone path which helps to make the approach to Loders Church so beautiful, has been re-laid by Mr. William

Gill, of Uploders, and evokes much praise from the people who use it. He has also repaired the altar tombs which needed it, and the churchyard is now in apple-pie order, except that the moles still contrive their unsightly mounds. Our churchyard moles are a law to themselves. They spring every trap without getting in it, and they seem to appreciate an occasional dosage of arsenicated worms. A recent article in *Country Life* gave the times of day when moles of sober and righteous habits throw up their mounds and can be rewarded with a heavenly crown, but our moles are nonconformists whose times of mound-making are when nobody is about. Anybody who can think of a solution has the freedom of the churchyard to try it out.

August 1957

Chrysanthemums and cyclamen for Christmas

Christmas in Church was a satisfying experience for the many who spent some of it there. The sight of Messrs. David Crabb and Horace Read struggling from the school to the church with a large spruce was a reminder to the residents of Loders High Street that Christmas had come again. The same tree, festooned with fairy lamps, was the focal point of the decorations in church, and the delight of the large congregation who looked at it in the dim light of the midnight service. On Christmas morning the gales that were lashing the seas into mountains of fury were also sweeping the roads with rain that stung; yet practically all the junior population of Loders turned out to sing carols in the chancel, and to receive sweets from the tree at the hand of the Enroling Member of the Mothers' Union. The carol service of the nine lessons, on the evening of the following Sunday, was not quite as well attended as usual – presumably because it came close to Christmas – but the singing was excellent, and the reading of the lessons by representatives of parish organisations was clear and with feeling. At Dottery the Christmas morning service escaped the rain, which was a good thing for those esteemed old friends of the church who had come a mile or two on bicycles. Their presence was all that was needed to make the service complete. At Askerswell a nice congregation got to church dry, but were not so dry when they reached home. In spite of the shortage of berried holly, all the churches looked thoroughly christmassy. There were some prize chrysanthemums at Askerswell and Dottery. At Loders red cyclamen were the feature of the chancel.

January 1960

The luck of Askerswell departs

For some years the roof of Askerswell Church has had bees in it, which was considered extremely lucky for Askerswell, and the probable reason why this little parish was so good at raising big sums for various projects. Now, alas, the bees are no more. Several slates were blown off the roof in the Christmas gales, and when the builders came to put them back on, they found this could not be done without opening up part of the roof, and putting in new timbers first. The affected part of the roof was where the bees were, and they did not thank the workmen for their intrusion. The blood of the workman most concerned, a fine Dorset type from Little Bredy, must be entirely alkaline, for the scores of stings it rendered neutral would have been enough to kill an ordinary mortal twice over. Mrs. Aylmer, who came to his rescue with a powerful squirter of 'Flit', was surprised to see him at work next day, apparently none the worse. As a reward for his pains, he got out of the roof a bucket of honey. There was much more, but this had atrophied, and was useless. With clusters of bees still sticking to it, this was put on the rubbish heap, where the poor bees fought a protracted but losing battle against night frosts, which killed them.

March 1960

Harvest fruit, veg and corn

Harvest Festival is pleasant to look upon. At Askerswell the business of preparing, the day before, was almost as impressive as the day itself. The road outside the church was conjested with cars, and inside, the church itself looked something like Covent Garden market, as the decorators got busy on the masses of flowers, fruit and vegetables at the strategic points. The Saturday preparations for Loders harvest looked less opulent than Askerswell. The cars outside were few. Parked near the church porch were the ancient push-chair and the sugar box on wheels used by the veteran decorators for carting their materials. But the inside of the church reflected none of this poverty. There was a wealth of colour. Thanks to the nice farmers who remember church when they put in the sickle, there was the display of sheaves in which Loders specialises, augmented by the corn dollies made by the village thatcher, the late Mr. Harry Legg, the loss of whom is felt anew every time they are brought out.

November 1961

Barnacled with honeysuckle

Askerswell Fête was an instance of how pleasantly money can be raised for a deserving object by this ancient device, given good weather and the right place. The June afternoon was perfect, and so was the home of Group-Captain and Mrs. Newall, under Eggardon, where the ladies could serve tea against sun-drenched old walls barnacled with honeysuckle. At Mr. Millington's bottle tombola the winning numbers seemed to have sunk to the bottom of the barrel, out of sheer inertia: indeed, your correspondent drew thirty-two blanks, and wondered whether there were any numbers at all in the barrel – until he saw Mrs. Fooks making off with the sherry and a couple of less desirable beverages, all for half-a-crown. Mr. Millington had obviously been caught napping. He was even larding Mrs. Fooks with the usual condolences, and assuring her of better luck next time.

July 1962

October colours

Loders was blessed with an auspicious day for its harvest on the following Sunday. There had been no late frosts, so there were flowers in profusion, and vegetables to make the church seem like an old tithe barn all set for harvest supper. The floral beauty of the nave was crowned by the chancel, where the scheme was of monstrous yellow dahlias nesting in brown bracken, and sheaves of all kinds of grain, and a small hayrick, and a Dorset corn dolly.

November 1962

Pigeons for breakfast

The 'Shell' Petroleum Company has more than once been commended for producing lovely glossy pictures of the English countryside as it looks in each of the twelve months. The Company gives a set to every school, and teachers like to have the picture of the month hanging on the wall. The picture for January is one of the most engaging of the lot. It shows a father and his children sporting on a frozen pond, against a parklike background of winter trees, and with a happy concentration of all the birds one notices in the snow. In normal times a delightful picture. But it was not without significance that in one of our schools the January picture vanished from the wall before the month was out. True, the children, and not a few grown-ups, have had a glorious time tobogganning – and even skiing by moonlight as well as sunlight; the shooting men have wrought great slaughter on fields of kale and rape crawling with pigeon. But there can be too much of a good thing, pigeon for breakfast, pigeon for lunch, pigeon for tea, and pigeon with a cup of cocoa before bed is no stimulant of the hunting instinct; and coming back home to frozen milk, burst pipes, and a grate where two poor little coals try to do the work of ten, is apt to damp the tobogganist's ardour. When the great frost ends, and the snow with which we have lived for a month has melted, and neighbours get together again, there will be wonderful tales to tell. Askerswell will have most. Its remotest farm, Nallers, is still asking how Farmer Tom Foot managed to drive the milk cross-country over the lynchets and the ravines to the collecting point without breaking his neck. South Eggardon is still chuckling over the sight which greeted Group-Captain and Mrs. Newall on their return from the winter sports in Switzerland – a sight causing them seriously to consider whether their journey had been necessary. Uploders now has a high opinion of the County Council, who saw the seriousness of the situation, and sent a snow-plough when they were cut off from The Crown. Dottery noted with satisfaction that not even snow of these Alpine proportions could stop their Miss Pearson from walking into Bridport.

February 1963

Of snowdrops and storks

Snowdrops may or may not be blossoming beneath the snow, but the stork has been working overtime in bringing us other harbingers of spring and new life in the form of six babies. At Dottery Mrs. Oxenbury has a daughter (the day she went to hospital was Dec. 29th, and as the ambulance could not get nearer to her than The Blue Ball, she had to walk to it).

March 1963

Of wallflowers, ageratum and marigolds

Loders congregation is grateful to Mrs. Audrey Green for employing her skilled needle on the altar draperies. It was good of her to spare the time when illness made her so busy in her own home. The mystery about the organist, Mr. Tiltman, is how he manages to shine as an organist as well as a carpenter. One would have thought carpentry would have spoilt his hands for playing. That it does not is apparent to all who hear him on Sundays. Evidence of his carpentry is now to be found in a bookshelf for choir music in the glory hole beside the organ. He made it out of an old door. The wonderful display of wallflowers up the church path is now over, but Mr. David Crabb has spent hours of his leisure time taking advantage of the rain and warmth to replant it with 450 ageratum and marigolds, at no cost to the church. Kindnesses like these are worth several collections.

June 1964

S.O.S.

There ought to be some countryman among our readers who can catch moles. If there is, would he consider doing a good turn to Loders churchyard? All three parts of it are infested with moles, and the trouble they cause is not confined to unsightliness. Before the rotascythe can cut the grass, the operator has to go round with bucket and shovel collecting molehills. When the moles are active this can take well over an hour. But this done, one has not finished with them. There remain the network of runs just beneath the surface. The wheels of the machine sink into these, pushing becomes hard, the blades chain up the soil, and the soil clogs the engine. Last year the new rotascythe had to go back twice to the workshop for repairs, which were not cheap, and the engineer says that if the moles continue to make its work as a rotavator instead of a rotascythe, it will continue to incur heavy repair bills. Would that the parishioners of Loders were as attached to their church as those moles! Poisoned worms they either avoid or devour with impunity; traps they fill with earth and eject; cartridges of gas which put paid to Mr. William Graves' moles, ours seem to relish the scent of. We gather that spring is the best time to deal with moles. So will some kind son of the soil come quickly to the rescue? Already the shrubs and plants have been furbished up, and the grass awaits its first cutting. To the question, What can I do for Lent? here is one answer.

March 1965

P.S.

As to the moles, our *cri de coeur* brought a quick response from Mr. Jack Greening, a retired sexton of Loders, who now lives in Bradpole. He had done battle with the 'little varmints' in his day, and regarded their recent eruption as a personal affront. His rheumatics could not keep them off the warpath. Armed with a dozen traps lent him by Mr. Tom Foot of Nallers, he has already caught seven of the 'little varmints' who eluded everybody else. To the satisfaction of slaughtering his old enemies is added the gentler pleasure of afternoon tea with his old friend Mr. David Thomas, parish clerk, when the round of traps is done. May we also thank those who tendered advice, from Brigadier Hammond's mothballs to Miss Hayward's shooting, via Mr. Geoffrey Glazeby's milk bottles poised on the runs to catch the wind and make frightening noises?

April 1965

Of church mice, and cats

A plague of mice is afflicting Askerswell Church. They have eaten large quantities of mouse exterminator kindly supplied by Mrs. George Bryan. She goes on and on putting it down, but there never lacks a mouse to dispose of it. At first they were very partial to the organ. Now they have taken a fancy to the sawdust of the sound-proofing in the belfry. We would rather them in the belfry than in the organ, for what might happen if Mr. Harold Spiller saw one while he was playing is too awful to contemplate. The organ people at Taunton say Askerswell is by no means unique. They are receiving complaints of mice in organs from many churches. A church cat is indicated.

April 1966

Of Brussel sprouts, snowdrops and barley in February

The hay harvest is not being easy. In spite of the dryness of the ground, the hay seems to get wet and has needed much work in the saving, although conditions have improved in the last few days. If anybody needs advice as to how to cope with a late harvest of any kind, he could do worse than consult our Mr. Charlie Wilkins, of Cloverleaf Farm. The *Gloucestershire Echo* has been telling how he harvested a good crop of barley one February! It says, 'We have been reminded that fifteen years ago Mr. Wilkins still had some barley standing at Coberly Farm in February. In the wet autumn of 1950 he tried to bring in the harvest but was hindered by unfavourable conditions and an undergrowth of clover among the barley. The crop was, therefore, garnered by instalments. Mr. Wilkins found December to be a good month. In two days he collected 128 cwt. of grain. By the New Year only one of his 35 acres remained uncut and he abandoned it. Then a cold spell in late February withered the clover, hardened the ground, and enabled Mr. Wilkins to make a last attempt with a combine harvester. He finished on February 23rd, and the grain was none the worse for wintering out'. The paper goes on to visualise a harvest festival in Lent in a Church decorated with snowdrops and Brussels sprouts.

July 1966

Still a mystery

Mr. and Mrs. Vicary, of Meons Farm, are still pondering the cause of the fire that robbed them of twenty tons of excellent hay. They disagree with the *Bridport News*' theory of spontaneous combustion. They think that trippers may have been responsible, as remnants of food were found nearby, and yet Mr. and Mrs. Vicary were about the farm when the fire broke out, but did not see anybody. They now incline to the theory that as the sun was very hot, it might have struck through a bit of glass.

September 1966

Rat poisoning

At Uploders Farm the newcomers are Mr. and Mrs. Roy Sheppard, who come from Portesham Farm, where Mr. Sheppard worked with his father until the latter's retirement. They have three children – four years, three years and six months. They had the misfortune to lose their highly prized golden retriever shortly after arrival. He died of poisoning from the bite of a rat he killed.

November 1966

Out of season

Mothering Sunday is on March 5th and there will be the usual mothering service in Loders Church at 2 p.m. With Easter so early there would normally be no flowers for the children to take to the senior citizens afterwards, but the mildness of the winter has brought on primroses, violets and daffodils. Indeed, one gardener has a peach in blossom and this does not please him.

March 1967

Of hay, silage, and lamb sandwiches

The licensee of the Loders Arms had a good measure of success against our awful June weather when he tried to get us celebrating the Longest Day. A lamb was roasted over an open fire behind the inn by Mr. Albert Wells. A large number of villagers watched. Then the rain descended, and the delicious lamb sandwiches had to be eaten under cover. Since that day the rain has scarcely stopped. Cut grass lies rotting in the fields and the uncut grass will not be much good. The season seems to have converted some staunch advocates of hay to silage.

July 1968

CHAPTER 7

Ring out the old, ring in the new

This chapter is devoted to the way in which the Vicar stuck staunchly to past customs, whilst entertaining anything new that was life-giving. His bell-ringing pulled him backwards and forwards because he loved tradition and any chance for new jaunts. He accused – rather harshly – Loders people of being 'as musical as turnips'. Hence the heavy influence of bells which he would agree with Samuel Taylor Coleridge are 'the poor man's only music' ('Frost at Midnight' 1798). Ringers' Out-Ins were notoriously enjoyable. But when anything else took off, he was an enthusiast – even if it was hassock-making, so long as someone else made the hassocks. He was a man of paradoxes. He himself only wanted to stay put, but he always relished moving on into new avenues of entertainment and enterprise. He knew about change and tradition and where to stand. (He admired the ringer who could make the tenor bell 'stand' on the dot of 11.00 a.m. on Remembrance Sunday.)

Harry Crabb, who nine times out of ten was this ringer, was the epitome of this spirit which could be defined as a deep-rootedness in the past, with an impish sense of fun about the present (and perhaps no particular relish for the future). Again, detractors might pull out the label 'conservatism', with a small c. It was just the country way of life. Harry's gnarled body fitted into Loders like a hawthorn in a hedge. Like David Crabb, the gardener at the Court, he was always preceded by a cigarette which emerged smokily from under his felt hat. When lubricated by gin and peppermint at The Crown he had a sweet nature, until about closing time when his spirit went somewhat acidic and his eyes began to roll. He was a past-master of table-skittles, and he always ran the outside skittles at the Fête. Although his eyes were impaired by a tragic farming accident and poor eyesight generally, they always had a twinkle in them. His laugh came from deep within his small frame, accompanied by tobacco-inspired splutters. It might be surmised that he was the Vicar's best friend. They were both Dorset shepherds in their way, and were always side by side, through all the ups and downs of their different lives. Harry had an infinite capacity in the bell tower to frighten off young ringers by bellowing – 'You s'll never make a ringer' – whilst a terrified apprentice was clutching at a flailing rope, and awful clangs were being made above, but he shared with the Vicar a heart of gold. (In *Yours Reverently,* p. 80, there's the story of the Vicar asking Harry to bequeath him his bladder if he predeceased him.)

The chapter ends on a note of sadness, for the Crabb family and the village. As Celia Andrews wrote in her review of *Yours Reverently* in *The Grapevine* – the diocesan magazine for Bath and Wells – 'Rev. Willmott creates a world of church fêtes, carol-singing, outings and shared joy and sadness you can almost touch and smell.' (July 1998)

The pull of the bells

Bellringing, which used to be the preserve of the beer and skittles type, is now being poached by the learned professions. There has existed for some years a guild of parson bellringers, and in consequence, bishops, and even archdeacons are occasionally to be found at the rope's end. Now there is an incipient guild of doctor ringers. Eight doctors, including a Harley Street specialist, are shortly to attempt a three-hour peal on the bells of Great Barrow, Essex.

October 1953

The Old Bell at Loders

Too strong

The bell which Sunday by Sunday proclaims to the neighbourhood of Dottery Church the imminence of Divine service is tolled by Mrs. George Gale. The other Sunday the bell suddenly stopped speaking. Thinking this to be somewhat unnatural (bells being females), Mrs. Gale gave the rope a good shaking, without effect. Looking rather nettled, Mrs. Gale suggested to that part of the congregation already assembled that the bell must be suffering from old age, having been 'up there seventy years and more'. But somebody remembered that the bell on the chancel step at Loders was 300 years old, and could speak as well as ever. So the congregation trooped out of church, and looked up at the open bell turret. Nothing appeared to be wrong with the bell, except that it had no clapper. The congregation returned to their pews, mystified. A Bridport firm were successful in finding the missing clapper and fitting it to the bell. But it would take more than that to convince Mrs. Gale that it was other than 'contrariness' on the bell's part. Mrs. Gale knows more of the ways of females – and bells are females – than she does of the strength of her right arm.

December 1953

Human entanglements

Dottery people flocked to church, although the bell did not summon them. When the bell fails to sound, they presume that Mrs. Gale and it have fallen out again, and on this occasion they were not surprised to find Mrs. Gale entangled in yards of rope. Her looks were saying things about the bell that tongue dare not utter in church. The bell seemed to be excusing itself by replying, 'She was shaking me, so I let go the rope'. Several car loads of Dottery people joined the mother church of Loders for the carol service, and round the vicarage fire afterwards Mrs. Gale yielded to a universal demand that she should sing her Christmas serenade to Mr. Barnes of Bilshay, who, from the depths of the biggest armchair, made a sign that he was not unwilling to hear it [p. 17, *Yours Reverently*].

January 1954

Captain amongst many

The late Mr. George Miller, of Askerswell, was a reminiscence of the heroic proportions of 19th century families. He was one of twenty-one children. In those days of high infant mortality it was considered no mean achievement for their mother to have got eighteen of them to the font. Until his sudden fatal illness, Mr. Miller had been very robust, and much in demand for odd jobs. For some years he had also been captain of the ringers.

March 1954

Raising the bells

Choosing a date for Askerswell Fête was a task which the recent Parish Assembly found none too easy. To every suggestion somebody managed to raise an objection. One date would clash with haymaking, and another with corn harvest. Another date was no good because The Ladies would be away. A long process of elimination proclaimed May as the only possible month, and the 22nd as the only feasible date. So Saturday, the 22nd May, it is to be, and the invitation of Wing-Com. and Mrs. Newall to hold it at South Eggardon has been gladly accepted. Mr. Allsop, the carrier, has kindly agreed to ferry passengers from the Square to the fête. Experience has proved darts and skittles to be efficient money-raisers. The landlord of the Travellers' Rest has consented to run a dart week at his establishment, with a bottle of whisky given by Captain Aylmer as top prize. The landlord of The Three Horseshoes, has agreed to a skittle week at Spyway, with the top prize of a pig given by Mr. Biss. Two hundred pounds is the target which the fête committee hope to hit. This is the minimum that a Bell Fund will need.

May 1954

Early birds

The Dottery churchwardens came to Loders for the Easter vestry a week too early. They adjourned to The Crown, and debated whether they should wait – there, of course.

May 1954

In a class by itself

In most villages and towns the prominent building is the church. In Dottery the prominent building is the newly completed public house, the Blue Ball. The little tin church makes a poor showing beside the splendid edifice that has arisen on an eminence in the middle of the hamlet. At first sight the new hostelry is palatial enough to be a police station, and the big blue ball which is its chief ornament fosters that illusion. The relative sizes and conditions of the church and the public house are no reflection on the character of the sober, God-fearing people of Dottery. The Blue Ball is obviously aimed at the passing motorist. When one looks at the photograph of the original Blue Ball, with its long low outline, and its thatched roof, a bit of old England, one cannot but regret the fire which burnt it to the ground in 1947.

July 1954

The escaped convict

Loders ringers took a large coach full of supporters with them on their annual outing, and shewed them Dartmoor in one of its savage moods. So skilfully had the ringers timed their outing that, to the delights of rolling mists and blinding rains was added the thrill of an escaped convict, who had broken gaol the night previously, and was still at large on the moor. The ringers had with them their physician, the landlord of the Farmers' Arms and thanks to his potent injections they were ready for all comers. It was merciful for the convict that he never met them. One ringer turned up for ringing next morning with his arm in a sling. But this was not, as one might have suspected, anything to do with the outing. From which some of our readers may infer, and rightly, that times may change, but ringers' outings do not.

August 1954

Nearly banned

Mr. Ronald Cornish and his bride, formerly Miss Jean Rogers, are living for the time being at Yondover. Theirs was a pretty wedding, with Loders church still full of harvest flowers, and a large congregation. The groom paid the bride the compliment of being so excited about the wedding that he forgot to bring his banns certificate. The bride didn't take it as a compliment that she arrived at the church gate just as the groom was rushing out and making for Bridport. Luckily the Curate of St. Mary's was at home, and the groom was back at the altar with his bride and the vital certificate in no time.

November 1954

Academic distinction for a lady

Dr. Kathleen Hughes, a penultimate occupant of The Old Cottage, Loders, has been accorded the high distinction, for one so young, of election to a Fellowship and Lectureship of Newnham College, Cambridge. Until her recent move to Cambridge she was lecturing in medieval history at Royal Holloway College, in the University of London. Dr. Hughes was, and still is, a great lover of Loders Church. She will have the good wishes of those who remember her as she takes up her new responsibilities.

November 1955

The husbands of the parish

The ladies' organisations of the parish have continued their round of gaiety. The Mothers' Union so enjoyed their festival at Sherborne Abbey that they went to another in Salisbury Cathedral, and being free of the epicure's aversion to anti-climax, followed up the cathedral festival by going to the deanery festival at Bradpole, where, for the edification of its readers, the local newspaper photographed them taking tea. The Women's Institute, not to be outdone by the wonderful tea partaken by the Mothers' Union in honour of their twenty-fifth birthday, put on another wonderful meal to celebrate the Women's Institute ninth birthday, and Mr. Fred Taylor, and Mr. Barker the only husbands to turn up among the many guests, were handsomely rewarded for their bravery. There were savouries of many kinds, luscious conglomerations of jelly and ice-cream, and a truly magnificent birthday-cake from the fair hand of Madam President herself. The husbands of the parish endure it all with a shy hope that those diminishing occasions when they do not have to get their own tea will benefit by all the practice their ladies are getting.

July 1956

Ringers' outing

Rain which had been falling most of the night was pelting down when Loders ringers, at seven o'clock in the morning, boarded the coach that was to take them to Salisbury, Winchester and Bournemouth. Some expressed their contempt for the English climate by a look, and others pinned their hopes to the adage, 'Rain before seven, shine before eleven.' Landlord Maddison of the Farmers' Arms saw many crates of liquid comfort into the back of the coach, and came aboard with the calm and confident look of one who knew that he was backing a winner either way – if the sun did not come out and make the ringers thirsty, the rain would dispose them to drown their sorrows. It transpired that the rain cleared long before eleven and the weather behaved itself for the rest of the day. At Salisbury some of the party who had never seen it visited the Cathedral, and with commendable patriotism declared that, while it was a fine bit of work it did not quite come up to Loders Church. Winchester Cathedral in its immensity did wring from them an admission that it beat Loders Church, but only by a hair's breadth. At Bournemouth most of the party went to a variety show. The secretary, Mr. George Hyde, had booked the seats *en route*, but not without difficulty, for every time he made for a telephone kiosk to ring the theatre, his charges made for the nearest 'local' and took some winkling out. As the coach was about to leave Bournemouth, the driver of a 'Royal Blue' delivered into their care a little Weymouth girl who had been in Bournemouth with a choir party and had got lost. The ringers' coach overtook a Weymouth bus and transferred her to that. Mr. Hyde has since received a letter of thanks from her parents, who received her safely. She was home well before the rest of her party, who had been searching Bournemouth for her, and did not leave until they had learnt from the police that Loders ringers were seeing her home. The ringers had taken the precaution of phoning the police before they left Bournemouth.

August 1956

Ladies outings

Our Mothers' Union spent an enjoyable day in Bournemouth. The dull weather made the shops more attractive than the beach, and a glorious bout of spending was had by all. The party got safely home without losing any of the naturally errant members of the Women's Institute. At Tinley's coffee-house in Exeter some of them made a rendezvous with Mrs. Rudd senior, who used to live at Corfe Farm, but is now in Exeter.

August 1956

Servants above their master

The man in the street may be forgiven for finding the thought processes of Christians a bit bewildering at times. On Friday, Jan. 18th, he sees flashed across the front page of his *Bridport News* a spirited protest by the religious leaders of Bridport against the proposal to allow a glass of beer at a dance in the assembly hall of the new Alfred Colfox School, on the grounds that it might contaminate the children, and would so pollute the hall as to render it unfit for morning prayers ever after. On Sunday, Jan. 20th, the Second after Epiphany, he opens his Prayer Book, and reads, as the gospel for the day, how Christ himself not only attended a 'licensed' wedding feast at Cana of Galilee, but provided the equivalent of a hundred gallons of more excellent wine when the decanters dried up. The man in the street might remember, on further reflection, that Christ made wine an essential element in the Holy Communion, which is the most sacred act of Christian worship. If the man in the street were well up on his Bible, he might also remember that St. Paul said to Timothy, 'Be no longer a drinker of water, but use a little wine for thy stomach's sake'. The religious leaders of Bridport are sincere and honourable men. But is sincerity enough? They have put their own Lord and Master in the dock; they have made the assembly hall of the Alfred Colfox School more sacred than our churches (which all have wine in their cupboards), and more sacred than our homes, for we in these three parishes are unconvinced that a glass of beer with our supper sets our children on the road to ruin, and makes the home unfit for them to live in.

February 1957

Where males fear to tread

The fate of many a lovely flower is to bloom unseen. It is being whispered that the comic acting by members of the W.I at their monthly meetings is excruciatingly funny, the best thing in entertainment that has ever been seen here. But only a fraction of the local population have the pleasure of seeing it, and no male may look on it and live. If hearsay be true, there has been a pageant of the years, from the cradle to the grave. Mrs. Knight has been a most winsome baby in a pram, Mrs. Wells a youthful ballet dancer, Mrs. Harry Legg a pigtailed schoolgirl, Mrs. Taylor and Mrs. Spencer young-men-a-courting, Miss McCombie a blushing bride, Mrs. B. Osborne one of those engaging ladies out of *Country Life* who still ride side-saddle, and our perennially youthful Mrs. Mabel Crabb as *Age, sans eyes, sans teeth, sans everything*.

March 1957

2½ ton tenor in peal

The Abbeys of Sherborne and Glastonbury are two great shrines of the Christian faith in the West Country. A pageant of history was recently staged in the choir of Sherborne Abbey by the Youth Fellowship, and a party of young people from Loders went to see it. Afterwards they were shewn over the Abbey, including the tower, where they saw the 2½ ton tenor bell being rung in peal. Saturday, June 29th, is the day of the pilgrimage to Glastonbury Abbey. Allington Church have chartered a large coach, and are willing to take any of our people. It will start at about 8 a.m. and return at 8 p.m., the fare being children 5s. and adults 7s. Application for seats may be made at Loders Vicarage.

June 1957

A Franciscan addresses the mothers

A coachload of our Mothers' Union went to the deanery festival at Toller, which was so crowded with mothers that the service had to be relayed to those who could not get into the church, and tea had to be divided between the village hall and the vicarage lawn. The sermon was preached by a Franciscan friar from the neighbouring friary at Hook. A professional bachelor, in the rough brown habit of the Franciscans, might seem an odd choice of a speaker for mothers, but the mothers found to their delight that he knew as much about home life as they, and could make the truths of religion homely and real.

July 1957

Ringers at large

To choose Dartmoor for an outing, as our ringers did, is usually to cause that shy lady to blanket herself in fog and drizzle, but this time she elected to beam on them, and give them more than a glimpse of her beauty. Perhaps she was in this mood because she knew her guests were not in the best condition to admire her, they having been kept awake the night before by thunder and lightning, and had recourse early on the trip to sedatives frowned on by the Band of Hope. At Plymouth they were recovered enough to enjoy the sunshine and the new city centre that had arisen from the ashes of the old. Those who had had the unwisdom to bring their wives were hustled off to the sales, and came back to the coach weighted down with bargains and looking decidedly wiser. At Torquay the company bestowed its patronage on a variety show, and one of them, a son of the soil, won a smart leather briefcase, suitable for carrying sermons. The return journey to Loders was less melodious than usual. Obviously the previous night's disturbances had left an arrears of sleep to be made up. Nobody remembered to thank Mr. George Hyde for his efficient arrangement of the outing, and only one commended his skill in bringing together so many staunch supporters of the Exchequer under one roof.

August 1957

Campanology

Loders ringers, in common with others throughout the diocese, rang touches on the bells to mark the seventy-fifth anniversary of the Salisbury Guild of Change Ringers, of which they are members. They also attended the quarterly meeting of the West

Dorset branch at South Perrott, and went from there to Broadwindsor to test the rehung bells, which evoked their enthusiastic approval.

October 1957

Ringing the changes

Change-ringers are always glad of an excuse to practise their art. When some of them learnt that the father of a Loders ringer, Mr. Harry Crabb, was nearing his eighty-fifth birthday, and had himself been a ringer for fifty years, they decided to attempt a quarter-peal of Grandsire Doubles in his honour. Mr. Crabb senior lives at Powerstock, but Powerstock lacks one of the six bells needed to make a good job of Grandsire, so the quarter-peal was rung on Loders bells, in the hope that the grand old man's hearing might be as good as his walking. When our country correspondent met him swinging along the road to Loders, he pointed out that the *Bridport News* had made a grave error, and that he wished the universe to know he was eighty-six, and not eighty-five.

November 1957

'Thic thur stay-a-light'

One of the delights of pastoral visitation is that it sometimes shews what impact modern science makes on the ancient rustic mind – the Russian satellite, for instance. When the Vicar called on one of the magnificent grannies of Uploders he was met with something like this:- 'Now Zur, I be all for this yer science. I always have a-said, We must move be the times. You should 'ave 'eard what the professor told us on the wireless last night. It were a caution. That there Russian stay-a-light be just like a gurt white fish, swimmin' round an' round the wurdle. 'Er be stuffed full of powder from 'undreds of pints of dried petrol, and that gives 'er the gee-up and lights 'er up at night. There's a rod what comes up out of 'er nose, and it's the rod what plays the toons. Bain't it wonderful zur? As I sez, We must move be the times.'

November 1957

Male knitter to join the ranks

A sewing meeting has come into being at Askerswell, in preparation for the fête, which is hoped to be another big heave towards the goal of the bell fund. Offers of help will be readily accepted by Miss Edwards, or Mrs. Aylmer. It has come to our knowledge that the male knitter and sewer is not an utterly unknown phenomenon. If Askerswell should contain any such creature, it would be well for the ladies to admit him to their circle, and so take him out of circulation for an hour or two each week.

February 1958

Six vicars on the bells

The Parish Clerk of Loders and Mrs. Thomas celebrated the fortieth anniversary of their wedding last month. Two events conspired to mark the occasion. First, their son George flew from Canada to join the celebration; and second, the Guild of Clerical Ringers, whose annual tour was based on Bridport this year, and who happened to be ringing Loders bells on the wedding anniversary, dedicated a touch of Bob Minor to Mr. and Mrs. Thomas. Few people can say, as Mr. and Mrs. Thomas can now, that the bells for their fortieth anniversary were rung by six vicars.

The student touch

A party of students from the University of London rang touches of minor and grandsire on Loders bells after morning service on St. Mary Magdalene's day. It was fitting that the bells should ring so tunefully on the feast day of Loders' patron.

August 1958

The veteran touch

The annual outing of Loders ringers was to Southampton and Bournemouth, and for once the weather left nothing to be desired. On the outward journey they rang at Ringwood, and called at Romsey Abbey. At Bournemouth they saw a variety show. On the way home they exhausted their stock of songs, and had to eke out the rest of the journey on hymns. The company were grateful to the ringers' secretary, Mr. George Hyde, for his excellent arrangements.

August 1958

The chiming apparatus

Loders Church is indebted to Mr. Charlie Gale, of The Forge, for mending the chiming apparatus of the treble bell, and for declining payment. Had the machinery been repaired by the bell-founders in London, the job would have cost a good Sunday collection. In these days of high labour costs, a bit of work done *gratis* for the church is worth its weight in gold, and should command the gratitude of those who are responsible for the state of repair of the church, namely, all parishioners.

December 1958

A dying art

Somebody who obviously had no knowledge of what he was talking about referred to bell-ringing in a letter to the *Daily Telegraph* as 'a dying art'. This evoked a spirited reply from the chairman of the West Dorset Ringers, Canon Cox; and the *Bridport News* followed it up with a front-page picture of a team of young lady ringers at Beaminster. We would have our readers know that Beaminster is not alone in having an infusion of young ringing blood. Throughout the winter a bevy of local youths have practised in Loders tower, and are shewing promise of becoming good ringers. They are Tommy Dennett, Brian Hyde and David Gill, of Loders, and Peter, Bill and Robin Hansford of Askerswell. This will ensure that when the bells of Askerswell are rehung (which should be soon) they will not lack ringers, and young ones to man them. Of course, bells practised on by learners are no more melodious than fiddles and pianos, and are apt to be painful to those within earshot. We have had no complaint from neighbours about our practices, which suggests that we have their sympathy and encouragement, for which we are grateful. In justice to the learners, it must be said that not all the clangs which emanate from the tower are of their making.

May 1959

Dry without and wet within

For their annual outing Loders ringers rather charily chose a route which on a previous occasion had taken them through fog and drizzle, but this time the weather was perfect and Exmoor made up to them. They went to Lynmouth, and then along the coast to Minehead. On the return journey they made a detour to Wellington, and spent the evening at the inn which Mr. Jim Follett, formerly of Uploders, keeps there. By the grace of God they got home safely, and next morning were manning their ropes as if nothing had happened. Although they rarely say so, they are deeply grateful to Mr. George Hyde for his excellent arrangements, and to their landlord, Mr. Bill Maddison, who ministered to their needs *en route*.

August 1959

Climbing the ramparts

Thanks to the glorious weather, and to the captivating route across the heather chosen by an obliging coach-driver, Loders Sunday School were able to vote this year's outing to Swanage the best they had ever had. A party of children, their parents and friends, numbering seventy-four in all, crowded into two coaches, and on reaching the sea, got into it and scarcely left it until the time came to go home. Their old flag, a bit of white sheeting, with 'Loders Sunday School' daubed on it in creosote, again proved its worth as a rallying point on the crowded beach, and ensured that nobody was lost or missed the bus. Indeed, the only anxiety the organiser suffered this time was at Corfe, when some of the weightier ladies in the party, renowned for tired hearts and indifferent boilers, determined to see the view from the castle, although it meant climbing the upper reaches of the ramparts on all fours.

September 1959

Not the same

The ritual of ringing in the new year at Loders followed the established pattern. The ringers rang a few touches early in the evening of the last day of the old year, and adjourned to their appointed snuggery for comfort. (Long past are the days when they could broach a keg of smuggled brandy in the tower itself, and wake to ring in the new year when it was some hours old.) At a quarter to midnight they returned to the tower, rang until a quarter past, and then yielded to the spell of their snuggery once more. This year, though, things felt different, for they were missing their captain, Mr. Harry Legg, who was out of the ritual for the first time in thirty-two years. He is in hospital. As a ringer Mr. Legg is valuable; as the only thatcher in the district he is almost indispensable; and everybody wishes him a speedy return.

January 1960

Johnnie Walker

Monday, Jan. 25th, was a red letter day for Askerswell, although most of the parishioners were unaware of it. For something like thirty years they have been wanting their sweet-toned bells restored, and on Jan. 25th the work was begun. By the time these *Notes* are out, the five bells will have been lowered to the ground, ready to be taken by rail to the Taylor foundry at Loughborough. They will be away for several weeks, then they will return, with a new sixth bell, and a new wooden frame of iroka, and be rehung. Which means that for some weeks there will be no chimes to summon the parish to church. We enjoin the faithful, during 'the silence', to be observant of the times of services in the *Notes*. The tackle for lowering the bells arrived a few days before Taylor's man. British Railways seemed to know by instinct who is the good angel of Askerswell Church, for their van-driver went straight to Mr. Adams to enlist his help in unloading. Finding accommodation near the church for Taylor's man was a problem until Mr. and Mrs. Sidney Fry came to the rescue. The engineer's name, by the way, is John Walker. When he announced himself as 'Johnnie

Walker', Mr. Sidney's face lit up, and he asked, 'Where's your bottle?'

February 1960

The passing of a thatcher and a ringer

Mr. Harry Legg, Captain of Loders ringers, and the one and only thatcher in the neighbourhood, died in Dorchester Hospital on March 27th, after having lain there nearly four months from an operation. His passing has plunged us all into a gloom, and evoked heartfelt sympathy for his widow. Every owner of a thatched house in this district is wondering what he will do about repairs in future. Harry had always been at beck and call, obliging, conscientious, a master of his craft, and one whose nice quiet ways made his employer almost regret the completion of the job and Harry's departure. His one real hobby was bell ringing, and for thirty-two years he was the staunchest member of Loders tower. Not being given to annual holidays, he would go for years on end without missing a Sunday ringing or a week-night practice. And he was there in good time, as if he secretly prized his record of being always the first arrival. The ringers' annual outing was perhaps the event in the year he most looked forward to. He was of a serious disposition, and this was the one day we found him quite relaxed and boylike. Only a few hours before his death, he was reminiscing over an outing to Lynton and Lynmouth. Loders ringers honoured his memory with half-muffled peals on the evening of March 28th. He was laid to rest in the grave of his niece, in Loders churchyard, not far from the tower he loved.

April 1960

Salmon for the ringers

When the West Dorset Guild of Ringers made history for Askerswell church by holding their first meeting there, the mothers and friends of the Askerwell ringers made history for the Guild by offering them Scotch salmon at the tea, which is also a vital part of the proceedings. The salmon was that which Mrs. Ernest Samways won at the Christmas Fair, and Mrs.

Newall had kept it in deep freeze. It was cooked at the Vicarage, and served on a big dish with the appropriate garniture. For all the time the fish had been dead, it ate as though it had been hooked yesterday. None of it went begging, and to the ringers the haloes of Mrs. Samways and Mrs. Aylmer (who killed the fish) were bright. The Guild shewed their gratitude by passing round the hat to help Askerswell ringers provide permanent sound-proofing for the belfry floor, which at present is proofed with sawdust.

August 1961

Ringers relaxing

Loders ringers revived their former customs of supping together on New Year's Eve. They, and their wives (or mothers) attended the carol service, and then made for the Farmers' Arms, where Bill Maddison, their treasurer, and his wife, served an excellent hot meal, one which everybody, even the captain, could enjoy because there were no speeches. Towards midnight they returned to the tower to ring out the old year and ring in the new. This they did in an amiable mood. Food, taken with liquor, prevents the latter from making its imbibers quarrelsome. Askerswell ringers, being of too tender an age to visit inns, went together to a film, and called at the Vicarage to supper on the way home.

February 1962

Changes at Loders Court

There has been a lord of the manor of Loders since before the days of King Harold, who is the first recorded lord. When Sir Edward Le Breton died last December, we feared that the days of the manor might be over, and that it might be the fate of the Court to become a block of flats or offices. But with a nice care for our well being, Lady Le Breton and Mrs. Laskey have contrived that the old order should continue. We are to have another squire, and one not unknown to us. He is the Honourable Alexander Hood, heir presumptive to the sixth Viscount Hood (his elder brother). He is a product of Dartmouth Naval College and of Trinity College Cambridge.

During the war he served in the Royal Navy, and left with the rank of Lieut. Commander. He has since made his mark in the world of industry and finance, being a director of Schroders, Associated Electrical Industries, Wimpey, Blaws Knox, and other concerns. He used to stay with Commander Streatfield when the latter lived at Matravers, and he developed a liking for Loders Church and its Sunday matins. He is forty-eight years old, and is married with three small boys, the youngest of whom is only weeks old. He intends to reduce the Court to its original Georgian proportions by demolishing the Victorian extension. But he says he will try not to disturb the staff and tenantry.

May 1962

At last!

The public water supply which has been coming to Loders for years and never arrived, is now only just round the corner. Loders Parish Assembly were informed that water from the new reservoir at Dottery will get to the railway bridge in Loders by the autumn, and will there be met by water from the reservoir above the Travellers Rest, perhaps a bit later than the autumn.

April 1963

In to dry

The shape of things to come is now emerging from the chaos of building activity about Loders Court. Freed of its Victorian accretions, the fine outline of the Georgian mansion is clearly discernible, against a new vista of Boarsbarrow Hill. But there is a spot in the park whence on Mondays the washing of Court Cottages looks to be hanging on a yard arm from one of the Court walls. When this is brought to the attention of the Hon. Alexander Hood, we can see the wives of Court Cottages being presented with spin driers.

April 1963

Woodworm in the belfry

Loders harvest was blessed by traditional Loders weather. An autumn sun suffused the windows and touched the labours of the decorators with harvest gold. Choir and organist were in fine form, and there were the usual large congregations morning and evening, including visitors who make a point of coming every year. The ringers rang touches after evening service, until the demise of the fifth bell's slider brought their efforts to a sudden conclusion. The slider was full of woodworm, which raises anxious queries as to whether the little beasts are anywhere else in the belfry. The report of the tower warden, Mr. Reg Dennett, will be awaited with crossed fingers. Woodworm in a belfry can be mighty costly. Fortunately the bell frame itself is of steel, and that has been well and truly covered with red lead by Mr. Spillman and Mr. Bradshaw.

November 1963

Success at last

A quarter peal of Grandsire Doubles was rung on Loders bells in honour of the late Mr. Alfred Crabb, who, on his death at 92, was Loders' oldest ringer. The team consisted of Treble, Mrs. Jessie Davis; Second, Mrs. John Mead; Third, Rev. O.L. Willmott; Fourth, Mr. John Mead; Fifth (and Conductor), Mr. Jesse Davis; Tenor, Mr. Harry Crabb. The tribute cost more effort than appears, for it succeeded at only the third attempt, the previous two having gone awry within a hair's breadth of the goal.

May 1964

Will it?

A visitor to Loders Church has written in the visitor's book: 'Too near Bridport for comfort. When that place grows a bit more, this church and village will go the way of all old things in a new world'. From the top of Boarsbarrow one can see the gradual approach of the tide of new urban dwellings which has already washed the rural nature out of Bradpole. Which makes us more thankful that at the death of Sir Edward Le Breton,

Loders Court became the country seat of the Hood family, and Boarsbarrow farm its annexe. These are a bastion against the urban tide that the writer in the visitor's book, being from Middlesex, was unaware of.

June 1964

A great occasion

The labours of many Loders ladies, and of a few gentlemen, in making hassocks for their parish church, concluded in a memorable service of dedication on a Sunday evening in June. As the bells pealed overhead, a steady trickle of worshippers flowing down the path to the church grew into a stream, and by seven o'clock the church was well filled. Some of the new hassocks were on show in the windows and on the chancel pavement. An evening sun beaming on them and on the flowers made the scene very colourful. Soon the organ and the meaningful singing of 'We love the place' and 'Pleasant are thy courts' added delights of the ear to those of the eye. The hassock-makers were mostly sitting in the Ladye Chapel. At the appropriate time they filed up the nave, each holding a hassock, which they delivered to the Vicar at the chancel step, and he added them to the hassocks already on the chancel pavement. Then, kneeling on one of them, he dedicated them to the divine service. In the sermon he pointed out bits of the church which were the handiwork of long dead Loders' masons, carpenters and blacksmiths, and said that in his seventeen years ministry in the parish nothing had given him greater pleasure than the adding of this fine workmanship of Loders women, to the work of Loders men of the twelfth and thirteenth centuries and onwards. After service the congregation moved over to the vicarage lawn for refreshments. A mild diversion was the spectacle of Vicar, Organist and Bass trying to coax the ale out of a keg whose tap was choked with hops. Nobody doubted that they would succeed, if it took them all night, but they struck oil before that. The hassocks are now in their appointed place, high on the backs of the pews, four to a pew. A Roman Catholic priest on holiday from Lancashire was admiring them the other evening, and remarked how to a visitor they gave the church the air of being loved and used.

July 1964

Recital on the vicarage lawn

The lay vicars of Salisbury Cathedral Choir will be giving a recital of glees and madrigals at Loders on Wednesday, June 16th, at 7.30 p.m. if the evening is fine, as we very much hope it may be, the recital will be on the vicarage lawn; if wet, the Hut. For those who do not know what lay vicars are, they are the men of the cathedral choir. The charge for admission will be five shillings (tickets obtainable at Askerswell Post Office and Loders Vicarage). The idea of making a charge is not the lay vicars, but ours. They sing for the joy of singing, but we saw in their visit an opportunity to help the mother church of the diocese. The boys of the cathedral choir are boarded at the choir school, and the school is now wrestling with rising costs. So the proceeds of the recital will go to the school fund. The musical tradition of English cathedrals is second to none in the world. It makes wonderful use of air, but cannot live on it.

June 1965

On their knees

Loders' ringers chose a lovely day for their outing. They went by coach over the Plain to Salisbury, down to Southampton for shopping and on to Bournemouth for a variety show, which they enjoyed, except that some regretted they were in the back row instead of the front when the amiable mezzo-soprano, Miss Yana, descended from the platform, and continued the trilling on some of her patrons' knees. Rather oddly, those of our ringers whose knees seemed least likely to bear her weight were the most energetic in trying to gain her attention! At the end of a perfect day the company felt grateful to the secretary, Mr. Bill Maddison, for all his good offices.

August 1965

New industry

The old forge in Uploders has become the home of a new industry and an expert one at that. A young couple from Hove, Mr. Douglas Baggott and his wife, Carole, are making old-fashioned leather firebuckets there. At present they are going all out to satisfy orders from America.

December 1966

Ringing in the year in 1900

One donation from Mrs. E.M. Norman and another from a kind 'Anonymous', has brought the appeal fund to £500. Mrs. Norman's donation was from her 86-year-old father as well. He lives with her. He was once a Loders ringer. He 'rang-in' the year 1900. Those were the days before the bells had been re-hung, when it took two men to pull up the tenor. He recollects that the tenor then bore the inscription, 'Ring me well and ring me right: thirty hundred weight is my weight'. The tenor seems to have slimmed down to nineteen hundredweight and to have grown in piety, for the present inscription is,

> 'Ay may I sound glory to God on hie,
> Thanks to my friends, in sweetest harmonie'.

July 1967

A short cut

A party of ringers from Kentisbeare, Devon, who were on a coach outing, and were due to call at Loders tower, were directed off the Dorchester-Bridport road via Lea Lane as a short cut! The coach was a forty-seater. When it neared Whitehouse Farm, having gingerly negotiated the narrow tunnel of overhanging bushes and the blind corners, it found itself at the narrow humped bridge over the stream. To advance was impossible, so it backed all the way up the tortuous lane it had come down and without an accident. The ringers' nerves were as good as the driver's, for when they eventually got to Loders by a wider road they performed superbly on the bells.

July 1967

* * * * * * *

Harry Crabb

A thirst-promoting day

The ringers' idea of a good outing alters somewhat from the choir's; the preference of the former is for a long journey in a comfortable coach, frequent halts for refreshment, and lovely scenery whose claims to attention may be rejected in favour of the darts board of a cosy inn. This year Loders ringers made the long trip through the Wye Valley on a hot, thirst-promoting day. Their objective was the high ground of Symond's Yat, commanding a view of several counties and the looping of the River Wye, but instead, in a manner unaccounted for, they found themselves in two motor boats, racing down the Wye listening to the tall stories of the boatmen about this season's catch of salmon. The young bloods of the party made a purchase of grey Edwardian toppers, and put them on. The effect of this on the captain, Mr. Harry Crabb, was interesting to observe. It is worth recording that the party got home safely, for which they may be grateful to the steadying influence of Mr. Churchwarden Lock.

August 1955

Harry takes over

Much sympathy is felt with Mr. Jim Steel, of Uploders, who has been forced by ill-health to give up his post as shepherd at Upton Farm, after working there for fourteen years. Shepherding is in Mr. Steel's blood. His father and his grandfather were shepherds before him, and he is gloomy at the prospect of life without sheep. To the modern suggestion that it is a lonely job he makes the laughing rejoinder that there are always the dog and the sheep to talk to, and that the shepherd is nothing like as lonesome as is a worker in a big factory, who is only a number among thousands of other numbers. Mr. Steel, who was born at West Stratton, began to follow sheep at the age of thirteen. His eyes light up when he recalls the twenty years of shepherding that he did in the Highlands of Scotland round Inverness. In imagination he still sits among the mountain heather and picks out the streams in the glen below, and his heart warms when he recalls the friendly

Harry Crabb

crofters, who would never let him pass their door without a cup of tea and a chat. Immediately before coming to Upton Mr. Steel was shepherd at Beaminster. His sheep at Upton are now in the care of Mr. Harry Crabb, which pleases Mr. Steel, for, says he, 'There ain't much anybody can tell old Harry about sheep.'

August 1955

The way of ringers

There is a touch of Thomas Hardy's 'Under the greenwood tree' about the way in which our ringers do their business with a fine contempt for orthodoxy. Captain Harry Crabb sent word to the annual meeting that since he had become a shepherd, watching his flock by day as well as night, he could not be as dependable as he could wish, and wanted to be relieved of his office. Harry Legg was therefore elected captain. But Harry Legg thought it was time George Hyde did a spell as captain. George, however, was re-elected secretary, a job he knows from A to Z. But George contended that Bill Maddison was just the man for secretary, and that he would try to get him to take over. Whereupon Harry Legg said that if George managed to pass on his job to Bill, then George must be captain. We learn that Bill has fallen to George's blandishments and become secretary, but whether George has yielded to Harry, we know not. Only one thing we know, and that is that Frank Good is now tower warden. Were this a matter of election instead of appointment, this also might be in doubt.

January 1957

Ringers relaxing

Loders ringers and their friends took this year's outing off the beaten track. Avoiding the traffic on the main roads occasionally landed them in delicate manoeuvres with lime lorries in country lanes, but close-ups of villages like Martock made this worth while. After a halt in Wells, they made for the Castle of Comfort, in the Mendips, which used to be presided over by a widow in a white linen costume and an Ascot hat. A notice saying 'No coaches' greeted their thirsty eyes, and a landlady who was not the widow came out and shoo'd them off as she saw Mr. Harry Crabb getting out of the coach. But when she saw the Vicar following, she called them back, and Harry's life was saved. The route thereafter lay through Cheddar and Wedmore to Burnham-on-Sea, thence to a little old inn under the Polden Hills, and finally to the village of Trent, where the former Archbishop of Canterbury, Lord Fisher of Lambeth, has just taken up residence. But it was not his lordship's house that the coach parked outside of. (Harry could not have seen the recent picture of the present Archbishop [Arthur Ramsey] broaching a gherkin with the Durham miners who called on His Grace.)

Ringers' outing

When Loders ringers take to the moors they usually choose a day of pea-soup fog and see little more than the insides of various hostelries. But this year they had the perfect day for Exmoor and Minehead, and do not remember an outing they enjoyed more. The high light of the day was when somebody saw a rabbit, but not everybody was convinced that he had. At their old haunt, 'The Crown', on Catcott Moor, they saw a van pull up outside the inn, and three long-haired beatle-type youths get out. Before going into the inn, one of the youths retired to the back of the van, pulled out a comb and mirror, and adjusted his flowing locks and tittivated his eyebrows. One of the ringers' ladies remarked that distinguishing between the sexes made topless dresses a necessity nowadays, and Mr. Harry Crabb agreed.

August 1964

Ann Haines

A shadow was cast over the fête by the untimely death of Mrs. Ann Haines, at the age of 39. Deep sympathy was felt for her husband and children and for her parents, Mr. and Mrs. Harry Crabb. Mrs. Haines died at her home in London and was cremated there. The funeral service was in Loders Church and the ashes were buried in the grave of an uncle. A mass of floral tributes included several from the factory where she used to work and from neighbours who had been very helpful during the long illness.

August 1965

Loders Organ

CHAPTER 8
Wit and mystic

The Articles of Faith of Chapter One have already demonstrated the Vicar's capacity for distilled thought, independence of opinion and conciseness of expression. We end with a mixture of the witty and the profound which always stood side by side in the *Parish Notes*. Chapter Five concentrated on his fascination for worldly events and issues. But here is where two other rich seams in his character come to the fore. He was a conscious stylist, and by wit is meant not just the cleverly humorous but the well-crafted phrase or paragraph. Once or twice he imitated the great diarists like Pepys or John Evelyn. 'Page from a preacher's diary', p. 243, is a *tour de force* of literary control as well as being absurdly funny (he was an ardent fan of the *Carry On* films). Then, without warning, comes a reflection worthy of the great mystics, as if he had been transported into the world of George Herbert or Thomas Traherne. Only such a concentration of spirituality could have come up with the phrase 'The evensong hour' (p. 239).

The lasting impression of the *Parish Notes* is their intense, driving interest: they were always very readable, whether you lived in Loders or not. But close study and attention to detail provides the reader with delights of style and, even more importantly, the occasional inspiration of saintly communication from a person with deep religious conviction. His homilies on Lent, for example, always had a benign sternness: 'Lent is early this year. The thought of Lent is hardly one to warm the cockles of the heart. It is too cluttered up with its long tradition of mortification. But it ought really to be a heart-warming thought.'

February 1964

The final note is one of humour. Harmoniums in church 'scream like a scalded cat' (p. 250); successful mothers are classed as 'Athletes in maternity' (p. 249); undertakers in the great freeze of 1963 are described as having been 'hankering after the warmth of the crematorium' (p. 242); and in the same year, 'When the snow came, the tree, lighted by night, made us look like the home of the sugar-plum fairy somewhere in the Black Forest' (p. 241). The Vicar practised the art of literary surprise. He didn't believe in excessive piety.

The church militant

Extract from provincial daily paper: 'A disturbance was caused in St. James' church, during evensong yesterday. A man at the back of the church shouted something and advanced towards the chancel, throwing off officials who tried to stop him. When he reached the Vicar, he assumed a menacing attitude. The Vicar replied with a straight left. The intruder was carried out by three sidesmen. He is now in custody, and will appear before the magistrates when sufficiently recovered.'

August 1953

Domestic chaplain

A legend of the Middle Ages tells how the domestic chaplain in a castle, having tried in vain to persuade the household to pause in its Christmas revels while he held a service, was determined that there should be a Christmas service in that castle. So he went down to the stables and held a service for the domestic animals telling them the story of Christ's birth. It speaks well for our parishioners that they were not so taken up with the Christmas feasting that they left Jesus Christ out of it. On the contrary, congregations tended to be larger than

Loders East Window and Easter Sepulchre

ever, and 161 people made their Communion (Loders 107, Dottery 28, Askerswell 26). The midnight service, at Loders, made a new record in attendance, and the Christmas morning service drew another full congregation, who heard a delightful selection of carols by the Sunday School children. Parishioners who have to leave us and live in other parishes can never seem to rid themselves of the feeling that Loders Church is their spiritual home, and we do not wish them to. It filled our cup of joy to have with us the Scotts, the Streatfields, the Hydes, the Bishops, and relatives of the late Eli Lenthall.

January 1954

An inspired answer

The Vicar was taking Scripture lesson in one of our two village schools. He asked which was the greatest festival in the Church's year. The class looked at each other dubiously, and there was no answer. Then the face of a small boy lit up, his arm shot up, and he said, 'Please, sir, the Cup Final'. One swallow does not make a summer, and 'Abide with me' sung at the Cup Final does not make a religious festival of it. The class knew this, and laughed. Then one child got what he thought was the right answer. A whisper went round, hands beat the air, and from a dozen small throats came the chorus, 'Harvest Festival'. Most adults in a country parish would endorse the children's opinion that Harvest is the greatest festival, but those who are familiar with the church calendar know that Harvest does not as much as appear on it. Easter, of course, is the greatest festival, the 'Queen of Seasons'. Without the Resurrection there would have been no Christianity. The Apostles called themselves 'witnesses of the Resurrection', and the Resurrection was the corner stone of all their preaching. So the Prayer Book is on sure biblical ground when it names Easter as the occasion above all others when loyal churchmen shall join in the Lord's own service of Holy Communion. A glance at the list of Easter Day services will show that there are times to suit all tastes.

The children in our two schools are now clear as to which is the greatest festival. They also know that Good Friday is not a holiday, but a holy day on which we lament what the world did to the only true Man. It is to be hoped that parents will not confuse the children by making a gala day of Good Friday, but will rather set them a good example by joining one of the devotional services at Church.

April 1954

Working under difficulties

Those familiar with their bibles know that times were so dangerous that the masons who rebuilt the walls of Jerusalem after the Babylonian exile had to work with a trowel in one hand and a spear in the other. Uploders contains, between the Travellers' Rest and Stony Head, one of the most dangerous bits of road in the West Country, the scene of accidents unnumbered, and, as we write, the most dangerous bend in it is in process of being straightened. Motorists who chafe at the slowing down imposed on them by all the cautionary signs of 'Road Works Ahead' might give a thought to the difficulties the men are working under. The road that these have constantly to cross and re-cross is now teeming with summer traffic. Sometimes thick fog adds to the danger, and when the sun is out it strikes on the white chalk they are moving as on virgin snow, and makes their eyes ache. The critically-minded are inclined to ask, Why couldn't a job like this be done in the winter when there is less traffic about? If the local roadmen had their way, the job would probably not be done in the height of the summer traffic. But theirs is to do and die, theirs not to reason why. Projects like these have to await the approval of Highest Authority before they can begin, and if approval is not given before the summer traffic begins, the work cannot begin till then. If the local authority thinks to defer the work till the traffic has abated, it is up against the hard fact that the work must be finished within a certain time to qualify for the government grant which alone made the work possible. So, from our own roadmen's point of view at any rate, the goings-on at The Travellers are not mere midsummer madness.

July 1955

'Season of mists'

We move into the fogs of November fortified by a radiant summer and a mellow autumn. The choicest experience that this summer offered was the early morning communion at Loders Church. You went along the sleeping village street with the jovial sun patting you on the back. Before you got to the church gate you smelt them – roses, a mass of them, covering the churchyard wall; roses that dropped in a few hours if you picked them, but, left on the wall, looked and smelt divine. You went along the gravel path through a floral guard of honour, lines of purple ageratum on your left, and ceanothus on your right. To the soft chime of the minute bell, you followed the crazy paving into church, where you found a pew, and knelt. You felt that the great coloured window in the east was giving you a look of welcome; you scented honeysuckle, and located a shy pot of it in Mrs. Harry Legg's window. The bell stopped; the voice of the priest broke the stillness of the chancel; the holy thanksgiving had begun. No, there is nothing sweeter than Loders Church in the early summer morn, and if next summer is as nice as this has been, you can see for yourself.

November 1955

Local elections

These might be highly popular if they followed the fashion of our recent Mothers' Union election. The members met over a sumptuous tea at Loders Court, where they were guests of Lady Le Breton, and in the feelings of mutual goodwill engendered by china tea and walnut cake, proceeded to the election of officers. It will give no surprise that in these auspicious circumstances the election rose to the level of a male election. No feminine nonsense of bits of paper and the veiled malice of the secret vote here! The Enroling Member was re-elected for a further three years on a healthy show of hands, with no opposition, and the committee got back without a scratch. Our diplomats might learn a thing or two from Lady Le Breton. The difficulty with which our Agricultural Discussion Club is annually faced is the election of a secretary. There is never any difficulty about the coveted dignity of chairman, which Mr. Charlie Gale had bestowed upon him in five seconds by a unanimous show of hands. The secretaryship is different. It is associated with writing and the keeping of accounts, to which the true farmer is allergic, and the Club gets a secretary only by marking the victim beforehand, seeing he is at the meeting, and frog-marching him into the job. This time the victim marked beforehand was Mr. Bob Hawkins. But at the meeting the utterly unexpected happened. As Mr. Hawkins was doing the bucking and kicking proper to secretaries before they are impounded, somebody idly suggested that Mr. Ward would not make a bad secretary – and he accepted like a lamb! There was a breathless hush. The first to find his voice was our Mr. Gray, a local farmer of renown, and a light of the Methodist community. He put the situation exactly. 'Friends,' he said, 'this is wonderful. We were Abraham, come to sacrifice Isaac, and we have found a ram caught in the thicket'.

November 1955

Broken in

Mrs. Hilton, of Vinney Cross, is in hospital at Weymouth for two operations. Her spouse is one those domesticated husbands who can do anything in the home. It was music to our reporter, who has not yet been 'broken in,' to hear Mr. Hilton, with a (rueful) eye on the dishes, hope that she would soon be back.

December 1956

An eye-opener

In that mood of despondency which can afflict thoughtful people at times, the Psalmist once said, 'There is not one godly man left; the faithful are minished from among the children of men'. And that is exactly how the faithful feel now, on occasion. But those of Loders and Askerswell who joined the recent pilgrimage to Glastonbury came back electrified by their experience. They found Glastonbury crowded with thousands upon thousands of fellow members of the Church of England who had come to worship in the place where the first church in England was built. 'I had no idea there were so many churchpeople,' said one Askerswell pilgrim. Which is a reminder that when Elijah, in a welter of self-pity, said he was the only one left who had not forsaken God, God replied, 'I have left me seven thousand in Israel, all the knees which have not bowed to Baal' [1 Kings, Chapt. 19, vs. 18].

July 1957

The W.I. at large

We have heard it said that if you see chocolate made, you will never eat another, but this is clean contrary to the experience of our Women's Institute, whose summer outing was an inspection of Fry's factory at Bristol. Samples of what they saw being made were offered them, and gladly eaten, in every department, and nobody refused the selection box with which they were speeded on their homeward journey after a sumptuous tea in the canteen. Their only regret seems to be that chocolate is not more amenable to smuggling, for it shewed an over-ready tendency to melt and combine with photographs and compacts in handbags. So fascinating was the tour that the ladies were oblivious of their feet until the guide told them they had walked two and a half miles in the factory, but there was no oblivion about their figures among the rounder ladies when they reached a narrow stairway, and were advised by the guides to descend sideways. ...

The comment of our most distinguished reader on our paragraph last month about the W.I. celebrating their tenth birthday was: 'Tenth birthday my foot! Feminine vanity! They must be at least forty'. And so, we suppose, they are, if they be dated from when they began. The ladies prefer to date themselves from when they revived.

August 1957

Impounded

The village pound at Askerswell is being tidied up by Mrs. Aylmer, Miss Edwards, Miss McCombie and Mr. Swaffield, and Mrs. Adams has made a professional-looking signboard for it. Their motive is purely antiquarian, and has nothing to do with the recent urge of some of the local cattle to stray.

What was once the old pound in Loders is now a pretty garden with a well in it that looks romantic enough to be a wishing-well. Bradpole pound has been less lucky, even if it is more used. Night by night it stables an Adam Lythgoe lorry.

August 1957

Now we know!

Mother, explaining things to her child in Dorchester market: 'That black and white one there is a bull. Black and whites are always bulls'.

August 1957

Higher service

Mr. Horace Read, the under gardener at Loders Court, was married to Miss Molly Pavitt, of Allington, at Allington Church, in early August, and he and his bride have set up home in the cottage lately vacated by Mrs. Hyde (who now lives with her daughter, Mrs. Wilfred Crabb). Loders Choir were quick to note that Mrs. Read is a member of the Bridport Operatic Society, and without a doubt are eager to promote her to higher service.

September 1957

Compliments of the season

We would like to wish our readers a happy new year, and we are thinking not only of the two hundred and ten who cheerfully pay for a copy of the *Notes*, but the large family scattered all over the world to whom a copy is sent by their friends. We do not know why, but it is pleasant to feel that our simple everyday doings are compassed about by a cloud of invisible witnesses who are deeply interested in us, and that the *Notes* get as far as the military hospital in Singapore, the farthest reaches of the Canadian Pacific Railway and the steamy jungles of the Amazon. Any pride that the Editor might have in this is sobered by the recollection that once in 1957 the *Notes* were threatened by a libel action, and that very occasionally they tread on an unsuspected corn. May we plunge into 1958

proclaiming with Peter Quince that, 'If we offend, it is with our good will?'

January 1958

An Askerswell wedding

It gave Askerswell people much pleasure to see Miss Eileen Norman, of Walditch, brought back into the parish as the wife of Mr. Michael Biss, of Medway Farm. The Norman family have their roots in Askerswell, and used to provide a good proportion of the choir. A combination of circumstances, of which not the least was to have the wedding before Lent, made the 13th of February the nuptial day. The significance of this date was not lost on the rustic congregation, who made great use of horse-shoes and black cats to put things right. The charms had no perceptible effect on the driving rain, but when the large congregation rose to the notes of 'Here comes the bride', it seemed a miracle that such a vision of beauty as the bridal party made could have come out of such weather. They took up their stand in a chancel where the first primroses and violets peeped out of the moss. The wedding feast was at Medway Farm. We owe it to the honour and reputation of the bridegroom's father as a District Councillor to assure our readers that the severe disability of elbow and neck to which he fell victim after the feast came quite exclusively of an encounter with a frisky cow. At the time of writing, he is still under the doctor, but making good progress.

March 1958

Fête jottings

Overheard at the jumble stall: saleswoman to gentleman, 'Can I interest you in this pair of boots? Excellent quality, exactly your size, only worn once or twice – sixpence the pair for a quick sale.' Gentleman, 'You're telling me. They were mine.' In the week before the fête, housewife to lady collector, 'No, I'm not giving to the fête this year. The Vicar never does anything.'

September 1958

The cuckoo

Your editor was flattered at being informed by the local statistician, Mr. Malcolm McDowall, that he first heard the cuckoo on April 5th, and saw the first swallow on March 24th, which is early. Usually intelligence of this calibre is communicated to *The Times*, by telephone. Mr. McDowall informs us that the dandelions are also early. This last piece of research deserves an appropriate comment, but we cannot think of one. O, for the ready wit of a Mr. Punch, who, when told of the new style dining-cum-drawing room known officially as a 'combination-room' (as seen in the new rectory at Bridport) presumed that it was 'a kind of vestry-cum-pantry'.

May 1959

It's an ill wind ...

Seeing that he does not pay Mrs. Roper danger money for living there, the landlord of her cottage, which stands on the awkward Blue Ball crossroads at Dottery, has no cause to regret the accidents which have lately befallen the said cottage. The wind blew down the television aerial and the chimney with it. The television people had to build the landlord a new chimney. Later a bus backed into the porch, knocking it askew, and the bus people have to build the landlord a new one. The next-door-neighbour, Mrs. Reynish, whose porch is a sort of Siamese twin with Mrs. Roper's regrets that the impact was not sufficient to knock her porch dizzy too. It was unsteady before, and she is fearful of what may happen – and not at the bus people's expense this time – when the builders operate on Mrs. Roper's porch.

February 1960

A happy Easter

People always have a merry Christmas. But not always a happy Easter. The weather can make or mar Easter. When the first holiday of the year is a matter of driving rain and windswept promenades, nobody can be happy. This year the weather left nothing to be desired, except perhaps a little more warmth, and in view of the large congregations all over the country, the Church, as well as the holiday resorts, can look back on Easter as happy. We in these three parishes are a small population of less than eight hundred, spread over a large area. It was therefore gratifying to have nearly two hundred communicants, and for all the Easter services to command an attendance of over five hundred. But numbers are not everything. Much of the joy of the festival lay in having with us former parishioners home on holiday, and in worshipping in churches which loving hands had turned into temples of flowers. We marvelled at the painstaking which had gone into some items of decoration – for instance, into the pavement of flowers round the font at Askerswell, with the words 'Christ is risen' picked out in primroses; and into the Easter sepulchre in Loders porch, which had taken one little pair of hands a day to do. It is a comforting thought that had there been no crowds to admire these works of art, they still would have caught the eye of God. The matins congregation at Loders, where the church was tight-packed, was also grateful for the impetus given to their singing by choir and organ, and for the brisk and cheerful anthem.

May 1960

Savile Row comes to Uploders

The sale at Loders School on a hot Saturday afternoon had West Bay and the Saturday shopping to compete with. Yet it raised £16 for the school fund, provided a couple of pleasant hours for those who like jumble sales, and was timely for those who rely on such sales to replenish their wardrobes. Uploders now looks a little less unlike Savile Row in consequence.

July 1960

Happy New Year!!!

Because it is the nature of these *Notes* to be a diary of local events, and because there is much to record this month, your editor will forego his undoubted right of propounding a new year solution of all the world's problems, and will only ask whether it is proper for a christian to desire a happy new year?

Happiness, if directly sought, is a will-o'-the-wisp that always eludes. The thing to wish for is that we may put duty first, duty to God and then to our neighbour. From duty done will come the happiness that was not asked for, deep and satisfying.

January 1961

Mrs. Sarah Hyde

The oldest inhabitant of the civil parish of Loders is Mrs. Sarah Hyde, of Yondover, who was 91 on July 5th. Her long life has all been spent in Loders, and been tied up with the church. She is the widow of Albert Hyde, for forty years the sacristan; sister-in-law of the late John Hyde, sexton, and daughter-in-law of the late David Hyde, 'the old sexton'. Many times she has scrubbed the church from end to end, to help her husband, whose pay was a shilling a week. She is a monument to the old saying, 'Hard work never killed nobody' – an oracle quite Delphic in its ambiguity. Her memory is clear, her health good, and she is well cared for in the home of her daughter, Mrs. Wilfred Crabb.

August 1961

Mr. and Mrs. Baggs

Changes have lately come thick and fast at Dottery, which was once as constant as Julius Caesar's northern star. Mr. and Mrs. Baggs and family have (not surprisingly, as their cottage was no credit to the parish) gone to Toller, leaving nobody to sweep the Dottery chimneys nor scythe the churchyard.

November 1961

A thousand years are but as yesterday

Memories in the countryside are long, and retentive, but is any in Loders long enough to assist a lady who is writing an article on a former Vicar of Loders, John Jones? It appears that he was also tutor to Legh Richmand, who became an eminent divine and an intimate of Wilberforce. The lady writing the article says: 'It may be that he is still remembered by stories in the parish'. If anybody remembers anything about John

Jones would they please tell the Vicar? We see that Jones was in Loders from 1783–1813, which is not so very long ago for the countryside, where a thousand years are but as yesterday.

March 1962

Detergents not needed now?

For some weeks Askerswell has been altogether in the hands of those gentlemen who put up the sign 'Road Works Ahead', and the legend 'Men Working'. How to get to the Post Office, or away from the Church, has occasionally been a problem as roads have been opened up to insert the intestines of the new water supply. At five minutes to nine the school playground looks as if it had never seen a child, and Miss Grigg can get on with her preparations for the day's lessons in heavenly peace. When the bell goes, the children cover the distance from the road works to the school in an incredibly short time, and prayers begin when they should. The parishioners say that the men are working well, and against difficulties, but their efforts have produced some unexpected results at this transitional stage. Some of the pipes at the council houses at Leggs Mead appear now to have been suffering from hardening of the arteries. They had been able to cope with the leisurely flow from Mr. George Bryan's spring, but when they had to contain the pressure of the public supply, they bulged and burst – and doesn't Mrs. Burt and her neighbours who were flooded know it? Householders newly connected but undeluged were able to note that the public water had a marvellous effect on clothes in the wash and prunes-at-soak. They were thoroughly bleached by the chlorine that conscientious authority puts in the water to kill the bugs and help the teeth. This may be all right where clothes that lack the Persil touch are concerned, but it is a serious matter when prunes, which turn a decent stomach anyway, are made to look like anaemic gooseberries.

June 1962

Vandalism, or act of God?

After morning service one bright Sunday in June, the Askerswell congregation gathered round an altar tomb on the south side of the tower, to try to figure out how one of its sides had come to be stove in, and another to be badly cracked. (The tomb belongs to the Chick family, formerly of South Eggardon.) The charitable were inclined to think the damage had been caused by the vibration of the pneumatic drills working nearby in connection with the new water supply; the religiously-inclined put it down to lightning, although nobody could remember when Askerswell last had any lightning; and the realists saw the handiwork of hooligans with a lust for destruction. It may be relevant to recall that some of the altar tombs in Loders churchyard had their walls knocked in and tops lifted a few years back, and this turned out to be the work of mischievous young men.

July 1962

The evensong hour

The Feast of St. Mary Magdalene, patron saint of Loders, falls this year on a Sunday, July 22nd. To make the event there will be another of the summer evensongs, and at 7 p.m., which suits some of those with farm work to do. The last evensong was well attended. There is a restfulness and a wistful beauty about Loders Church which the evensong hour, and no other, captures on a nice summer's day.

July 1962

The return of a native

The Vicar received the following letter from Mrs. Annie Laurie Peck, of Sturminster Newton, whose maiden name (which might help Loders people to identify her) he does not know: 'My husband and I would like to thank you, and the choir, not forgetting the organist, for the really lovely service we enjoyed in Loders Church this morning. Fifty five years ago I used to come to Loders Church with my Grand-father and Aunt, who undertook my up-bringing after my father's sudden decease. He and my dear grandparents lie at rest in the churchyard. You can imagine how my thoughts wandered back to the morning when as a small girl of 4½ I wriggled round in the same pew to admire a large ruby ring on the finger of a gentleman in the seat behind. Thank you all so much for a very happy morning. I think you were brave over the sermon on "Visiting". I loved it.' Comment: All sermons have to be brave. They are merciless self-revelations of the preacher.

September 1962

Of mothers and Sunday Schools

Loders Sunday School hadn't the best of days for their coach outing to Swanage, but at least it was dry, and the fog patches *en route* were of short duration. Everybody enjoyed themselves – the mothers perhaps a little too strenuously for their liking. The proprietors of the paddle boats refused to let children out in them without an adult. The attraction of forbidden fruit is well known. This embargo prompted many children to want the paddle boats, and once out, they were loth to come in. Poor mothers were kept at it like ducks all the afternoon, and some were forced into port by exhaustion.

October 1962

The Black Angel

The Black Angel was busy in October. He robbed Loders of three of its most valued parishioners. First was Mr. George Crabb, an invalid of years and yet surviving to the ripe age of 84. He was the last of the old-time shepherds of the parish, who had lived here nearly all his long life, and given it exclusively to sheep. Nobody knew this countryside as he did, in the changing seasons, and in all its moods, by night as well as day, and nobody had a deeper reverence for nature than he. In a sophisticated and greedy world it was a delight to have one who prized the simple and abiding things, and who was an infallible weather-prophet to boot. George Crabb was quickly followed by his near neighbour, Mrs. May Poole, who had been devotedly nursed through a long illness by her daughter Betty at Dorchester. People of a sunny and neighbourly disposition like hers are not so plentiful that they are not missed. Her special significance to Loders Church was in her being the wife of a husband who once combined the offices of sexton, chorister and bellringer, and mother of a daughter who was a chorister. She herself was invariably one of those who served teas at fêtes and socials. She was buried in her mother's grave in Loders churchyard. A muffled peal was rung on the bells on the evening of her funeral, which is the local custom for a ringer's wife. Finally there was Mr. Robert Newberry, who lived, as it were, in the suburbs of the parish at Uploders Farm, but had a firm place in the citadel of its affections, as was appropriate to one so shy and yet so transparently good. His legacy to us was the example of his doggedness in meeting and overcoming a succession of misfortunes, which, instead of souring him, made him all the kinder to other unfortunates, and deepened his faith in God. The extreme discomfort of the malignant illness which carried him off could not extinguish his wry humour, nor dampen his affection for his sheep, which used to gather outside the window of his sick room at his whistle. He died at Weymouth Hospital. One of his messages home was to be sure to send corn to Loders Church for harvest.

November 1962

The scene of the century

We live in rare times. The wireless tells us as we write these *Notes* that Bridport's road communications with the outside world are cut off, and that the blizzard which kept us and the West Country under thick snow for days on end was the worst for eighty-two years. Those of us who haven't to tackle the problems this has made for the farms, may be able to admire samples of nature's artistry which have not been seen here before in the twentieth century (and which many hope will not be seen again). It is at night-time that Loders is most picturesque. Mr. Wells had put a Christmas tree outside the post office, and hung it with baubles and coloured lights. When the snow came, the tree, lighted by night, made us look like the home of the sugar-plum fairy somewhere in the Black Forest.

January 1963

Who are the heroes of the great freeze?

When we mentioned the roadman, the coalman treading the ice with hundred weight sacks, the newspaper man, the milk man, the bread man, the postman, and the railwaymen who kept open our only link with civilisation, the gentleman with whom we were conversing said, 'How about the undertakers?' (He happened to be one.) Our own parishioners were too well-behaved to die at a time like this, but in less Christian places it seems that people did die and undertakers had the dickens of a job to locate the proper grave site beneath the churchyard snow; a harder job still to dig the frozen soil, and the hardest job of all to fill in the grave with soil that froze harder on being brought to light. Hankering as they were after the warmth of the crematorium, it is to the credit of undertakers that they did not limit their services to cremations-only during the emergency.

February 1963

Steering clear

Mrs. Wilkins, of Cloverleaf Farm, is back from Portland hospital, showing little outward sign of the ordeal that put her there, and able now to laugh at it, although she was lucky to come through alive. She and her husband were near the auctioneer's ring at Yeovil market when a twelve hundredweight steer took fright and broke loose. He knocked Mr. Wilkins down, but it was Mrs. who got the real savaging, resulting in a broken arm, a gashed leg and a damaged nose. It seems that she has to thank the leather coat she was wearing for her life. By all accounts she was more scared of losing her new hat and handbag than she was of the stampageous steer, and she saved these, though she didn't her arm. Wondrous are the ways of women.

February 1963

Question and answer

Question: 'Hey, Vicar, why did you omit the farmers from your list of heroes of the Great Freeze?'
Answer: 'Personal modesty.'

March 1963

Page from a preacher's diary

'And so to Dottery Church, where I delivered my Lenten sermon. I endeavoured to take my flock in imagination of an aeroplane flight over the Wilderness of the Temptation. They being of a specially earthbound disposition after Sunday dinner took much endeavour on my part to get airborne, but no sooner were we nicely in flight than I noticed from the overt agitation of their countenances that something was gravely amiss. A matron in the back row had me pierced by her eye as she whispered to her neighbour; another in the front row was endeavouring to concentrate attention on me by a reverent use of the toe; another was motioning the children not to panic; and the churchwarden's wife was getting redder and redder. Never had I known such a focus of interest on my humble person, and I could not think why. Had a bat alighted unperceived on my head? Or was there one of those church mosquitoes on my nose, about to launch his dart? Then I perceived that it was something slightly to the right and rear of me that was holding all eyes so awfully enrapt. At the same time a wisp of smoke impinged on the confines of my vision, and a smell of burning assailed my nostrils. Taking a crafty glance to the right of me, but not stopping the sermon, I beheld the altar, and lo, two wooden candlesticks thereon were afire, the candles having burnt out, and the altar draperies were much imperilled. In aeronautical parlance, the sermon looped the loop and nose-dived to a sudden conclusion. With all the outward composure I could command, I announced a hymn, and made for the altar. My powerful blowing only increased the conflagration at first, but what can altogether withstand a clerical gush? The fire went out, and clouds of tallowy fumes came in but a judicious snuffing with the fingers ultimately separated these from their *fons et origo*. A discreet cough at my rear betokened that the alms needed elevation. I hoisted them high, then turned me about to bestow the Church's blessing on my little flock. With one accord, they dropped on reverent knee, and vanished beneath the clouds. But I, declaiming the benison from above, knew that they were somewhere beneath. And so to bed!'

March 1963

Marriageable daughters

Loders people have been uncharacteristically wedding-minded of late. Interest focused first on Mr. David Crabb Junior, who married Miss Patricia Tuck in St. Mary's Bridport. David has left his old home in Vicarage Lane for a brand new bungalow in Bridport. If he does not already know it, the wedding reception won full approval of Uncle Harry Crabb, but not of Mr. Reg. Dennett, who suffered more than usual when Harry put the ringers through their paces next morning. Miss Anne Frapple, of Lower Pymore, shewed that a church wedding may be as quiet and inexpensive as any other if the parties so wish. She married Trooper Brian Jackson by licence in Loders Church. She met the bridegroom in Benghazi, where she was nanny to an officer's family. The weddings reached their climax on the eve of Michaelmas. A large congregation saw Mr. Hamilton Barnes, of Loders Mill, lead the last of his four daughters – Janet Mary – to the altar, and the significance of, the last hymn, 'Now thank we all our God', was not lost on them. Gone are the days when daughters commanded a dowry. Father has now to give the bridegroom a banquet to take her away. Fathers with marriageable daughters, being fathers still at the 'Lead us heavenly father' stage, marvelled that Mr. Barnes could give all his daughters such a splendid send-off and remain solvent. At the reception in the Greyhound the guests were moved to stand and sing, 'For they are jolly good fellows' in Mr. & Mrs. Barnes' honour, and Mr. Barnes, who has never been known to make a speech – of this sort – unfurled a typed manuscript, and most suitably replied. The authorship of the speech will long remain one of the mysteries of literature. The lucky bridegroom was Mr. Tom Billon, of Barton Farm, Toller, whose brother married the former Miss Thelma Cleal, one-time organist of Dottery.

October 1963

Keeping your faculties

Dottery Church has solved its heating problems. A tin hut lined and floored with wood is nothing like as absorbent of heat as a stone church, and the newly purchased electric fires are satisfactory. Dottery's problem is to get water into the churchyard for flowers on the graves, and to keep it out of the church. While rain fell only in the vestry and on the vicar nothing was done, but it now falls on the churchwardens, and without bothering architects and faculties they have embarked on an excellent scheme which will keep everybody dry for £70. If the Archdeacon roars about faculties, Dottery can let him roar again, for it is a mission church and not a parish church.

November 1963

'Once more into the breach!'

As with Shakespeare, whose fourth centenary it is, so with Askerswell Church. Having just put the organ in order at a cost of £300, it is now faced with the urgent necessity of putting in a new heating apparatus. The old Gurney stove is coming to the end of its tether. So are the noble army of stokers enslaved to it every winter. So are the congregation, who run the risk of getting gassed in the divine service. A small committee has been nosing round other churches, seeing how they cope with the heating problems, and it is the system at Chideock Roman Catholic Church that takes their fancy. Here is something up-to-date, which the Chideock R.C.s have tried out and found as satisfactory as church heating can hope to be. The attraction of the system is that it does not attempt the costly business of heating the church. It aims at giving the congregation the impression that they are warm, which is the essential thing – and succeeds. At Chideock the committee had Colonel Weld's assurance on this and their own experience. They had tried out the system for themselves before he arrived at the church, and they managed to look completely innocent when he also demonstrated it. The principle is that of an electric hair-dryer. Cold air is sucked into a machine, hotted up, and blown on to the congregation's feet. When the feet are warm, the rest feels warm, and fortunately the way of heat is to rise. The running cost at Chideock has been about £20 per winter, with no dirt and no labour. The running cost of the Gurney is about £50 per winter, with much dirt, prodigious labour, and often a poisonous smell. As one would expect, the capital outlay is considerable. The cost at Chideock was £450. But there the church is really the private chapel of the Weld family, who were not obliged to get faculties and employ architects. As a parish church, Askerswell has first to obtain a faculty, and this requires a plan drawn up by an approved architect. Also, Askerswell Church is bigger than the Chideock chapel, all of which means that a similar system in Askerswell would probably cost about £600. Nothing daunted, the Church Council have decided to get estimates and to run a fête in June. Fortune favours the brave. One good parishioner promised £100, in the hope that the gesture would be infectious, or spread like wildfire. £600 seems a lot for a community of 120 to raise. But it is chicken-feed to what the 120 cheerfully spend on their own domestic arrangements. (Oh dear! What a mixing of metaphors is here – infection, wildfire and chicken-feed).

May 1964

Loders village hall

This was crowded the other night for a jumble sale of the grand variety to raise money for the improvement fund. The pleasing sum of £38. 10s. 0d. was taken. Gilbert and Sullivan would have enjoyed the situation. To read these *Parish Notes* one would imagine that Loders was split in two camps – church versus hall. Yet the same crowd as attend the church fête were thronging the hall, and the same cheerful faces that run the fête were manning the grand jumble stalls. Like Poo Bah in the Mikado, these public-spirited ladies combine in their persons all the parish offices except that of parish councillors. One day they function as Women's Institute, another as Mothers' Union, another as Church Council, another as Dr. Barnardo's agents, and so on, and so on. To quote The Bard again, 'What's in a name? That which we call a rose, by any other name would smell as sweet.'

May 1964

All glorious within

The *Notes* are early this time to give Loders and Dottery readers a reminder that Mrs. Cecil Marsh and the Vicar are about to start collecting for the fête stalls. What Mrs. Marsh's plan of campaign is we do not know. The Vicar will begin operations in Uploders on Monday, July 27th, and will work down to the other end of the parish terminating in Mr. & Mrs. Jack Dare's, which he usually reaches on Thursday evening. Their home, Hole Farm, is a kind of winning post which these good souls never let him pass without appropriate celebration. Some kind folk have already left offerings at the Vicarage, and one unfailing source of support has presented enough ice-cream to ensure that it does not run out as it did last year. Loders Court will be open to view under the guidance of the Hon. Alexander Hood. Like the king's daughter in the Psalms, the Court is now all-glorious within.

August 1964

Winning salmon

Askerswell Fête was held in the school playing field in early September. The day was perfect. Once again it was seen that as a means of combining the business of raising mnoey with pleasure this old-fashioned institution has much to commend it. The takings were £164. 0s. 6d. and the profit £153. 6s. 6d. And everybody enjoyed themselves. The village was out in strength. Loders also was well represented, but the most pleasing feature was the number of old Askerswell boys and girls who turned up. About twenty of Mr. & Mrs. Sidney Fry's well-spread family were there. Music was provided without charge by a local group of young musicians who, by the way, like to be known as 'The Falling Leaves' and NOT 'The Fallen Leaves'. Among the competitions the keenest interest centred on a salmon lunch. This was a handsome steak from a 27lb Scotch salmon killed by Mrs. Aylmer. When the tickets were put in a box, Mrs. Skeats of Uploders drew the winner for Lady Williams of Bridehead. Lady Williams had delayed her departure in the hope of taking the salmon home for supper that night, but Mrs. Skeats was not to know this. May this opportunity be taken of saying that the press were at fault in omitting the names of some of the helpers from the report? A reporter did the reporting.

October 1964

Confirmation

Confirmation qualifies the candidates to attend Holy Communion. Already some candidates have made their first Communion. It was pleasing to see them accompanied on this great occasion by their parents. It is to be hoped that the remaining candidates will also have this help and example from their parents and that both together may be regular at least one a month. An hour a month is little enough in all conscience to return to the God who gives us our every moment.

October 1964

The ice-cream man cometh

The pupils of Askerswell School have settled easily into their new quarters in Loders School. They like the set-up, and the daily ride in a minibus. Juniors and seniors each have their own teacher in a nicely sized class, and get the undivided attention which was impossible in a one-teacher school. Parents from Askerswell had a chance to see their offspring's new environment when they attended the school harvest festival. This service was a great success, producing a collection of £4 for the Save the Children fund. It was also an unexpected exercise in restraint for the children – while they were at their devotions the ice-cream man arrived outside, and doubtless wondered what was wrong when his siren did not bring down on him an avalanche of children.

November 1964

Carol party

On two exceedingly cold nights before Christmas, the younger members of the choir, well wrapped up, and one with a lantern on a pole, sang carols through Uploders, then Loders, collecting nearly £13 for the Children's Society. They enjoyed themselves hugely in the process. In Uploders Mr. & Mrs. Harrison, helped by Miss Armitage, plied them with red and white wine and two-tier sandwiches. At Uploders Place Mr. & Mrs. Sanctuary, Mrs. Rust and Commander & Mrs. Danis in a combined operation put on a Christmas revel for the carollers and immediate neighbours. Hot soup issued from a downstairs window. Beer, home-made wine, hot dogs and mincepies seemed to rise up from the ground. Further along at Upton Peep Mrs. Lenthall can always be relied on to fortify the inner man. When she heard of the great gorging at Uploders Place she cast a pitiful eye on the delicious coffee and hot sausages she had prepared. But the pity was wasted. The effort of singing between the Place and the Peep had consumed much albumen [white of an egg], and the carollers were as ready for the coffee and sausages as if they had had nothing. Thereafter they were joined by other songsters, so that they looked like the French Revolution descending on Matravers. Mr. & Mrs. Bartlett received them calmly, even picturesquely, framed in the doorway of their bungalow. In Loders on the following night the first call was at the Court, where they sang indoors to the house party, and quaffed sherry and cordials. The tour of Loders ended at the Vicarage with 'eats' round a hot fire of churchyard yew and holly in the big Tudor fireplace of the dining-room.

January 1965

Athletes in maternity

Congratulations to Mr. & Mrs. Reg. Kenway on the birth of a daughter. Mrs. Kenway achieved motherhood with all the efficiency one expects of the ladies of Loders Choir. One Sunday she was singing matins; the same night she was in hospital; and on Christmas Day she was back in church. What athletes in maternity these ladies are, taking it all in their stride and continuing with the Lord's work as if naught had happened.

January 1965

Looking forward

As one looks out of the study window, across the vicarage lawn to Boarsbarrow Hill, noting the slight flurry of snow flakes, and feeling the draught of a biting wind, it needs an effort of imagination to picture the scene that that same lawn should present on the evening of June 16th. A letter has just come from Salisbury to confirm that Mr. Christopher Dearnley (the cathedral organist) will be bringing the lay vicars of the cathedral choir to give us an open air concert on that date. The concert will be of madrigals, glees and solos, and will prove that the men of the choir may be excellent in the sacred, but are certainly *excellentissimus* in the profane. It pleases the cathedral choir to say that they have a soft spot for Loders, and this occasion will doubtless give us a soft spot for them. But the essential business will be to raise funds for the choir school, not to compare spots. Rising prices make the maintenance of the choir school quite a problem. The problem is all ours to solve if we will. Loders is a wee bit like Nazareth: unexpected good comes out of it at times.

February 1965

S.O.S.

Does anybody know of a serviceable harmonium that might be acquired for Dottery Church? There seems to be plenty of them about, that their owners would even pay to be rid of, but Dottery cannot make the acquaintance in the hour of need. So short of breath has the old harmonium become that the organist has to pump furiously to produce the thinnest of sounds. Some notes do not play when they are touched, and others play when they are not touched. This state of affairs has obtained for a long time. It must have been about 1952 when a note refused to stop playing during the prayers. This so irked the then churchwarden, Mr. Fred Cleal, that he crawled on all fours to the chancel, and gently pulled an appendage of the soft underbelly of the harmonium. It screamed like a scalded cat, and Mr. Cleal returned with haste, not on all fours. The prayers were not exactly helped when the Vicar saw some sixteen stone of churchwarden crawling through his line of vision.

March 1965

Thanks

These *Notes* began last month with an appeal for a harmonium for Dottery Church and for somebody to deal with the moles in Loders church-yard. That the *Notes* are read, and read quickly is apparent. Mr. Albert Wells was awakened by a telephone message from Mrs. Forbes that she had a suitable instrument at Eype's Mouth. He at once offered to fetch it in his van. Mrs. Forbes thought it ought to be tested first, which the Dottery organist promptly did, and found it excellent. Now it is enthroned in the church, looking far too dignified to have come out of a cottage, and too big even to have got into one. The note it gives for 'O Lord, open thou our lips' is a deep, full-bellied growl that wakes everybody up. Many thanks to Mrs. Forbes, to Mr. Wells and to Mr. John Marsh for removing the defunct harmonium. The latter was to have been killed, but the Marsh children delight in keeping it alive.

April 1965

Records in the deep freeze

A wedding at Askerswell is a rare event. The last was in 1961. So it was not to be wondered that the wedding of Miss Valerie Gillingham, of Legg's Mead, and Mr. Michael Phillips, of Bridport, should be a village occasion, filling the church, ringing the bells, and inspiring the sun to shine warmly. The marriage register emerged from the darkness of the church safe for signing. At the present rate of marriages it will need to be immortal if its potentiality is to be realised. It was brought into service in 1837, and the first entry is of William Bryant, inn keeper, and Katherine Way. In the 128 years from then till now there have been 181 weddings. The book has room for 319 more entries. Being 128 years old already, it is beginning to look its age. If the Askerswell rate of marriage continues at one in three years, the book will be over a thousand years old by the time it gets to the last entry. By then it will have to be kept in deep freeze.

April 1965

Mothers' Union fogbound

One does not take fog into one's calculations when arranging a midsummer deanery festival of the Mother's Union. Those who know the capacity of Eggardon and the Dorchester Road for serving up fog should have, but did not. So when the first Deanery gathering of mothers at Toller in many years coincided with the best that Eggardon could do in the way of fog there were bound to be unplanned incidents. Mrs. Penfold, the new Enroling Member for Loders, was taking a party to Toller but did not know the way. It had been arranged that Mrs. Cecil Marsh, who was bringing a party from Dottery, should be guide to the Enroling Member's party. But Mrs. Marsh never got out of the fog at Dottery. Mrs. Penfold gratefully accepted the offer of one of her own party, Mrs. Thomas, to guide, blissfully unaware of Mrs. Thomas's infinite capacity for getting lost on M.U. outings. Strange to say, Mrs. Penfold's party got to Toller without incident, whereas parties from Bothenhampton and Burton landed first at Hooke. But the whole congregation managed to come together before the service was quite finished, only to find that parts of the church were wetter than outside, owing to the roof being under repair. Water was falling on the vicar as he preached, but that did not damp the sermon, which the veterans said was the best M.U. sermon they had ever heard. And the vicar is a bachelor. He pointed out that fathers have as much responsibility as mothers for the religious upbringing of their children. So conditioned are we to the contrary view that this simple fact came like a revelation from Sinai.

The festival ended festively in the village hall, where the Toller mothers obliterated memories of the fog with a truly memorable tea.

July 1965

'After the ball was over'

When Miss Hornsby and Miss Wallace got home to Dottery from the M.U. social they found themselves minus their door key. Not being athletic types, it was no use eyeing their bedroom windows. The willingness of a neighbour to fetch a ladder was not all that useful either, for the windows were not made for anybody to get through. The problem was happily solved by another neighbour, Mrs. Scadden, who went through a bunch of old keys and found one that would fit. A similar misfortune befell another member of the Dottery congregation, Miss Male.

She arrived home to find her sister awaiting her outside. The sister had been taking a constitutional and had accidentally locked herself out. She had been waiting in the cold for half an hour, thinking Miss Male had the key. But Miss Male hadn't. It was locked inside. These ladies did not think of bedroom windows and ladders. Luckily their house has a basement and one of the ladies fitted the basement window!

February 1966

Shouting it down the street

Congratulations to our police officer and his wife, Mr. and Mrs. Ronald Parham on the birth of a daughter, their third. Daughters are the fashion in Loders this year. We owe an apology to Mr. and Mrs. Raymond Crabb for not noting their new daughter in January. We did not hear at the time, although the clothes-line was shouting it down the street.

April 1966

An outing to Pilsdon

The glorious September weather made our Mothers' Union visit to the Rev. Percy Smith's community at Pilsdon an event to be remembered. Members made their way there in their own cars, those with giving lifts to those without. Mr. Smith was away, but a service was taken by his wife in the church. After tea in the refectory, the manor house and the farming and the gardening departments were thoroughly explored. Mrs. Thomas tells us that one of the cowsheds has been converted into bed-sitting rooms. The two half-doors have been left as they were, and this seems to have tickled the members' sense of humour.

October 1966

Of burglaries and fires in Dottery

The Dottery scene was enlivened last month by a burglary and a fire. Strictly speaking, the burglary was not in Dottery. It was at the house of Mr. and Mrs. Sorsen, which is only a few yards from the church and yet in the parish of Netherbury. While these two elderly people were watching television one night the thief borrowed a ladder from our churchwarden, Mr. Cecil Marsh (unknown to the latter, of course), put it to a bedroom window and took from a wardrobe a tin containing £400, the deeds of the house and a marriage certificate. At the time of writing, the police had not caught up with him. Certainly this was not for lack of trying. Dottery is impressed by the thoroughness of the police investigations and by their courtesy, even when things looked suspicious. When the police called on Mr. Cecil Marsh he happened to be having one of his rare days off, with 'flu, and it was not easy to prove that he had not caught it at the top of a ladder on a cold night. The ladder had none of his finger prints and fortunately he has no gloves. When the police called on Mr. Roper he was home with a black eye and a swollen fore-arm. He found it harder than he thought to prove he had fallen off a bike and not out of a ladder. With a night prowler still at large, the devout ladies of Dottery are taking no chances. They successfully petitioned the Vicar to cancel the evening service on Ash Wednesday and came to Loders to the morning commination instead. National Savings in Bridport went up the week after the robbery and we cannot say whether the mattresses or long stockings of Dottery helped. But we do know that fire insurances have been taken out and browsed over. Poor Mrs. Oxenbury got home from Bridport to find two fire brigades extinguishing her living room. They confined most of the damage to this spot, but the misfortune follows weeks of agony, Mr. Oxenbury suffered from a bad arm. He had only just gone back to work.

March 1968

Historical background (1945–1968)

THE ROYAL FAMILY

1947 King George VI substituted the title of Head of the Commonwealth for that of Emperor of India after the Labour Government had granted independence to that sub-continent

1949 Prince Charles born

1951 King George VI opened the Festival of Britain: brocade from his coronation to Loders Church (p. 91)

1952 King George VI died suddenly of coronary thrombosis: Sir Edward Le Breton attended as a member of the Corps of Gentlemen-at-Arms

1953 Queen Elizabeth the Second crowned

1957 Queen makes first Christmas television broadcast

1958 Edward Laskey plays football with Prince Charles (p. 153)

1960 Prince Andrew born; Princess Margaret marries Anthony Armstrong Jones

BRITISH POLITICS

1953 Winston Churchill resigns as Prime Minister – replaced by Anthony Eden

1957 Anthony Eden resigns: Harold Macmillan is Prime Minister (pp. 159–160, 'Changes at Uploders Place')

1958 First Life Peerage awarded in Britain

1959 Conservative Government elected under Harold Macmillan (p. Rab Butler's Budget compared to Askerswell's)

1960 UK applies to join European Economic Community

1964 Labour Government elected under Harold Wilson
Vote to end capital punishment (pp. 34–14 the Vicar's faith in corporal punishment)

1965 Sir Winston Churchill dies (pp. 170–1 the State funeral service: Bill Tiltman and Mr. Dykes Bower)
Harold Wilson talks with Ian Smith

1966 Labour Government wins a substantially increased majority under Harold Wilson

1967 Abortion Bill passed

NATIONAL AND INTERNATIONAL EVENTS

1945 Foundation of the United Nations

1953 First meeting of the Economic Coal and Steel Community

1954 End of all rationing (p. 90 the luxury of a sugar-lump at the Court Party)

Communists capture Dien Bien Phu in Vietnam
US Supreme Court outlaws racial segregation in schools (p. 12, A smell of Nazidom, Articles of Faith)
Algerian earthquake kills 1,500
1955 Warsaw Pact signed
Malenkov resigns: Bulganin becomes USSR Premier
Riots in Cyprus: EOKA action (p. 129, 'An intelligent appraisal': Police Constable Edrich reports)
1956 Suez Crisis
Soviet troops enter Budapest (p. 152, Hungarian refugees)
Eisenhower wins 2nd term as President of the U.S.A.
Olympic Games open in Melbourne (p. 153, Roy Taylor of Uploders by bike to the Sahara)
Hurricanes in the West Indies (p. 150)
1957 UK explodes first H bomb
USSR launch first space satellite (p. 207, 'Thic thur stayalite')
Treaty of Rome signed to form the Common Market
1958 Formation of Campaign for Nuclear Disarmament
Race riots in Notting Hill
De Gaulle becomes president of France
1959 Castro forces President Batista to flee Cuba and declares new Government
European Court of Human Rights has first meeting
Dalai Lama goes into exile in India following Tibetan revolt against China
1959 US U-2 bombers shot down in USSR
Sharpeville massacre in South Africa
Kennedy elected US President
Olympic Games in Rome (p. 67, The Traveller's Rest takes on Bridport F.C.)
1960 UK applies to join EEC
1961 East Germany erects Berlin Wall
1962 Cuban missile crisis
1963 Great train robbery
John Kennedy assassinated
1964 Olympic Games in Tokyo
Nelson Mandela given life imprisonment
1965 Soviet cosmonaut's first walk in space
Rhodesia's Unilateral Declaration of Independence, 1966 Winter Olympics (p. 174)
1966 Aberfan disaster – 147 die (mainly children)
1966 Winter Olympics (p. 174, 'Olympic Awards')
1966 Unmanned US spacecraft lands on moon
Hendrik Verwoerd (born Amsterdam), South African P.M., assassinated
1967 Torrey Canyon disaster
Mrs Ghandi re-elected P.M. of India
6-Day War began in Middle East
Che Guevera killed in Bolivia
1968 First decimal coins

Ronan Point disaster
Martin Luther King assassinated
Soviet attack on Czechoslovakia
Richard Nixon elected as U.S. President
Robert Kennedy assassinated

PEOPLE

King Abdullah Ibn Hussein 1882–1951, first king of Jordan (1946–51) (p. 148)
Clement Attlee dies (P.M. 1945–51 in post-war Labour Government) (p. 150)
Roger Bannister runs mile under 4 minutes 1954
Christian Barnard performed first heart-transplant operation in Cape Town – his first patient died of pneumonia after 18 days 1968 (p. 136, Max and Hilda Jones go as medical missionaries to Africa)
George Blake, British spy, sentenced to 42 years 1961
Rab Butler (1902–1981) MP for Safron Walden. 1955 introduced thee emergency 'credit squeeze' budget (p. 149–50, 'Other parishes please note')
Donald Campbell breaks water speed record at 202 m.p.h. 1954
Francis Chichester's solo yacht world trip in *Gipsy Moth IV* 1968
John Reginald Halliday Christie (1893–1953) hanged for the murder of his wife, having confessed to the strangulation of five other women. In 1966 Timothy John Frans was granted a free pardon for the murder of Mrs. Frans. The trial of Christie affected the legislation affecting the death penalty (pp. 15–16)
Diogenes of Sinope founded the Cynic sect, based on an austere asceticism – he was said to have lived in a tub ('like a dog'); Savonarola would have approved (p. xii)
Sir Francis Drake 1540–1596, the first Englishman to circumnavigate the globe (and compose prayers in Cadiz, p. 2)
Empress Faustina perhaps bore Marcus Aurelius 12 children (p. 63)
David Heathcoat Amory 1958–60, Chancellor of the Exchequer (p. 164)
Doctor Edward Jenner, the discoverer of vaccination, born in Berkeley Vicarage, Gloucestershire. Believed that cowpox could be efficacious against small-pox 1749–1823 (p. 93)
Martin Luther King awarded Nobel Peace Prize 1961
Lord Northcliffe 1865–1922 'one of the pioneers of mass circulation journalism' ran *The Times* for 1d in 1914 and used up lots of forests in Newfoundland (pp. 154–5)
Kim Philby defected to USSR 1954
John Profumo resigned over Christine Keeler 1963
Erwin Rommel, 1891–1944, Nazi supporter, as the 'Desert Fox' drove the British back to El Alamein in 1942 until Montgomery defeated him there: died by self-administered poison to preserve his estate (p. 152)
Baron John Selwyn-Lloyd (1904–78) Foreign Secretary 1955–1960 (p. 151, Secretary to Selwyn Lloyd)

ENTERTAINMENT

1953 Dylan Thomas' radio play 'Under Milk Wood' (with some similarities between Rev. Eli Jenkins and Rev. Oliver Willmott, and echoes of Thomas' enthusiasm for local characters in the *Parish Notes)*
1954 Bill Haley's pop song 'Rock around the clock'
1956 John Osborne's play *Look Back in Anger*
1957 Leonard Bernstein's musical *West Side Story*
1958 Henry Moore's bronze 'Two-piece Reclining Figure'
1964 Beatles' film *A Hard Day's Night* (p. 5; p. 223, Harry Crabb and topless dresses)
1964 M.B.E. for the Beatles (p. 174, 'Death-watch beatle in Loders Church')
1966 England wins the World Cup at soccer
1968 Tony Hancock commits suicide
Rock musical *Hair* opens

THE CLERGY

1943–1961 Geoffrey Fisher, Archbishop of Canterbury (p. 148)
St. Aldhelm, (*c.* 640–709) first bishop of Sherborne (p. 67)
1961–1974 Arthur Ramsey, Archbishop of Canterbury
1949–1962 William Louis Anderson, Bishop of Salisbury
1963–1972 Joseph Edward Fison, Bishop of Salisbury (pp. 169–70, 'Nothing to do with fertilisers')
1947–1959 John Maurice Key, Bishop of Sherborne (p. 27; p. 80)
1960–1976 Victor Joseph Pike, Bishop of Sherborne (p. 144)
1961 Coventry Cathedral consecrated
Archbishop Michael Ramsey and Paul VI met in Rome to strive towards Church Unity: at home he failed to forge reconciliation with the Methodist Church

Copies of the complete *Parish Notes*, 1948–1982, photocopied and bound in two volumes, may be obtained from the editor at:
8, Bishop Street, Shrewsbury SY2 5HA at a cost of £50, which includes packaging and postage. (Cheques should be made payable to The Bishop Street Press.)